Haynes
Restoration Manual

Land Rover Series I, II & III

Lindsay Porter

© Lindsay Porter 1992 and 1999

First published by G. T. Foulis &
Co. as *Land Rover Series I, II & III
Purchase and Restoration Guide,*
1992
Reprinted 1993, 1994, 1995 (twice),
1996 (twice) and 1997 (twice)
Reprinted by Haynes Publishing,
with new cover and minor
amendments as *Land Rover
Restoration Manual* 1999.
Reprinted 1999, 2000, 2001,
2002 (twice), 2004, 2006 and 2007,
2009 (twice), 2010, 2011, 2013, 2014
and 2015 (twice)

A catalogue record for this book is
available from the British Library

ISBN 978 1 85960 622 3

Library of Congress catalog card
number 91-76132

Haynes Publishing, Sparkford,
Yeovil, Somerset BA22 7JJ, UK

Tel: 01963 440635
Int. tel: +44 1963 440635

Website: www.haynes.co.uk

Haynes Publications Inc.
861 Lawrence Drive, Newbury Park,
California 91320, USA

Printed in the USA.

**Other Haynes Publishing titles of
interest to Land Rover enthusiasts:**

Land Rover: Simply the Best
(ISBN 978 1 85960 437 3)
*Land Rover Defender Restoration
Manual* (ISBN 978 1 85960 600 1)
*Land Rover II, IIA & III petrol (58-85)
Service and Repair Manual* (0314)
*Land Rover II, IIA & III diesel (58-85)
Service and Repair Manual* (0529)
The Car Bodywork Repair Manual
by Lindsay Porter
(ISBN 978 1 85960 657 5)

Contents

Introduction & Acknowledgements

The Land-Rover must be one of the most hands-on vehicles on the road today. Of all vehicles it is one of the most honest and unpretentious, and is in every sense down to earth. Designed to be simple in construction it is also relatively simple to maintain and compared with most classic cars, bodywork replacement and repair is incredibly simple to carry out. When you add to this the fact that the parent company Land-Rover and its offshoot Land-Rover Parts can still supply virtually every part for every vehicle they have produced for over 30 years, you have one of the most ideal restorer's vehicles around today. What it all means is that it is quite within the bounds of possibility to buy any of the Land-Rovers that have ever been built and to restore them in to anything, from good, usable condition, through to better-than new concours order using parts supplied by Land-Rover Parts. These are available through the many hundreds of Land-Rover dealerships throughout the world, or by purchasing specially reproduced parts for the Series I Land-Rover from one of the numerous specialists catering for them.

All the photographs in this book are of actual restoration work being carried out on Series I, II and III Land-Rovers and with most being taken at Dunsfold Land-Rover whose address is shown in the back of this book. Not all that many people know about Dunsfold Land-Rover and yet they are a proverbial mecca for those with a special interest in the marque. The Dunsfold Land-Rover museum is the largest of its type and contains examples of many rare, prototype and specialist vehicles, many of them having passed directly from Land-Rover themselves. The Dunsfold workshops, situated among the most idyllic of southern English countryside attract customers from a far wider radius than most Land-Rover dealerships, simply because of the enthusiasm and dedication of father and son team Brian and Philip Bashall, the proprietors.

The Bashalls reflect the sort of enthusiasm found at the parent company and that is found at only a small handful of vehicle manufacturers in the world. Miles Kimberley at Land-Rover Parts has been extraordinarily helpful and sympathetic to this project and so have the Press Office and Engineering sections at Land-Rover Ltd. The integrity that goes into producing every Land-Rover can be deduced from the enthusiasm which those involved have for the history and background of the marque.

A number of key people have been involved with the author in the production of this book including Brian and Philip Bashall who took a number of the photographs and who dictated copious notes in connection with the work being turned out. In my office, Tricia Lees-Milne, Sarah Weller, Kath Tickle, Catherine Larner, and Paul Guinness all made significant and invaluable contributions and, as ever, my warmest thanks go to my wife and business partner, Shan, who had an input at every stage and without whom none of this would have been remotely possible.

Thanks are also due to Ken and Julie Slavin of 'The Land-Rover Directory' for their permission to use some of the research material on Land-Rover production figures published in their excellent guides.

Using this book

The layout of this book has been designed to be both attractive and easy to follow during practical work on your car. However, to obtain maximum benefit from the book, it is important to note the following points:

1) Apart from the introductory pages, this book is split into two parts: chapters 1 to 6 dealing with history, buying and practical procedures; appendices 1 to 6 providing supplementary information. Each chapter/appendix may be sub-divided into sections and even sub-sections. Section heading are in italic type between horizontal lines and sub-section headings are similar, but without horizontal lines.

2) Step-by-step photograph and line drawing captions are an integral part of the text except those in chapter 1) – therefore the photographs/drawings and their captions are arranged to "read" in exactly the same way as the normal text. In other words they run down each column and the columns run from left to right of the page.

Each photograph caption carries an alpha-numeric identity, relating it to a specific section. The letters before the caption number are simply the initial letters of key words in the relevant section heading, whilst the caption number shows the position of the particular photograph in the section's picture sequence. This photograph/caption 'DR2' is the 2nd photograph in the section headed "Door Removal".

3) All references to the left or right of the vehicle are from the point of view of somebody standing behind the car looking forwards.

4) Because this book concentrates upon restoration, regular maintenance procedures and normal mechanical repairs of all the car's components, are beyond its scope. It is therefore strongly recommended that the Haynes *Land-Rover Owner's Workshop Manuals* should be used as a companion volume as appropriate.

5) We know it's a boring subject, especially when you really want to get on with a job – but your safety, through the use of correct workshop procedures, must ALWAYS be your foremost consideration. It is essential that you read, and UNDERSTAND, Appendix 1 before undertaking any of the practical tasks detailed in this book.

6) Before starting any particular job it is important that you read the introduction to the relevant Chapter or Section, taking note of the 'safety' notes. It is recommended that you read through the section from start to finish before getting into the job.

7) Whilst great care is taken to ensure that the information in this book is as accurate as possible, the author or publishers cannot accept any liability for loss, damage or injury caused by errors in, or omissions from, the information given.

1 Heritage

Background

It is often the case that the biggest success stories in automotive history come about almost by accident. The Land-Rover is a case in point, being a product of circumstance rather than the result of a long-standing desire by Rover management to produce an all-terrain vehicle.

Imagine being in charge of a car manufacturing company in the immediate post-World War 2 days; a company with an excess of production capacity and a severe restriction on the amounts of sheet steel available to it.

Rover's situation looked almost hopeless after the War. With raw materials in such short supply, the British Government of the time was allocating the largest quantities of sheet steel to those car companies who could offer relatively large levels of exports. With Rover's existing and essentially outdated range of cars unlikely to capture any major share of overseas markets, there simply wasn't the money available to develop another fairly upmarket model in keeping with Rover's new-found image of quality.

What Rover *really* needed was a stop-gap model that could be developed and launched both quickly *and* cheaply, yet would appeal to large numbers of buyers in Britain and elsewhere. This could then tide the company over until the launch of a *true* post-War Rover (which turned out to be the highly successful "P4" a few years later); the stop-gap model, having served its purpose by then, could easily be discontinued and would have proved useful by earning a few pennies for the Rover piggy bank.

It had been thought that Rover might rush into production a new 700cc economy car, code-named the M-type, but such plans were dismissed when this model was deemed unsuitable for export. Meanwhile, Rover's application to build 15,000 examples of its pre-War design "P2" series cars each year was turned down, the Government explaining that only enough steel could be allocated for the production of 1,100 examples. The company's problems seemed never-ending ...

At the time, Rover's troubles were resting on the shoulders of Spencer Wilks, the company's Managing Director ... but it was to be Spencer's brother, Maurice, who was eventually to prove the inspiration for Rover's route back to recovery.

Maurice Wilks owned a 250-acre farm in Anglesey, his land including woods, sand dunes and some coastline. His cross-country transport at the time was an old and battered Willys Jeep, and when it was nearing the end of its useful life Maurice was forced into thinking of buying another ... despite the idea of purchasing a non-British vehicle again, displeasing him somewhat! It suddenly dawned on the Wilks brothers that there existed an enormous gap in the market for a British-built four-wheel-drive utility vehicle that would appeal primarily for its agricultural potential.

Although they could not have known it then, the inspiration for such a model was timed perfectly. Mechanised farming was proving popular by now; and in these post-War austerity years surely an ultra-basic workhorse would prove a popular mode of transport with a great many people?

That the American Jeep was *the* major influence throughout the development of Rover's new project is undeniable. After all, if it were not for the fact that the Jeep had no equivalent, the "Land-Rover" idea would probably not have materialised.

The Wilks brothers were convinced they were on to a winner. So much so that work on the project started almost immediately and continued at rapid pace. By the time a Board Meeting had been called in September 1947, the first prototypes were already up and running. At the meeting it was agreed that "... the all-purpose vehicle on the lines of the Willys-Overland post-war Jeep was the most desirable". There was also the advantage that the Rover P3's engine, gearbox and back axle could be used and there would be no need for body dies as most of the panels would be crafted from shaped aluminium. Even the name Land-Rover was decided on at this early stage.

The speed with which the Land-Rover took shape is truly remarkable. It *had* to be a swift development, simply because Rover had the overheads associated with large-scale production but hadn't the opportunities to produce in big numbers due to the export factor. The sooner the new Land-Rover could be launched, the better it would be for Rover's long-term prospects.

An interesting set of guidelines were laid down for this revolutionary (for Rover) new model. It had to be useful to farmers as a *proper* farm machine and a real, and more versatile alternative, to the tractor; it had to have uses as a power source, with power take-offs *everywhere*; and it had to have all sorts of bolt-on accessories available to further widen its usefulness.

Public acceptance

The Land-Rover was first shown to the public at the opening of the Amsterdam Motor Show on April 30th, 1948 ... just one year after the initial idea for the

vehicle had first emerged. During that year, the project had gone from the idea stage, through the drawing board phase and quickly on to the point where nearly fifty prototypes were working hard in order to prove the Land-Rover's worth. These prototypes were performing widely varying roles; the fact that the Land-Rover's chassis incorporated a central power take-off enabled the vehicle to be harnessed to a whole range of machinery, making a lot of tasks much simpler and quicker to carry out. Its cross-country abilities were also developing, thanks to almost weekly improvements to the prototypes – their abilities at crossing ploughed fields, tackling amazingly steep inclines and fording streams were becoming quite superb.

The original Land-Rover of 1948 was aesthetically similar to the later models, but in reality the Land-Rover design has changed greatly over the years, whilst still retaining its strong, visual, family identity. Mechanically, the '48 Land-Rover was based heavily on what was already in the Rover range, hence the adoption of the 1595cc engine from the Rover P3 after deciding that the 1389cc Rover 10 engine lacked sufficient power. The idea employed on one of the prototypes of using a central steering wheel and centrally positioned driver's seat was never taken as far as the production stage, despite its obvious advantages of needing no alteration for overseas markets.

At the 1948 Amsterdam Motor Show, Rover exhibited two examples of the new Land-Rover – and eagerly awaited the comments from both press and public alike. The response was sensational, with the motoring magazines of the time giving Britain's latest innovation nothing but rave reviews. *Autocar*, introducing the

newcomer, said: "There is now something to describe which can either be regarded as a private car able to perform many most valuable duties other than sheer transport, or as a general purpose countryside worker which is also capable of providing comfortable and efficient transport". *Motor* summed up the Land-Rover by calling it a "... go-anywhere vehicle with a plain utility-type body, a portable source of power, and an alternative to the light tractor". This was exactly the sort of response that Rover had been hoping for, and the public's reaction was equally optimistic. The Land-Rover wasn't being seen as simply an agricultural workhorse; it was viewed by many as a genuine alternative to the standard car, no doubt partly due to its basic launch price of just £450, though buyers paid extra for such "luxuries" as a passenger seat, heater, sidescreens, spare wheel and a starting handle.

American influence

It was no coincidence that, at 80 inches, the Land-Rover's chassis was the same length as the American-built Jeep's, whose chassis was the basis for the Rover product. Major improvements *were* made to it however, mainly involving adaptations that enabled the Land-Rover to power as much extra machinery as possible. The National Institute of Agricultural Engineering tested an early Land-Rover, using it in field trials that included ploughing, harrowing, muck spreading, potato harvesting, rolling and pulling a reaper; the Land-Rover passed such tests with flying colours.

The Land-Rover was Britain's first four-wheel-drive vehicle of its type, and it is a credit to the company that the

design was so right . . . particularly when you consider the speed with which the development was rushed through. The Jeep that inspired it was an extremely well designed vehicle though, therefore giving Land-Rover something of a head-start.

Like the Jeep, the Land-Rover boasted a separate box-section chassis frame, front-mounted engine with a gearbox in unit with it, transfer gearing behind the 'box, and propeller shafts running backwards and forwards to live front and rear axles. Semi-elliptic road springs and telescopic dampers provided the suspension system. Performance was reasonably lively for the time, the 1.6-litre engine fitted initially developing 50bhp.

Construction

Due to Rover's financial problems of the time, the body had to be produced using an absolute minimum of new tooling, and so it was decided to produce the body panels from aluminium alloy, thereby requiring no press tools. In fact, the production of body panels was made all the more easier by their actual design, with only the bonnet and front wings having any real "shape".

The part of the Land-Rover that caused the most problems from a cost point of view was that chassis. If money had not been in such short supply at the time, the chassis frame would have been constructed from deep-drawn steel channel section, carefully shaped where required and built on a proper jig. To save expense, each chassis box section was actually made from four long strips of sheet steel with the edges all welded together in long seams. Despite this somewhat haphazard way of producing a

box section (something with which Rover had little experience anyway), the idea worked, producing a box section of great strength that was capable of withstanding some pretty torturous treatment.

Value for money

The Land-Rover seemed extremely good value at £450 when it was launched in 1948, and indeed it was. It had one great advantage over most "normal" cars in that it was not liable to purchase tax – the authorities weren't too sure how to class the Land-Rover, although its general agricultural uses ensured that it certainly could not be classed as a passenger car.

At the time of the Land-Rover's launch, Rover were faced with two main headaches. Would the public have the confidence to place orders for such a new model? And would the Government of the time allow Land-Rover enough raw materials to produce the 5,000 examples that the company thought it might sell in the first year? The good news was that the orders started to *flood* in; the bad news was that the Ministry of Supply would only allow enough sheet steel for the production of 1,000 Land-Rovers per year. Fortunately, Rover were able to persuade the "powers-that-be" that the new Land-Rover should have a great future as a profitable export, and production was allowed to continue at the planned levels. In fact, it soon became clear that *extra* production would be needed; so much so that in the first year of production, the original hope of 5,000 units was *exceeded* by an extra 3,000!

It is true to say that for most of the time since 1948, each and every Land-Rover

produced has already had a customer ready and waiting for it. Such success, particularly in the Land-Rover's early years, enabled the company to carry out steady development and improvements . . . though never simply change for change's sake.

Variants

The improvements started as early as October 1948, when a Station Wagon version of the Land-Rover appeared for the first time; it featured new doors, a horizontally split tailgate and inward facing rear seats, allowing seating for up to seven passengers. The problem was the price; unlike the existing Land-Rover, this new model would have to be taxed as a conventional, passenger-carrying vehicle, forcing the price up by about £200 due to the resultant Purchase Tax. Compared with the £450 price tag for the open-top model, the new Land-Rover derivative *was* expensive at £960 . . .

By 1952, it was decided that the Land-Rover could handle extra power. As a result, its engine was bored out to 1997cc, before giving way to an identically sized but further improved unit in 1954.

The same year, the original 80-inch Land-Rover was replaced by a new 86-inch model, while a 107-inch variant (initially available only as a pick-up) was also added to the range. These new models incorporated such "luxuries" as a redesigned fascia, improved seating and, in the new De Luxe model, even a headlining, door trims and floor covering! And at last, the previously compulsory dark green paintwork was joined by grey and blue paint finishes . . .

In 1957, the Land-Rover that so many commercial users had been awaiting for so long, finally

appeared – the diesel version. By now the Land-Rover had grown up into a slightly more refined but still incredibly capable vehicle, having been "extended" once again in 1956, this time offering 88-inch and 109-inch variants. The new diesel engine was a 2052cc all-iron wet-liner unit with overhead valves. New features included roller tappets in the valve train, proving a great improvement over the conventional pad-type that were so prone to wear. Aluminium alloy pistons were fitted on the conrods, specially shaped to allow easy withdrawal up the bores for servicing.

Not surprisingly, the diesel Land-Rover proved an instant hit, particularly with those companies or farmers running fleets of vehicles for whom it was highly inconvenient to possess a petrol-engined vehicle when all their other commercials were diesel-powered.

World wide success

Ten years after the introduction of the Land-Rover, it was clearer than ever that it was no longer simply a stop-gap model. A total of 200,000 examples had been produced by 1958, compared with "just" 100,000 Rover saloons. Of this total Land-Rover production, more than 70% had been exported, with the model now available in 150 different countries, with several countries even building Land-Rovers locally from CKD kits. Despite the introduction of several new rivals in the 1950s and '60s, the Land-Rover still reigned supreme, and even replaced the Austin Champ as the British Army's favourite vehicle.

Series II

The 10th Anniversary of the Land-Rover coincided with the launch of the Series II versions, which retained the 88-inch and 109-inch wheelbases. A major feature was the 2286cc version of the existing petrol engine ... but the most obvious aspect of this latest model was its updated styling. For the first time ever, Rover's styling department was asked to take a look at the Land-Rover, and the Series II is what they came up with. The difficulty was that as the existing shape was so ideally suited to the Land-Rover's image and demands, how could it be improved? The styling team finally decided upon minor refinements and revisions rather than any great restyling job; such changes included "modesty skirts" on both sides to cover up the exhaust pipe and chassis frame, more rounded body sides, a reshaped bonnet and neater door hinges. A more varied range of colours was also introduced, emphasising the Land-Rover's appeal to the private motorist as well as the commercial user. Softer road springs and modified dampers were now incorporated, giving a softer, more comfortable ride *and* increased stability – the Series II Land-Rover could be driven at an angle of 45 degrees to the vertical with few problems ...

Although the Land-Rover had sold strongly from day one, Rover pursued a policy of gradual improvement to the model. The next stage in the evolution came about in 1961 with the introduction of the Land-Rover Series IIA. Changes were relatively minor, apart from the adoption of a more powerful diesel engine, now sharing the petrol engine's 2286cc capacity.

One problem that Rover simply *had* to tackle was that of Purchase Tax on the Land-Rover

Station Wagons, these being the only Land-Rovers subject to this tax simply because of their passenger-carrying abilities. The answer was to launch a *12*-seater Station Wagon, which was possible due to the extra length of the standard long-wheelbase models by now. Unlike the existing 10-seater models, the new 12-seaters were classed as "buses", hence commercial vehicles, and were *not* liable to Purchase Tax. This enabled Land-Rover to market the 12-seater on the home market at a lower price than the 10-seater (just £950 as opposed to £1,293 in 1962), increasing Station Wagon sales dramatically.

More power

By the mid-1960s, Land-Rover customers were once again asking for more power from their vehicles ... and it was up to Rover to oblige. The Forward-Control models in particular were criticised for being underpowered. These models were strange looking devices introduced in 1962, based on the standard long-wheelbase chassis but with purpose-built bodywork and vastly different styling. They were aimed fairly and squarely at the commercial vehicle market where there was a demand for a tough, go-anywhere, four-wheel-drive workhorse capable of carrying a load of up to 30cwt. The newcomer was initially sold only in dropside lorry form. Because of its extra weight, the Forward-Control variant was understandably lacking in power, being fitted with the 2286cc diesel and petrol engines.

To answer this question of urgently needed extra power across the whole of the Land-Rover range, Rover sought a smaller-capacity version of the

six-cylinder engine used in the Rover 3-litre saloons. This 2625cc petrol engine was ideal in that it offered the required extra power but was also available "off the shelf" thanks to its use in this form in the more powerful of the Rover P4 series saloons.

This 2.6-litre six-cylinder engine was particularly successful in the Forward-Control Land-Rovers, where it provided enough power to propel even a fully laden version with reasonable gusto. The same engine was eventually to find its way into the long-wheelbase versions of the "standard" Land-Rover and remained there until the adoption of the 3.5-litre V8 in 1980.

Before the Series IIA Land-Rover was finally superseded, Rover were forced into making one of the most obvious changes to its styling so far. Due to new lighting regulations in several export markets, the Land-Rover's headlights were moved (for the first time in twenty years!) from their position next to the radiator grille to the front of the wings – more prominent and more likely to get damaged, but at least they complied with the regulations! This affected export models from 1968, although the change wasn't introduced to UK-spec versions until February 1969 when supplies of the old-type front wings were finally exhausted.

Here to stay

By now, it was apparent to everyone that the Land-Rover was here to stay. It was a market leader in so many countries, and production was reaching record levels. The 500,000th Land-Rover had rolled off the lines in 1966 (it took eleven years to build the first

250,000 examples, and just seven years to build the *next* 250,000!), and by then the factory was almost at bursting point. It was only Land-Rover's keenness to develop overseas production that enabled the company to expand its manufacturing still further, with more and more countries now producing Land-Rovers from kits of parts. By the late 1960s, no less than 30% of Land-Rover's export vehicles were leaving the factory in kit form for local assembly in any one of 29 countries. Rover's association with MSA of Spain, which had evolved over the years, proved most useful, with some of the Spanish-built Land-Rovers being shipped to other countries to supplement those going abroad from Solihull. By the time the Land-Rover's 21st birthday was being celebrated in 1969, the vehicle was being sold in 182 different countries, with exports now accounting for 80% of annual production. As the 1970s dawned, total Land-Rover production was edging towards the 650,000 mark.

In terms of the history of the Land-Rover, 1970 is probably best remembered for the launch of the all-new Range Rover... more of which later!

The Land-Rover wasn't being neglected though, for in 1971 came the Series III, consisting of a package of improvements to increase the consumer appeal of the evergreen Land-Rover. From a cosmetic point of view, modifications included a new injection-moulded radiator grille, flatter door and bonnet hinges, and a new heater air-intake on the nearside front wing.

The Series III changes were more than skin deep though, for the Land-Rover now boasted a fully-synchromesh gearbox (although it had been fitted to the last few Series 11A vehicles), plus an uprated clutch on all models. Brakes were also altered, with new brake drums,

re-routed brake pipes and now servo-assisted brakes as standard on all Station Wagon and six-cylinder variants.

It was in the late 1960s and early '70s that the future of Rover as a company, and in particular its mainstay Land-Rover, took several major turns... which at times proved rather worrying for those who cared about the Land-Rover marque.

At this time, with several other manufacturers (mainly overseas companies) developing and launching their own 4x4 models in an attempt to gain a slice of the action, Rover were having to fight harder to retain their healthy share of the four-wheel-drive market... both in Britain *and* abroad. Indeed, it was primarily this new threat of increased competition that had led to the launch of the Series III Land-Rover. It is a credit to the company that Land-Rover's total production for the 1970-71 year reached a new record of 56,663 units, aided slightly by the introduction of the Range Rover (although this new model actually took some sales away from the top end of the Land-Rover range, as well as helping to boost total sales for the company).

British Leyland takeover

Despite such successes in most markets, all was not well with the Rover company at home, following a number of management and ownership changes that had taken place over the previous few years. At the same time, the various mergers had begun that would ultimately lead to the formation of the mighty British Leyland corporation, which in itself posed problems for Rover; with Rover relying on other companies for the manufacture

of bodyshells (enabling higher production levels without Rover requiring major factory growth themselves), the company was seen as something of an 'outsider' that needed bringing under the same, ever-expanding umbrella. As a result, a proposal by Leyland for the takeover of Rover was accepted and, by 1967, the company was 'swallowed' and no longer a separate entity in its own right. By 1968, this mixture of once-small companies had grown still larger, thanks to the further takeover of British Motor Holdings (resulting in the new title of British Leyland Motor Corporation) and the achievement of securing financial backing from the British government.

It was at this stage that a gradual process of separation of Land-Rovers from Rover saloon cars began, with British Leyland being split into 'divisions'; Rover became part of the Specialist Cars section, along with Jaguar and Triumph, but Land-Rover was rather more awkward to define. It really belonged in the Light Commercial sector, alongside Austin and Morris trucks, but with the launch of the Range Rover imminent by the late 1960s (and this new model *certainly* did not deserve to be placed in the same company division as its commercial vehicle 'cousins'), Land-Rover was allowed to exist more or less on its own, proving a valuable profit-earner for the group of which it was just a tiny part.

Land-Rover was left more or less to its own devices until 1974, when British Leyland found themselves in deep financial trouble; with a range of outdated and uncompetitive models, and all the problems that the 1970's oil crisis brought, British Leyland had hit hard times, though the Land-Rover sector *still* managed to remain profitable! When British Leyland appealed to the Government for a major cash injection at the end of 1974, the answer was a cautious "Yes"... as long as a government-appointed team could look into the running of British Leyland and make whatever changes it felt necessary.

An immediate effect of all these troubles was that Land-Rover found itself a part of the British Leyland division known as Leyland Cars. A less direct effect was that the Government decided to inject regular amounts of money into British Leyland on condition that any future expenditure in the company would depend entirely on the group's achievements and overall performance. Therefore, no matter how much profit Land-Rover itself could make, there was no guarantee that such profit would be ploughed into the development of new Land-Rovers, or even the continuous development of existing models.

Those involved with Land-Rover had some serious decisions to make to ensure that the marque had some chance of survival in the increasingly competitive four-wheel-drive markets worldwide. As a result, a series of cost-cutting exercises were embarked upon; the Forward-Control Land-Rover was discontinued (it was produced only in low volume anyway) and Land-Rover shortly withdrew from the North American market, mainly because of the cost of developing engines that would comply with the United States' increasingly strict anti-pollution laws. Even those modifications to the Land-Rover that *were* deemed essential, such as the development of an overdrive system to reduce fuel consumption in the light of the oil crisis, had to be carried out on a desperately tight budget. In the case of overdrive, the cheapest solution (but still a highly competent system) was developed for Land-Rover by Fairey, a company already well known for making winches for the company. By 1974, the Fairey overdrive was an official option and an approved after-market conversion, creating a significant reduction in fuel consumption *and* quieter on-road performance.

By 1976, Land-Rover had produced its one-millionth four-wheel-drive vehicle, amid much publicity and flag waving. But behind the scenes, things weren't running as smoothly as they seemed on the surface. To deter foreign rivals from achieving a firm foothold in the 4x4 market, an increase in Land-Rover production was considered in order to meet the still healthy demand. But because of the uncertainty over the future of British Leyland as a group, such increased production levels were shelved. It was inevitable that those customers who weren't prepared to wait possibly months for their new Land-Rover would look elsewhere for their off-road motoring... much to the advantage of the Japanese manufacturers. It is ironic that the very success of Land-Rover (and failure to take advantage of such success) was what led to its steadily diminishing market share over the next few years.

Unfortunately for Land-Rover, there were some pretty great priorities within the British Leyland 'empire', namely the development of new engines for its mid-range cars and the funding of an all-new small car (later to be known as Metro), the latter being vital to the group's future.

As a result, Leyland Cars was once again split into separate sections, with the setting up of two autonomous groups – Austin Morris Ltd and Jaguar-Rover-Triumph Ltd, with Land-Rover Ltd established as yet another company within the latter group. Part of this arrangement was that Land-Rover could have complete use of the Solihull factory, with

production of Rover saloons being moved elsewhere. And *at last* Land-Rover could look forward to some major investment under the ownership of this enormous (by Land-Rover's standards) group, of which it was just one tiny part.

One of the reasons for such heavy government investment in the future of Land-Rover was the company's enormous export potential. Throughout its history, Land-Rover had shown that exports were not just possible but were an essential part of the company's success, contributing substantially to the export totals of the whole of the British motor industry. Land-Rover was justifiably being seen as a valuable earner of revenue from abroad, although by this time its share of the overseas markets had diminished, mainly due to Land-Rover's inability to meet demand, plus the 'wilderness years' of the early 1970s which saw very little model development. By 1978, Land-Rover held just 50% of the home market for four-wheel-drive vehicles (down from a peak of 98%!) and just *15%* of the worldwide market...

The investment that was earmarked for Land-Rover totalled £280 million – a clear indication of the Government's commitment to the marque and its long-term future. First items on the agenda of expansion and development were the replacement of the six-cylinder Land-Rovers and a major increase in production, by 8.5% for Land-Rovers and by no less than 50% for the Range Rover.

The model that was to replace the six-cylinder Land-Rovers came as no great surprise. Rover had been using their ex-Buick 3528cc V8 engine in saloon cars since 1967, and even Land-Rover had made use of it in the Range Rover. What could be more logical than to shoehorn this lightweight but powerful unit into the latest Land-Rovers?

Like the six-cylinder Land-Rovers before it, the V8 version was available only in long wheelbase form. Its engine was heavily detuned to make it more suited to the needs of the average user, and could happily run on low octane fuels (particularly useful in those areas of the world where little else was available). Despite being detuned to offer a relatively modest 91bhp, the Land-Rover V8 could cruise happily at a steady 80mph, enough to keep most customers happy *and* managing this with a degree of quietness that earlier Land-Rovers lacked!

To squeeze in such a seemingly large unit, the Land-Rover's engine compartment had to be enlarged and this was achieved by modifying the front end of the vehicle. The front panel that had been set back behind the wings on previous Land-Rovers was now flush with the rest of the front end, with a new, modern looking grille to further emphasise the Land-Rover's new identity.

The rest of the range wasn't being ignored by the Land-Rover management either; a new pick-up body was introduced for the long wheelbase version (boasting a 20% bigger load area and a 45% increase in cubic capacity over its predecessor), and a new De Luxe trim package was launched, primarily for the Station Wagons, for those customers who were now demanding a little more in the way of creature comforts. Known as the County Station Wagons, these newcomers were intended to bridge the gap between the undeniably spartan Land-Rover and the increasingly luxurious Range Rover, and were available in both 88-inch and 109-inch forms. This County version was immediately recognisable thanks to its new, distinctive looks; it boasted more external trim than any other Land-Rover before it, with

smart new colour schemes, tinted glass, twin driving lamps, a spare wheel cover and (probably much to the disgust of the die-hard purists) the luxury of *cloth* covered seats finished in black and grey 'tweed' to complete the image. A lockable 'oddments' storage box could be specified to replace the central front passenger seat, but once again Land-Rover found themselves with a problem of taxation; on the home market, this option was not available on the long wheelbase Station Wagon as it would reduce the total number of seats from twelve to eleven, thus deeming the vehicle a 'car' rather than a 'bus' and therefore making it liable to Special Car Tax (this tax *and* VAT having replaced the Purchase Tax on cars some years earlier).

Despite such improvements, the Land-Rover company could not afford to become complacent. Their models *had* to be good enough to prove their worth the world over, mainly because production was now at such an increase that, unless Land-Rovers were continuously improved, the chances are that the demand-outstripping-supply situation that had been a feature of the company since day one might actually be *reversed*... something which had to be avoided at all costs!

One Ten and Ninety

At the 1983 Geneva Motor Show came the beginning of the end for the old 'series' Land-Rovers when the One Ten was introduced – the most dramatically revised Land-Rover in 35 years of production. By now, the world's best selling four-wheel-drive vehicle was no longer a Land-Rover but the Toyota Land Cruiser. Land-Rover were now pinning their hopes on the new One Ten – hopes of

regaining ground that was lost in the 1970s and of reversing their trend of a sliding market share.

The big news about the One Ten was that it used the coil-spring suspension first seen on the Range Rover, the long suspension travel provided by this set-up giving a comfortable ride both on and off the road. To implement this system on the Land-Rover though, its chassis had to be completely redesigned. Several ease-of-servicing ideas were introduced at the same time, such as a bolt-on crossmember below the gearbox to make removal and maintenance that much easier. Disc brakes were added to the front wheels, and servo-assistance became standard. Power steering was also available for the first time ever on a Land-Rover. Along with the chassis changes came an increase in wheelbase to 110 inches – obviously the source of the new model's name!

All three engines used in the existing Series III Land-Rovers were carried over into the One Ten, albeit in higher states of tune; the 2¼-litre diesel and petrol engines now developed 60bhp and 74bhp respectively, while output from the 3.5-litre V8 was now up to 114bhp at 4000rpm. Five-speed gearboxes became available on the four-cylinder versions, with the same option to follow for the V8s in due course.

Styling was similar to that of the 109-inch V8s, although a one-piece windscreen and deformable wheelarch guards made the One Ten instantly recognisable. The interior was also redesigned, with a functional but fresh and modern feel to it and, for the first time ever, the option of factory-fitted air-conditioning.

With the One Ten came the usual variety of different body styles available to the customer, from the Full Tilt Pick-Up to the Station Wagon, still available in County trim even in this form.

It was only to be a matter of time before the "One Ten treatment" was applied to the short wheelbase Land-Rovers too, this happening in 1984 with the launch of the Ninety. Like the One Ten, it appeared with the usual choice of body styles, although engine choice was limited to just two – the two-and-a-quarter litre petrol unit and a new 2.5-litre diesel engine that similarly found its way into the One Ten the same year.

In many ways, the Ninety looked just like a shortened version of the One Ten, with similar styling touches and trim finishes and, of course, another completely redesigned chassis. The Ninety's wheelbase actually measured 92.9 inches, though this would hardly have sounded tempting as a model name for the newcomer! Just like its 'big brother' One Ten, the Ninety represented the latest in Land-Rover luxury... without losing sight of the fact that it was still very much a hard-working vehicle.

More improvements

Throughout the 1980s, the Land-Rover came in for steady improvement, in both its long *and* short wheelbase forms. Mechanical changes included the eventual adoption of a turbocharged version of the 2.5-litre diesel engine, providing a welcome boost to power and, in particular, on-road performance. Thankfully, the ubiquitous Land-Rover met with widespread commercial success once again, with steadily improving sales figures worldwide as the 1990s approached. But it was clear that this much loved vehicle could not hold on to a major share of the world markets without some assistance from new designs; with more and

more customers now demanding sophistication as well as rugged, off-road appeal. The company needed something else along the lines of the Range Rover, but at a rather more affordable price. The answer was... Discovery.

There was certainly plenty of life left in the "old faithful" Land-Rover though, and for the 1991 model year the company announced yet another series of improvements across the range. In line with the expanding range for the 1990s, the "old-style" model was given a name in its own right – Land-Rover Defender. Outwardly similar to the V8 and County models that had gone before it (in fact, the 'County' model designation is still used on some Defender versions), the Defender incorporated minor, visual improvements like new seat trim, special badging and colour-keyed decals.

Under the bonnet, however, is where Defender *really* differs from its predecessors, with the adoption of the new 2.5-litre direct-injection intercooled diesel engine from the Discovery models, producing 26% more power than the old turbo-diesel unit. Maximum speed increased to 84mph (from 75mph), while the Defender 90 accelerated from rest to 60mph in just 15.7 seconds (down from the 'old' time of 22.5 seconds). Official fuel consumption figures also showed a dramatic improvement, with the 90 model now achieving 28.3mpg on the urban cycle compared with the previous figure of 23.7mpg. Those who did not want a diesel engine could still opt for the legendary 3.5-litre all-alloy V8 used so extensively by Land-Rover over the years.

With the Land-Rover's latest round of improvements and the adoption of the Defender title, hopefully this model can continue in production almost indefinitely, for surely there will always be a market for a *true*

Land-Rover – a rugged workhorse with relatively little in the way of luxury appointments.

Discovery

As mentioned earlier though, not everyone is prepared to put up with what can still be termed a 4x4 utility-type vehicle. The discerning buyer of the '90s wants a little extra, particularly with so many potential customers looking at vehicles like the Mitsubishi Shogun, Isuzu Trooper and Toyota Land Cruiser for everyday transport, which means 99% *on-road* driving. Land-Rover saw the need for a British rival to such established Japanese models; their answer lay in the 1989 launch of the Land-Rover Discovery, a model which, almost overnight, took the market by storm.

Launched in November 1989, Discovery met with immediate acclaim from the motoring press, most road-testers rating it as the best vehicle in its class. The public were impressed too, as soon as supplies started to build up. A quite lengthy waiting list had been necessary right from day one, but Discovery took little time in becoming the best selling 4x4 leisure vehicle in the UK – a clear indication that, once again, Land-Rover had come up with a brand new vehicle that people *wanted*...

Initially available only in three-door form, Discovery was a distinctive looking vehicle; it wasn't *excitingly* different to look at but its styling was attractive and unlikely to get confused with any of its rivals. A choice of two engines was offered, the 3.5-litre V8 in carburettor form and the 2.5-litre direct-injection intercooled turbo-diesel unit.

Based on a wheelbase of 100 inches, Discovery was about

the same size as most of its Japanese rivals. And, unlike the original Land-Rover, it was aimed fairly and squarely at the leisure market, for those people who wanted 4x4 everyday transport (whether for its usefulness or for its 'trendy' image that had developed throughout the 'eighties), with no loss in terms of standard equipment and comfort. The Discovery was certainly well equipped, with such luxuries as electric windows, central locking, electrically adjustable door mirrors, alloy wheels and seating for up to seven people. Its price was competitive at approximately £17,000; very similar to some of the top-of-the-range Japanese offerings.

The Discovery certainly was not "all-show-and-no-go" however, for it boasted superb off-road capabilities (as you'd expect from any new Land-Rover). Permanent four-wheel-drive followed the Land-Rover tradition, with high and low transfer settings for when the going got *really* tough! While the Discovery was pure Land-Rover under the skin, the refinement and superb driving comfort of this newcomer was a new experience for anyone used to the Land-Rover 90 and 110 models.

One of the few criticisms levelled at Discovery was the restriction of being available only in three-door form. Such criticism was soon answered however, when the 1991 model year Discovery was announced. In came a new five-door version, plus a whole host of other improvements to the Discovery in general.

For 1991, the 3.5-litre V8 petrol engine now came as standard with fuel injection, thus offering improved performance and top speed – up from 101.6mph to 106.5mph, with the 0-60mph acceleration time now taking just 10.8 seconds as opposed to 12.7 seconds. Impressive figures for a vehicle

of its type.

There is now doubt that, with the right sort of product development throughout the '90s, Discovery has a good future ahead of it and should help to boost Land-Rover's now-healthy sales figures still further, not just in Britain but throughout Europe too.

The Range Rover

There is one major model in Land-Rover's history yet to be covered in any great detail. As the flagship of the company for more than two decades, it is perhaps fitting that it is featured last, particularly as it also represents the most expensive standard-model passenger vehicle ever to roll off the Land-Rover production lines. That vehicle is the Range Rover.

In much the same way that Land-Rover saw a need for a less agricultural vehicle when it developed Discovery, so the Range Rover was conceived in the late 1960s. The concept behind the Range Rover actually goes back much further, to the early 1950s in fact, when it was suggested that a more comfortable, bigger and more stylish alternative to the Land-Rover could happily sell alongside its established, workhorse cousin. At this stage, the Road Rover (as it was then known) would be based on the chassis and components of the Rover P4 saloons and use only *rear*-wheel-drive. In effect, a purpose-built estate car with no cross-country abilities. Thankfully, such ideas were given up by the time the '60s dawned, the company then directing its efforts towards the development of the new Rover 2000 P6 saloons.

With the Rover 2000 not only launched but also proving highly successful by the mid-1960s however, it was time

to consider the idea of an 'upmarket' Land-Rover once again. It was now decided that this newcomer should employ *permanent* four-wheel-drive. It was to be a "station wagon" based around a 100-inch wheelbase and, it was decided, would use the six-cylinder 3-litre engine from the *big* Rover saloons. Few people were happy with this engine though, for such an important new model. And so it was with great joy that those working on the project heard that Rover had secured the rights to an all-alloy GM-designed V8 engine, the unit that was to become the highly successful and much respected Rover V8 mentioned earlier. It was almost as though the whole project had been given new meaning, now that there could be used, a powerful, lightweight engine in keeping with the proposed upmarket image of the vehicle.

Exactly what that image would be still wasn't too clear to many. There would be no competitors by which to judge the new Rover, so the planners were left to follow what few guidelines had been set; the vehicle had to be bigger, faster and more civilized than a 'normal' Land-Rover, but just as practical and still recognisably Rover. Such practicality dictated features like a high ground clearance, yet there was still uncertainty over how the styling should look. Two of the leading figures in the Range Rover development, Spen King and Gordon Bashford, set about building a mock-up of how they thought the newcomer should be shaped, rather than wait for the styling department to come up with ideas. The end result looked remarkably similar to how the finished Range Rover would be like at its launch in July 1970. It was always intended that the new model would be two-door only, to save on development costs and to ensure structural rigidity.

The Range Rover's development survived the company's merger with British Leyland in the late '60s with ease, the new owners being particularly keen for the development to continue (much to the relief of all concerned!). And so it was that, just before the 1960s came to an end, pilot production runs of the new Range Rover were under way, ready for the much publicised launch in the summer of 1970.

Introduced with a price tag of under £2,000, the Range Rover was considered remarkably good value at launch for a four-wheel-drive go-anywhere vehicle... but then it was never intended to be anything other than upmarket compared with the Land-Rover. Despite rumours of an average fuel consumption of around 15mpg, stories of production troubles and claims of poor build quality and even early rusting on those panels made of conventional steel (most were aluminium), the public *loved* the Range Rover. It boasted near 100mph performance and, with its exceptionally high driving position, allowed both driver and passengers a commanding view of the road ahead. It was an image vehicle that fortunately (for Land-Rover) portrayed the kind of image to which so many people aspired. In true Land-Rover tradition, the Range Rover immediately built up a cult following, with long waiting lists soon appearing, particularly once exports began. The situation became so intense that a black market existed for Range Rovers for quite a while, as demand continued to outstrip supply by a massive margin.

The potential for the development of the Range Rover has always been immense, but throughout the 1970s it was almost ignored by the decision-makers at British Leyland/Leyland Cars. It soldiered on, its popularity still strong, but changes to it over

the decade of the '70s were few and far between compared with its subsequent development.

Despite having been in production for nearly ten years by the time the 'eighties arrived, Land-Rover management was only now beginning to realise (or at least make use of) the potential that had been going to waste. Throughout the 1980s, the Range Rover went from strength to strength, being gradually moved further and further upmarket.

A four-door version was at last introduced, and soon began to outsell the two-door quite substantially; nowadays, something in the region of 90% of new Range Rovers are bought in four-door form. The Range Rover's interior was greatly improved over the years, becoming positively luxurious in the top of the range versions. In fact, for the first time ever, *several* variants of the Range Rover were available as official models from Land-Rover dealers, climaxing in the Vogue version – a particularly upmarket derivative that is still in production today, offering true luxury car appointments without losing any of the original's practicality and off-road abilities.

On the mechanical side, the Range Rover's development included the availability of automatic transmission, and at long last a turbo-diesel engine option.

The *ultimate* production Range Rover in terms of prestige was introduced for the 1991 model year... and just 200 examples were produced. Based on the two-door model, the Range Rover CSK (named after the initials of the original designer, Spen King) featured just about everything a customer could ask for... from anti-lock brakes and air-conditioning to American Walnut trimmings and a six-speaker stereo sound system (with the option of a CD player and

cellular telephone). Paintwork could be in any colour so long as it was black! Under the bonnet lay the company's latest 3.9-litre version of the venerable V8 engine, developing 185bhp and powering the vehicle to a top speed in excess of 114mph. And the price for such luxury when the CSK was introduced at the tail end of 1990? A cool £30,319.32 for the automatic-transmission version.

Both Land-Rovers *and* Range Rovers have come under the scrutiny of countless specialist coachwork and bodywork companies over the years, not to mention such mechanical conversions as after-market turbo applications for the petrol-engined Range Rovers.

In the case of the Range Rover, it was probably British Leyland's lack of model development in the 1970s that led to so many specialist conversions of the marque... ranging from ambulances and fire-tenders to convertibles and 'stretched' limousines. Probably the most famous Range Rover conversion was built in 1982 just before the arrival of the Pope on a visit to Britain; the subsequent 'Popemobile' gained worldwide attention and respect, despite some onlookers' claims that it bore more than a passing resemblance to an upmarket ice-cream van thanks to its "greenhouse" rear end in which the Pope stood behind bullet-proof glass.

Specialist modifications

Almost since its introduction well over four decades ago, the humble Land-Rover has also come in for its fair share of specialist modifications. Its adaptations as a farm vehicle are natural, bearing in mind the reasons for its introduction in the first place. But in those

uncertain days of 1948, when the success of the Land-Rover was still very much open to question, even the most optimistic of onlookers couldn't have predicted the diversity of jobs for which the Land-Rover would readily be used.

Ambulance and fire-engine conversions became fairly commonplace, and of course the Land-Rover quickly established itself as a more than competent Forces vehicle, with the British Army soon adopting it as their favourite means of transport and using it for innumerable tasks; in fact, with Land-Rover's export success over the years, the same can be said the world over and nowadays there are many, many countries using Land-Rovers as "official" vehicles.

Six-wheeled versions of the Land-Rover have also been around for a long time, as have specially modified Land-Rovers fully equipped for safaris. Because of the model's abilities at crossing treacherous terrain, safari-equipped Land-Rovers and even Land-Rover caravanettes have always seemed logical choices for anybody planning an expedition of some kind. The list of after-market conversions goes on.

The future?

It's impossible to know what will become of the Land Rover brand in the future, of course, though the iconic status of the Land Rover marque will surely live on for as long as there are vehicles on the road – and off it, naturally.

What can safely be said is that the original leaf-sprung versions of the Land Rover will, for some, be the only 'true' Land Rovers while for all Land Rover enthusiasts, they are the models that led to the extraordinary and, in many cases, historic range of vehicles that have carried the Land Rover name.

It is a remarkable history for a marque that came about mainly because of one man's reluctance to buy a *foreign-built* utility vehicle for his farm in Anglesey!

Model identification

by Brian Bashall of Dunsfold Land-Rover

PM1. Fifty pre-production Land-Rovers were built in 1947/48, all with 80 in wheelbases. Half were right-hand-drive, half left-hand-drive, and all of them had a galvanized chassis and were finished in Sage Green. The example shown here carries chassis No.8.

PM2. Three of the surviving pre-production Land-Rovers, all of them lovingly restored; almost half the pre-production run, is thought to survive. All the prototypes used 1.5-litre engines, plus permanent four-wheel-drive, making use of the Rover freewheel unit on the front of the transfer box.

PM3. Yet more Land-Rovers from the pre-production "batch". It is thought by many that the Sage Green colour was actually an ex-air force cockpit green, which had an egg-shell finish rather than a gloss. Anyone restoring a particularly early example may well need to recreate such a finish rather than go for the conventional gloss. The original-spec. paint is still available from Dunsfold Land-Rover who have had it specially formulated.

PM4. The classic "shovel" seat backs, as fitted to the very early models. The seat cushion was by Dunlopillo, providing reasonable comfort.

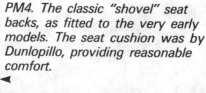

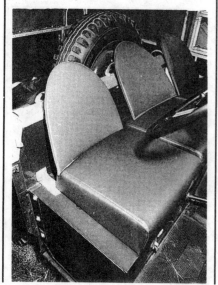

PM5. A general view, showing the pedal arrangement, grab handle right across the bulkhead, steering wheel with the horn push in the centre, and "crackle-finish" windscreen wiper motor. This particular vehicle is a military Land-Rover, identifiable by the two turnbuckles on the bottom of the windscreen, the bottom panel being an opening one unlike on the civilian models.

PM6. A well restored Series I, dating from around 1949. At this time, trafficators and a heater were optional extras at around £5 each! Exterior door handles weren't to appear until 1952.

PM7. The flat section of the hood hoops; the later ones had a slight bow in them to prevent water resting in the middle of the roof. The hood would have had perspex windows in the back flap which soon crazed over, so alternative replacements are now usually fitted. The agricultural plate on the rear crossmember was welded on to these early models.

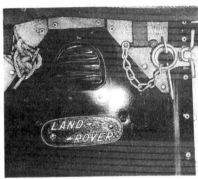

PM8. These D-shaped rear lights with the dividing bar on them are now strictly illegal, due to insufficient lens area, but were original equipment at the time. The later D-lights had no division. Needless to say, these early versions are now extremely rare.

PM9. This photograph shows the interior door lock arrangement (in the open position), the "shovel" seats, and the triangular flap in the door top through which you reach inside to open the door from outside! Also note the canvas flap down the back of the door top, with aluminium inside, to help keep the draught out. There are no door stays (apart from rubber "buffers" on the front wings!), and with the doors opened as far as possible the complete door assembly lifts straight off.

PM10. One of the very early, very rare estate cars produced from 1949 to 1951. This particular example, the earliest known surviving, is an export model.

PM11. Quite a rare model! An 80 in Hard Top, relatively few of which were made (this example, featuring rear windows, was built for export), dating from around 1951/2. Note the mud protectors on the exhaust – now quite an unusual feature. LSM was owned by the author until quite recently. ▶

PM12. A home-market 80 in Hard Top, featuring an early grille but is actually a slightly later-model Land-Rover, identifiable by the wing-mounted sidelights and external door handles. When the 86 in Land-Rover was later launched, it used the same 2-litre engine (complete with by-pass oil filter), but because of head-gasket problems with this bored-out-1.6-litre engine, the bores were changed before Rover changed over to a "full-flow" engine in the 88 in of 1957. Over-size tyres are fitted.

PM13. A detailed shot of the front badging, complete with the Station Wagon title that slips under the front badge and also appears on the rear of the vehicle.

PM14. An 86 in Hard Top, as opposed to a Station Wagon, with a lift-up flap at the rear – no "tropical roof" and no seats in the back. Note the more substantial door lock arrangement and better sealing. This particular vehicle has been re-registered sometime in the last few years.

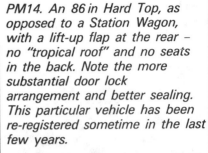

PM15. The cabin arrangement of the 86 in and 107 in models, complete with pedals that come through into the vehicle at a sensible angle instead of sticking up through the floor like a couple of stalks on the 80 in! These models still used the old worm-and-nut steering box system, whereas later versions used a recirculating-ball set-up.

◄
PM16. The burnished aluminium finish of this Land-Rover is obviously non-standard, but it's nice to see as a demonstration of how much of a Land-Rover is made of aluminium-alloy!

PM17. The 107 in Station Wagon – not the most attractive of Land-Rovers but certainly rare, and consequently of interest to the serious enthusiast. This example is thought to date from around 1957.

PM18. An 88 in Series I Station Wagon of 1956/57 vintage . . .

PM19. . . . superbly restored and in immaculate condition throughout.

PM20. One of the most popular Land-Rovers, the Series IIA, is typified by this all-original 1966 example. The IIA was introduced in 1961 to replace the Series II. This is the Land-Rover currently owned by the Author and restored by Dunsfold Land-Rover as the main project vehicle for this book. This is FVJ in 'before' condition: not bad at all!

PM21. Another 1966 Series IIA, albeit less original! Non-standard fitments include radial tyres, air horns and the like, but it does illustrate another version of the IIA – a Hard Top with windows.

PM22. A very late Series IIA with a six-cylinder engine (identifiable by a heavier exhaust that comes out through the wing), the six-cylinders being introduced in 1967. Note the headlamps now being fitted on the front wings for the first time, to comply with Australian lighting regulations. Shown here is a 109 in Station Wagon.

PM23. The front end of a Series 3, complete with plastic radiator grille, introduced in late 1971. Also new were an all-synchromesh gearbox, plastic dashboard, improved heater arrangement and a diaphragm clutch. Rumour has it that many Australians disliked this model because they couldn't remove the radiator grille and cook their steaks over it, like they'd been used to with the previous models!

PM24 Series III heater inlet grille, positioned in the front left-hand wing to avoid most of any debris that might be flying around. ◄

PM25. The headlamp and ► sidelight arrangement of the Series III. Incidentally, a headlamps-in-the-wings conversion can be carried out on any elderly Land-Rover, whilst still retaining the original headlamps as a pair of "spots". The wing-mounted lights ensure a much better lighting pattern for the road ahead.

23

PM26. A Series III seven-seater Station Wagon, with such standard luxuries as headlining, sliding windows and individual seats in the rear. With a little more in the way of creature comforts, this model makes an ideal family vehicle. Classed as a passenger car, it was liable for car tax as well as purchase tax/VAT when new. ►

PM27. A Series III 109 in 12-seater, featuring a central bench seat behind the front seats and a pair of sideways-facing bench seats behind that. Legroom in the back is strictly limited. This model escaped car tax by being classed as a bus! ▲

PM28. Still on the Series III ► theme, here is a 109 in Hard Top. This is an export model, with rubber-mounted side windows fitted as standard (they weren't standard fitments on UK-sale models as the vehicles would then have attracted car tax!).

PM29. If you decide to convert a Hard Top to a "Station Wagon" by fitting side windows and rear seats, you should inform Customs & Excise to enable them to charge you some tax! As far as they're concerned, you're turning a van into a passenger car and, as such, should pay 10% car tax (worked out on the value of the vehicle).

PM30. One of the last Series III models built by Land-Rover, in 1983, and used as a promotional vehicle complete with plastic panels in the bonnet and doors to let everyone see inside. This unique example is now housed safely in the Heritage museum. Alongside is the first of the County One Ten models, the first production Land-Rover to feature coil-spring suspension.

PM31. CWK 30Y is the prototype Land-Rover 90, with many different features to the production ones. The wheelbase is exactly 90 in, there are no "eyebrows" round the wheel arches, there is a 2 and 4-wheel drive gearbox (four-speed) and the whole vehicle is almost a pinned together hybrid based on a shortened One Ten chassis. Note imitation split windscreen to detract attention away from this prototype.

PM32. CWK 40Y is the No. 2 prototype of the Land-Rover 90 Series, an unusual combination of a $92\frac{1}{8}$ in wheelbase and a modified 88 in body and hard top. The petrol-filler is in the normal 88 in position.

PM33. The interior of a One Ten, from around 1984, complete with wind-down windows for the first time! Engine options now included the 3528cc V8, at first, and 2¼-litre petrol and diesel units later giving way to two-and-a-half litre units. Introduced in March 1983, 110 in models offered coil sprung suspension, five-speed gearbox and permanent four-wheel-drive á la Range Rover.

PM34. The Land-Rover Ninety Pick-Up, with Range Rover coil-spring suspension, a special chassis, five-speed manual gearbox and a choice of 2.5-litre petrol or diesel engines. For 1991, the 200 Tdi engine was introduced to this model.

PM35. Also available in the Ninety Series are the Hard Top 'van'...

PM36. ... and the rather neat looking County Station Wagon, bringing the traditional Land-Rover shape more up to date. The 90 Station Wagon has now been supplemented by the Discovery in the UK market.

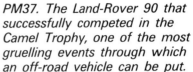

PM37. The Land-Rover 90 that successfully competed in the Camel Trophy, one of the most gruelling events through which an off-road vehicle can be put.

PM38. A One Ten County Station Wagon, criticised by some for being too luxurious – its list of equipment included tinted windows, side-stripes, halogen headlamps, cloth seats and so on. If you intend using your Land-Rover for high mileage, everyday motoring, this is one of the most user-friendly models available secondhand! Like the previous long-wheelbase Station Wagons, this vehicle is exempt from UK Car Tax at the time of writing. ◀

PM39. In 1986, the Diesel Turbo was introduced, providing 28% more torque, 25% more power but still with excellent economy. The engine shown here is the 200Tdi unit, easily the most reliable diesel engine that Land-Rover has ever built.

PM40. In September 1990, Defender model names were introduced; this is a 90 in Hardtop 'working' version. The name 'Defender' helped to differentiate the more traditional Land-Rover from the company's all-new 'Discovery' models.

PM41. The 110 in, this one a luxurious, Turbo Diesel Tdi Station Wagon, offering comfort a-plenty. The direct injection turbocharged diesel engine was introduced along with the Defender name.

PM42. A "stretched" One Ten, now known as the Defender 130, with a 127 in wheelbase and crewcab. A popular choice with those customers who need to carry a "crew" and require a large load capacity.

PM43. One of five 129 in one-and-a-half-ton prototype trucks produced, this one with a six-cylinder engine.

PM44. This 80 in chassis (No. 416) dating from 1948, and photographed alongside the latest Discovery production line, was rebuilt as a rolling chassis by Dunsfold Land-Rover. The production line is virtually where the first Land-Rovers were assembled all those years ago.

Land-Rover Variants and Military Vehicles

V&M1. An army Land-Rover of 1949 vintage, with a one-piece grille across the tiny headlamps, and sidelights mounted on the bulkhead. Army Land-Rovers looked like this up until 1951. In 1952, a 2-litre engine was fitted to the Land-Rover (in place of the 1.5-litre unit), together with wider front springs, external door handles plus other, fairly minor improvements.

V&M2. An ex-Ministry vehicle (identified by the "RGC" registration number), boasting much improved weather protection compared with the "standard" models. This particular model is a seven-seater station wagon with a "tropical roof" and the Station Wagon rear door. Quite a desirable little model! "RGC"s and "SXF"s were mostly civil defence contract models.

V&M3. Ever since the Land-Rover's launch, custom-built versions have been produced for special purposes. This Forward Control 110 IIB model (the IIB was available in four or six-cylinder form) was produced for the Fire service, although other public corporations also appreciated the merits of the Forward Control model.

V&M4. The Lightweight Land-Rover, a ½-ton model specially produced for military use, featured narrowed axles (the width was the same as the old Series I models to enable them to fit in "Andover" aircraft) and special lightweight bodywork, again with air-lifting in mind. This example has been customised slightly, with bigger wheels and tyres and a hard-top. The name Lightweight is somewhat confusing, as this model was actually heavier than the civilian Land-Rovers but lighter than the "usual" military ones.

V&M5. An interesting shot of a Lightweight Land-Rover and a very late Series IIa – compare the differences!

V&M6. Another variation, this time the 101 in Forward Control 1-Ton complete with V8 engine, (modified) Range Rover gearbox and permanent four-wheel-drive. More Land-Rovers destined for military use! The sides could be removed to provide an ideal off-road military platform; just 2,000 were produced.

V&M7. This interesting conversion, complete with caterpillar tracks, was carried out by Cuthbertson and was based on a 1959 109 in Land-Rover (short-wheelbase and Lightweight versions were also available). Ideally suited to forestry work, the tracks and running gear were detachable, enabling the vehicle to be used "normally" once again! Steering was a problem, with a lack of power steering (obviously!) on the early models. They were also criticised for lack of power and an overstressed transmission.

V&M8. Another Land-Rover ideally suited to forestry work was the logically named Forest Rover, boasting a very high ground clearance and excellent cross-country abilities. This model dates from 1964.

V&M9. Made in Spain under Rover licence for the Spanish army, this 1968 1-Ton Land-Rover Santana boasts a 3.5-litre straight-six engine developed from the four-cylinder Land-Rover engine. Other features included a lockable centre differential and lashing points on the wheels enabling the vehicle to be either air-lifted or tied down!

V&M10. This APGP (Air-Portable General Purpose) Land-Rover had air-bags that were inflated by the exhaust system, plus a totally different and sealed body. The chassis was full of "floatation foam" and a propeller was fitted to the rear propshaft. Just 21 examples were built and about four are thought to still exist.

V&M11. Portuguese assembled 1-ton Land-Rover with a specially produced pick-up body at the rear and a soft-top cab.

V&M12. A Shorland armoured car based on a Land-Rover 1-Ton military chassis, built for light patrol and airfield defence duties. Several hundred were made, many of them exported throughout the world.

V&M13. VXC 100F, an example of what is known as the "Big Lightweight", the proper title for which is the 110 Bonneted Control. It was fitted with a six-cylinder 3-litre engine. It was about 10 in wider than the normal Land-Rover and could boast truly excellent off-road capabilities. Just two were made, both of which survive today. (Courtesy Dunsfold Land-Rover Museum.)

V&M14. Nicknamed the "Pink Panther", this S.A.S. vehicle was converted by Marshalls of Cambridge and used mainly for patrol work. Many were exported to desert regions and were painted a sandy-pink colour to blend in with their surroundings, hence the nickname. Out of the 72 produced, more than twenty are still around. Three men could survive for up to ten days in a "Pink Panther", thanks to the on-board extra food, water and fuel supplies. Machine guns, self-loading rifles and smoke launchers complete the specification! (Courtesy Dunsfold Land-Rover Museum.)

V&M15. A beautiful example of a model recently restored by the experts at Dunsfold Land-Rover. (Courtesy Dunsfold Land-Rover Museum.)

V&M16. It arrived as a total wreck, with one side of the body completely missing, and finally emerged in its current pristine condition after a complete last-nut-and-bolt rebuild. (Courtesy Dunsfold Land-Rover Museum.)

V&M17. "CXC", the very first Lightweight Land-Rover produced and another example of a Dunsfold restoration. (Courtesy Dunsfold Land-Rover Museum.)

V&M18. An unusual conversion based on a 107 in model – a golf ball collector! This was one of the first long-wheelbase Series Ones, from around 1955/56.

V&M19. Another of the five 129 in one-and-a-half ton trucks that were built. This one was fitted with a six-cylinder engine, although some had intercooled turbo diesel units despite dating from as far back as 1961!

V&M20. A Forest Rover, one of eight still surviving, with its enormous tractor wheels, special axles and heavily modified bodywork. They were built by Roadless Traction in 1963 and 1964, especially for forestry use, being ideal for driving over tree trunks and exceptionally rough terrain. ►

V&M21. The Cuthbertson ▲ *conversion again, complete with caterpillar tracks and enormous ground clearance. Built in around 1960, the company also converted short-wheelbase versions.*

V&M22. Off-roading takes on a whole new meaning! A 1960 Series II diesel that was converted to railway use for 'shunting' duties.

V&M23. The APGP (Air Portable General Purpose) Land-Rover, was just one of several such conversions to provide amphibious motoring for military use.

V&M24. APGP's were designed for easy transportation, two of them stacked here ready for their forthcoming flight! ▼

V&M25. A much later (1988) ▲ amphibious Land-Rover, based on the standard 90 model. It still relied on the large, side-mounted 'floats' for buoyancy.

V&M26. The 1967 110 in bonneted-control model known as the 'Big Lightweight'. It had the provision for pulling a power-driven trailer, thanks to a twin transfer box.

V&M27. One of the very first Series IIA Forward Control 109 in models, whose claim to fame was that 70% of its parts were straight from the bonneted-control 109 in Land-Rover. To be able to use so many standard Land-Rover parts in the maintenance of a Forward Control model was (and still is) a great bonus to owners.

V&M28. A prototype for the Series IIB Forward Control Land-Rover, still using many of the IIA parts but with the IIB's longer wheelbase (110 in), wider front axle, anti-roll bars and a totally re-designed chassis. ►

V&M29. A six-wheel-drive ▲ Suntrekker conversion, modified in the mid-1960s and ideal for desert and safari work.

V&M30. A Land-Rover caravanette, courtesy of well-known converters Martin Walter. The four-cylinder versions were a bit 'gutless', although this particular example from 1973 used the six-cylinder engine. The tilting roof contained two bunks, with a double-bed conversion below to make this a four-berth vehicle.

Range Rover and Discovery

RR&D1. At its launch in 1989, the Land-Rover Discovery was available only in three-door form (the five-door didn't arrive until the following year).

RR&D2. The Discovery's interior was a revelation for Land-Rover, it being designed by an 'outside' company of stylists. The Discovery is short of nothing in the way of creature comforts.

RR&D3. Discovery was launched with a choice of two engines, the petrol model being fitted with the carburettored V8 engine shown here. (Fuel injection didn't arrive until the 1991 model year.) Also available was the new 200 Tdi direct-injection turbo diesel unit. ▼

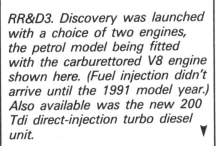

RR&D4. A front view of the ▲ Land-Rover Discovery, its smart styling and upmarket image enabling it to compete with the wide variety of Japanese models on offer.

RR&D5. Despite its upmarket ▲ profile, the Discovery is a useful vehicle; shown here are the optional two rear seats, enabling the vehicle to become a fairly roomy seven-seater family car.

RR&D6. A 1990 Range Rover ▲ Vogue, the ultimate in luxury from Land-Rover. Detail changes have been introduced throughout the Range Rover's life, this particular model being fitted with the viscous coupling transfer box. Simply select high or low ratio and let the vehicle do the rest!

The visually similar, Range Rover Vogue Turbo D relies on a 2.5-litre VM turbo-diesel engine for its power. Luxury and reasonable economy all in one!

◄

RR&D7. Goodies abound in this really upmarket Vogue SE! A few years ago, the idea of Land-Rover producing a vehicle with an interior as plush as this would have been considered ludicrous.

RR&D8. In its latest form, the venerable Rover V8 is a 3.9-litre unit with electronic fuel injection. A far cry from the de-tuned V8 Land-Rovers of a few years ago.

RR&D9. 20 Years of Range Rover. The vehicle on the left, YVB 172H, is owned by Dunsfold Land-Rover's Brian Bashall. Land-Rover made 22 pre-production launch vehicles, all with YVB registration numbers and with quite a number of odd features, such as aluminium bonnet and peculiar dashboard and gearchange arrangements. All the YVBs are recorded and there are about 12 out of the 22 still surviving.

RR&D10. YVB 153H is the earliest one still surviving today and shows the axle articulation.

RR&D11. Aerial view of a left-hand drive Range Rover. This one is actually in the Service School at Land-Rovers, being used daily by students. ▼

RR&D12. YVB 160H. A nice ▲ view of the pristine interior.

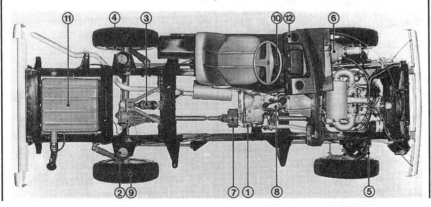

2 Buying

Which Model?

With so many different models of Land-Rover to choose from on the second-hand market, the decision of exactly which one to go for is not easy to reach. Any vehicle still in production after more than four decades will inevitably provide the purchaser with headaches and complications, simply because of the bewildering variety of different versions on sale.

The Land-Rover is no exception. It has certainly had its fair share of changes in specification over the years, even though Land-Rover have never been noted for alterations simply to follow fashions or trends. Potential purchasers of second-hand Land-Rovers should tread carefully and make a conscious decision about which Land-Rover best suits their needs before scouring the classified ads.

While it is the Land-Rover's unbeatable off-road capabilities that attract most people to the marque, it is a fact that a large proportion of Land-Rover buyers don't *need* such abilities for most of their driving time. It is essential that, as a potential Land-Rover purchaser, you examine your *own* needs and make your choice accordingly,

based on which model is most suitable for the demands you're sure to place upon it.

When the Land-Rover was launched in 1948, its designers would probably have laughed at any suggestion that it would ultimately become a fashionable vehicle to be seen in, rather than simply the agricultural aid it was intended to be. For those who *do* buy a Land-Rover for its now-trendy image, the ideal choice is one of two extremes – either an immaculately-kept, late-model County in Ninety or One Ten form *or* a particularly battered Series II or IIA short-wheelbase model, complete with dents-a-plenty and, of course, faded green paintwork.

For the rest of us, whether or not we admit to spending 99% of "Land Roving" time *on* the road, the purchase of a second-hand Land-Rover is a sensible and economical proposition. Nobody can deny that four-wheel-drive abilities *are* useful when we encounter the worst of the British winter, and it's most refreshing to own a vehicle that, in many cases, isn't greatly affected by the odd scratch or dent. Then there's the Land-Rover's rugged simplicity when it comes to maintenance, repair and restoration.

If off-road abilities are of paramount importance to you,

the obvious choice is a *short-wheelbase* example, simply because there is less length to get stuck on ridges, though if you do a lot of cross-country driving and would like a comfortable ride too, then a late-model One-Ten is ideal. Of course, for the ultimate in ground clearance, a Forward-Control Land-Rover is just the job, though this is a *true* commercial vehicle (a lorry in every sense of the word), with virtually nothing in the way of interior appointments.

If you anticipate mainly *on*-road driving, a petrol-engined Land-Rover will provide you with reasonable performance, though try to go for a six-cylinder or V8 version if possible – provided that you can stand the extra fuel consumption of the big 6 – as the four-cylinder models are slow by any standards! If money is tight, a diesel-engined Land-Rover will provide the best fuel economy by a large margin, but be prepared for a *very* leisurely drive . . .

While we all like to ponder on the best model for our needs, our eventual choice will depend very much on what we can afford. Still, *do* shop around as there is a surprising number of Land-Rovers to choose from even on a tight budget.

Whatever finances are available, above all be sensible – such rules as "Don't buy a Pick-Up if you regularly carry four passengers" and "Only choose a petrol-engined model if you can afford the petrol bills every week" should be self-evident!

Where To Look?

Once you've decided you want a Land-Rover, there should be no shortage of examples to check out. The money you have available will, of course, affect the age of the Land-Rover you can afford . . . and the age of the vehicle will, to a certain extent, affect where you see it advertised.

For late-model Land-Rovers, the obvious place to start is with an official Land-Rover dealer, who should have a reasonable stock of second-hand models in excellent condition, complete with service histories and warranties. These vehicles will certainly be at the more expensive end of the market though, simply because they will be comparatively young. Don't expect a *vast* choice of Land-Rovers of this ilk – people who buy brand new Land-Rovers tend to hang on to them for longer than a year or so!

If, like most potential purchasers, you're looking at models from the 1970s, '60s or even 1950s, you should find some on sale in the classified ads of your local newspapers. You may find that there's even a Land-Rover specialist local to you who buys and sells relatively inexpensive examples of the marque.

With the Land-Rover's increasing popularity as a slightly different "classic" vehicle, you'll find more and more of them appearing for sale in some of the popular classic car magazines. Then of course there are those magazines specialising in nothing but four-wheel-drive vehicles, so again it's worth checking the classified columns.

Finally, but certainly not bottom of the list of priorities, there are the clubs – whether they cater for nothing but Land-Rovers or simply for four-wheel-drive vehicles in general, they should provide Vehicles For Sale sections in their magazines and newsletters, and there will be the obvious benefit of personal contact with many of their members. Details of clubs can be found in the Appendices later in the book.

Golden Rules

If you're thinking of buying a Land-Rover for restoration, it is essential that you work out a personal budget – a *maximum* that you would want to spend in total. Knowing this limit, together with the asking price of the vehicle, a note should be made of the estimated cost of restoring the Land-Rover you're inspecting to the standard you require. And make sure you *over*-estimate the cost of restoration to avoid difficulties later on. If restoration costs plus purchase price exceed the budget figure, then it may be time to review the purchase price or consider an alternative example.

By doing research beforehand on the cost of replacement parts and the labour involved, you will save both time and money later. Then, while inspecting a vehicle of your choice, following the guidelines set out later in this chapter, you can methodically make a note of each and every fault and work out a rough guide to the cost of parts. You will also have a fairly thorough idea of what needs tackling for the restoration, enabling you to sit down later and decide on the "running order" of tasks.

Before going along to see any Land-Rover, get as much information as possible by telephone, bearing in mind that many vendors will exaggerate the condition of their vehicles enormously! Asking lots of questions over the 'phone will save time ultimately however, though it is a good idea to look at several Land-Rovers before you start the buying procedure, simply to get a "feel" for what sort of questions you need to ask.

When looking at any Land-Rover, you should take with you: overalls, a good torch, a large strong screwdriver for levering and poking at rust, ramps, a trolley jack and a flat board for lying under the car. Allow yourself plenty of time for the visit as you will miss the points if you are rushed or uncomfortable, and don't let the vendor's conversation distract you from the job in hand.

Safety First!
Remember: When inspecting a car, don't forget safety. NEVER rely on the handbrake to hold a car that is on a slope or up on ramps. Ensure that the wheels are chocked when using jacks or ramps. Use axle stands if you have to inspect the underside of the car. Do not use a naked flame when inspecting the underside of a car.

What To Look For!

One of the most popular versions of the Land-Rover to buy second-hand (and there are still a good many offered for sale, despite their age), is the Series IIA that ran from 1961 to '71, with almost half a million examples produced in that time. The IIA is also one of the most affordable Land-Rover variants available . . .

By detailing the points to watch out for on a Series IIA, we will be covering much of what to check for on *any* Land-Rover, though model-to-model differences will be mentioned where they affect buying procedures.

Bodywork

The key to buying a good, reliable Series IIA Land-Rover is to look at the vehicle's condition rather than the year of registration, the latter being used only as a guide. Most Land-Rovers will have spent their entire lives outdoors and are quite happy to do so; the paintwork will be faded and streaked in places but is soon rejuvenated with an application of "T-Cut" and elbow grease!

The bodywork, being aluminium, does not deteriorate as badly as would an all-steel assembly. It will often be dented, though this should only be of minor consideration as the panels are readily available and easily replaced. There are, however, *some* parts on a Land-Rover that are made of steel and these can (and do!) corrode. The door tops are particularly prone to rust, especially in the window runners, and may require the fitting of replacements.

The Land-Rover's bulkhead is also made of steel, and corrosion is common in the footwells. Other areas may similarly show signs of decay, such as the base of the door pillars, around the door hinges, in the frames of the door bottoms and (on later Series III models) in the headlamp area at the front of the wings.

Chassis

Special attention should be paid to the condition of the chassis as it is this, more than any other part of a Land-Rover, that determines how much life there is left in the vehicle. Some repairs to the chassis are not unusual and, if done properly, should cause no problems. Replaced outriggers are common, as can be a replaced rear chassis member which suffers badly from corrosion on the 88-inch model, while the long-wheelbase variants in particular tend to rot around the spring mounts. Larger areas of the chassis should be examined just as thoroughly, as extensive rot may result in removing the complete bodyshell to provide access to the top face of the chassis frame.

While the chassis is prone to rust (often due to blocked drain holes), it can also get *damaged*, depending on how much off-road work has been encountered. Damaged crossmembers are not uncommon; it's even possible for the crossmember under the gearbox to be partially torn off, while that under the clutch housing can get pushed up against the housing so that any engine vibrations will be felt right through the vehicle. If you inspect a Land-Rover on which some of the crossmembers and outriggers have previously been replaced, you should always ask yourself *why* they needed replacing in the first place. The answer may provide you with an indication of the sort of treatment the vehicle has received over the years!

Engine

The principle engines installed in the Series IIA Land-Rover are the 2¼-litre four-cylinder petrol and diesel units, although alternative replacements may have been fitted over the years. Beware of any engine swaps and check workmanship carefully!

This petrol engine is rugged and reliable and, if well maintained, will seemingly go on forever. It may sound a little tappety, coughing and spluttering at times, and may even use a little too much oil, but by and large most faults (except the latter!) are easily put right with carburettor repair kits, tappet adjustment or some attention to the ignition system. Much the same can be said for the 2625cc six-cylinder petrol unit used in a great many Land-Rover variants.

The diesel engine is a little more complicated and, contrary to popular belief, tends not to last as long as the petrol equivalent as more is generally asked of it. The diesel is noisy even when in good condition; therefore, the best guide to engine wear is to remove the crank case breather filter and, while slowly increasing engine speed, check the quantity of emissions that come from it. In a worn engine, the pressure of emission caused by "blowby" will increase with rising RPM and, in extreme cases, may even throw out droplets of oil. This is because, with the higher compression ratios of the diesel engine, piston ring wear and worn bores are more readily detected by this method. A smokey exhaust, especially when the throttle is first opened, is an indication of worn or badly adjusted fuel injectors; the only remedy for this is to have them cleaned and recalibrated. The DPA fuel injector pump is normally trouble-free and reliable and, like the injectors, is way beyond the scope of the "home mechanic". They require high pressure test equipment and, because of the fine tolerances in their parts, demand scrupulously clean repair conditions, making it best to leave overhaul to a qualified expert.

Considering the Land-Rover's exceptionally long production run, engine changes so far have been *relatively* few. Apart from the 2286cc petrol

and diesel units detailed above, other power-plants include the 1595cc and 1997cc four cylinder petrol engines (used very early on in the Land-Rover's life); the 2625cc six-cylinder diesel engine; the early-model 2052cc and late-model 2494cc four-cylinder diesel units; and, of course, the 3528cc V8 petrol engine. In later life, the latter diesel engine mentioned was also offered in turbocharged form.

Like the engines used in the Series IIA, *all* Land-Rover engines are renowned for their longevity and reliability. They are basically simple in design and the same sort of checks you would make to any car engine before purchase should be carried out on "your" prospective Land-Rover.

As mentioned earlier, the 2286cc Series IIA petrol engine can suffer from excessive oil consumption; this suggests worn rubber sealing rings in the valve guides. Four-cylinder engines have a different type of valve gear to the six-cylinder models, with pad-type cam followers instead of the six-cylinder roller type, these followers eventually wearing, leading to a knocking sound from the engine's top end.

The V8 petrol engine, though essentially as robust as the smaller units, is more difficult to keep in tune. It will also suffer more than most if its oil is not changed regularly. One of its weaknesses lies in the valve gear, where a build-up of sludge can affect the efficiency of the hydraulic tappets, leading to premature wear and, eventually, even wear of the camshaft. When cold, the V8 engine may give a slight "knock" from the top end; if this doesn't disappear when warm, all the signs point to camshaft problems. Repairs are expensive, especially as there are usually eight or 16 of everything.

Standard engine-bay checks to make before buying *any*

second-hand vehicle (and the Land-Rover is no exception) include:

1). Check oil and water levels, brake and clutch fluid and fan belt tension. Is there any "white emulsion" deposited inside the oil filler cap and the rocker cover?

2). Start the engine and listen for any untoward rumbles or rattles, as mentioned earlier.

3). Depress the clutch pedal with the engine running and listen for the whirr of a worn release bearing.

4). Examine oil and air filters for signs of fairly recent renewal – if not, the engine could well have been neglected.

5). Look around the engine for signs of new gaskets, evidence of recent dismantling or any other work – and ask what and why!

6). Check for oil and water leaks and examine water hoses – check radiator for signs of repair.

7). Check engine mountings for signs of wear.

8). Look at the condition of the battery and terminals.

9). Feel for leaks under the carburettor and fuel pump/piping.

Clutch

The Land-Rover's clutch is a heavy duty unit that is built to last and should give little trouble. A "slipping" clutch normally indicates that replacement is necessary, while a "juddering" clutch can point to other defects in the drive-line, such as worn or loose engine mountings and/or worn propeller shaft universal joints or could stem from a small amount of oil on the clutch plate. A one-off freak or (more likely) a leaking oil seal? The clutch plate is quite easily replaced by separating the gearbox from the engine and moving the box rearward as far as it will go. This leaves sufficient room to

enable clutch replacement to be carried out.

Gearbox/Transfer Boxes

The gearbox is a rugged unit built to take the heavy loads that are demanded of it. It is among the most difficult part of the Land-Rover to work on and involves dismantling the seat unit to remove it for repairs, so it's essential before you buy your Land-Rover that you ensure the gearbox is in good working order.

Potential gearbox troubles include oil leaks, jumping out of gear and noisy gears, all of which indicate a high mileage vehicle or one that has led a hard life. Check underneath for signs of a leak; and listen particularly well when the vehicle is driven in first gear as this is likely to be the noisiest of all the gears. The all-synchromesh 'box of later Land-Rovers is slightly weaker than the earlier type, and may lose its synchromesh on first and second gears, first gear even chipping teeth in extreme circumstances.

To check the common tendency for second and third gears to jump out of mesh, select each gear in turn and, whilst moving at a reasonable speed, dab and release the accelerator quickly a few times; watch the selector to see if it jumps out of gear. If all is well, stop the vehicle and select reverse gear, then sharply back-up for a few yards, listening for knocking noises from the gearbox. These usually indicate chipped teeth in the gear train.

The transfer box is invariably trouble-free and rarely causes any problems. To check, however, select high and low ratios in turn to ensure correct operation. The four-wheel-drive selector should be checked by depressing it on the move in high ratio; then stop the vehicle and pull the red control back

into low range. The yellow four-wheel-drive selector control should pop up smartly if all is well. If it doesn't the answer could be mud and corrosion; but it could be Trouble! You'll need to take a look underneath.

Propshaft and Differentials

Worn universal joints on the propshaft can normally be detected by clutch judder and excessive vibration; the UJs are easily replaced and should be of little consequence to the prospective buyer. The differentials may be checked for wear by placing chocks under the vehicle's wheels and, with the handbrake released and neutral selected, trying to turn the propshaft by hand. Any more than a quarter turn of the propshaft indicates a worn differential, the rear differential usually being the one to show the most wear. Even these units can be re-adjusted and, where necessary, new thrust washers fitted. Clunks and knocks in the driveline are quite normal, with gearbox and differential whine not uncommon. A prospective purchaser should not be put off if all else seems to be in good order.

One point to mention is that, with 88-inch and especially 109-inch Land-Rovers without heavy-duty axles, the rear half-shafts can snap at their inner ends but there is no way of telling whether this is about to happen!

Steering

Check the steering for excessive backlash, which may indicate worn swivel pins and bearings in the front wheel assemblies.

A certain amount of free-play in the steering should be expected and can usually be reduced by adjustment at the steering box. Check that the steering box is secure on its mounting bracket and that the steering relay is secure in its housing in the front chassis crossmember. Linkage is by tie-rod and ball joint and the latter should be checked for wear. The relay often leaks oil but this is not generally considered to be serious.

Although hard-wearing, the Land-Rover's steering components can, of course, get damaged so check carefully for this. Also, look out for leaks from the steering box, though this is not too serious a fault; on later Land-Rovers fitted with power assisted steering however, a major fluid leak from the power steering system can be expensive to rectify, so check carefully before purchase.

Swivel Pins and Universal Joint Housing

Check the condition of the swivel housings. They are chrome plated and should be clean and free from pitting; if badly pitted, they will be useless and costly to replace, both in time and parts. Some leakage from the housing seal is to be expected, but signs of excessive oil loss could mean worn swivel pins. These are visible from underneath and behind the wheels, emerging from a housing onto which the brake backplate is fitted; when the axle is *safely* jacked up (do not go beneath the vehicle), they can be checked by firmly grasping the top of the tyre and moving it sharply in and out. *Some* movement is acceptable but, if excessive, this usually indicates worn swivel pins or bearings. If this movement stops when you apply the brakes, then check out your bearings as the swivels are probably working well.

Brakes

The Land-Rover's braking system is of proven design and should give little trouble. Routine replacement of brake shoes is fairly simple and repair kits are available for the slave and master cylinders and also for the brake adjusters if these need attention. Check that the brake pipes are firmly anchored to the chassis and are free from corrosion or damage; it is possible for the brake pipe anchor plates to be "eaten away" by rust, leaving the actual pipes hanging loose and likely to get caught and torn away by the next bit of rough terrain you might encounter. The flexible pipes to the front brakes should be sound and free from cracks in the rubber.

Land-Rover brake problems are often connected with the handbrake, which of course is a drum type operating directly on the transmission and not on the rear wheels. (For this reason, the handbrake should *never* be tested by applying it when the vehicle is on the move.) Oil leaks from the drums are common but are easily cured with a new seal and linings, while the ratchet may also be worn but again is easy to replace.

Suspension

Apart from the Ninety and One Ten models (which were the first Land-Rovers to use coil spring suspension, and which are recent enough to still be financially out of reach for a great many Land-Rover enthusiasts), Land-Rovers use semi-elliptic leaf springs and telescopic shock absorbers, the latter mounted on rubber bushes at their top and bottom ends. They should be firmly attached but these bushes do wear and their replacement should be considered normal. Likewise the chassis and spring bushes may be worn and in some cases the shackle plate and spring securing bolts will

also need to be changed, but this is a straightforward and inexpensive operation. The springs, however, should be in good condition and free from rust, which tends to splay and distort them, eventually causing fractures. The swinging shackle on the front springs should be as near vertical as possible and the spring's leaves of equal thickness throughout their length.

The rear shackles should lie at about 15 – 20 degrees and, once again, the spring leaves should be of uniform thickness over their whole length. Look at the ends of each spring leaf, where most of the wear takes place, and check its thickness. If you need to change a spring it is essential to remember that they are handed, ie, the spring for the driver's side has more camber than that for the passenger's side. This takes into account the weight of the driver. Springs for the diesel-engined Land-Rovers are a heavier duty type than those for the petrol models.

It is not uncommon to find a Land-Rover fitted with wrong-spec. replacement springs and this could affect the handling quite badly.

Interior

Unless you're buying a top-of-the-range, late-model Land-Rover with all the trimmings, the Land-Rover you eventually choose will probably have an interior that is spartan in the extreme!

This lack of luxury is probably a great bonus to the buyer of a well-used example though. You needn't worry about scuffing the upholstery or damaging the internal paintwork if the interior is already well and truly battered; and, thanks to the back-to-basics approach of Land-Rover when it came to the interior designs of pre-V8 models, the fact that there are no carpets and no such

extravagances as cloth upholstery to worry about means the interior in general will have worn reasonably well, even if "your" Land-Rover has led a particularly tough life.

It is very much up to the individual to decide how fussy he or she wants to be about the condition of your prospective Land-Rover. If you don't care about torn upholstery or general tattiness, you probably won't be disappointed! But *do* check carefully any interior items that are essential to safety: look out for frayed or torn seat belts, severely cracked or damaged steering wheels, defective instruments and so on, all of which are potential MoT failure points and general safety hazards. While on the subject of seat belts, it is worth bearing in mind that, in the UK, pre-1965 cars do not legally require seat belts to be fitted, although if they *are* fitted they must obviously be in good condition.

UK Tax Exemption

Cars built before 1 January 1973 are exempt from UK vehicle excise duty ('car tax'). The important point here, especially for cars first registered in early '73 or later imports, is that the relevant date is the build date, *not* the date of first registration. If you provide Land-Rover with the chassis number (VIN), they will give you the evidence you will need to claim tax exemption from your local Driver Vehicle Licencing Centre.

Classic Car Insurance

If you own a 'classic' Land-Rover, you can save money and ensure that you aren't caught in the 'old-car-not-worth-much' insurance trap.

Classic car insurance is usually cheaper than private motor insurance. This is because classic vehicles are generally

used less than the main family vehicle and with extra care, making them a good risk as the likelihood of a claim is lower.

Naturally enough, most insurance companies will set some restrictions to qualify for this. Models considered to be 'classics', are usually supported by an owners club. In addition, all insurers specify that the car must be at least a certain number of years old, while in many cases, it must be not the main vehicle or be used for more than a specified annual mileage. Often, you can choose the mileage that suits you, but the lower this is the lower the premium is likely to be.

However, there is one cardinal rule that must be remembered before insuring your 'classic' Land-Rover. Make sure you can agree the value of your vehicle with your insurer before taking out the insurance. Some may have insufficient experience to be know what a vehicle's true value is and try to fob you off with a value that is too low. I know because it's happened to me! Agreeing the value before committing to the insurance is the only way to protect your investment, should the worst come to the worst.

One thing is for sure. If your vehicle is eligible, you really should consider an agreed value classic car insurance policy.

3 Bodywork

Bodywork restoration

More than almost any other vehicle on the road, the Land-Rover is just a giant kit of parts! It was deliberately made to be a vehicle that can be unbolted and bolted together at will and, although the aluminium outer panels are difficult to repair by virtue of the fact that they are of aluminium, they could not be simpler to remove. At least, that's the theory! In practise, the body panels on any older Land-Rover will be held in place with nuts and bolts that are well rusted in and so the first step in bodywork repair is to soak with releasing fluid, all the threads that you know you are going to have to undo. If you really want the releasing fluid to have a beneficial effect, carry this out several days before you intend to start work and then do the same thing again the day before. Even so, you will have to face up to the fact that some fixings will undoubtedly have to be drilled out. Equip yourself with a centre punch and a set of new, sharp drills. Take care not to slip sideways when drilling one of the obstinate fixings because the drill will cause severe damage in the soft aluminium panelling. Panels themselves are unlikely to be

corroded unless they are of steel – see later parts of this chapter – but they are quite likely to be damaged. Almost all Land-Rovers seem to have been treated roughly at some stage in their lives. However, you can take heart from the fact that all panels are still freely available for everything from Series II onwards, while many Series I panels are also available from specialists who also happen to be Land-Rover agents. Even the Series I panels that cannot be bought as original items are usually to be found as reproduction panels. You can't

expect these to be as good as the originals – and indeed they invariably are not – so some owners will set about repairing the originals or finding good quality replacements for their own damaged panels rather than buying repro. panels.

BOD1. The author's Series IIA Land-Rover prior to restoration – complete with the parts which will be used in its restoration. This particular Land-Rover was chosen for restoration because of the remarkable lack of damage to its inner and outer body panels.

Bodywork Notes

Land-Rover have always been aware of the needs of older-model owners, and as such pursue a policy of keeping as many spares available for all Land-Rover variants for as long as possible, although the Land-Rover company, Land-Rover Parts, is the *only* producer of official Land-Rover components. Of course, there *are* remanufactured and reproduction parts available elsewhere but, as always, it pays to buy the genuine article whenever possible. With a genuine front wing for your Series II supplied by your local Land-Rover dealer, you can rest assured that it will at least fit! You are strongly recommended to use only genuine Land-Rover parts. There must be no motor manufacturer that pays more scrupulous detail to engineering integrity. Non Land-Rover parts may look similar but it is almost certain that they will be of inferior quality.

"Our" Land-Rover

The model of Land-Rover we chose to restore in preparation for this book was 'FVJ', a 1966 Series IIA short-wheelbase. Many of the procedures shown and explained throughout the book will feature this model for illustrations, although much of what you see will be broadly similar, whether restoring a Series I, II, IIA or III Land-Rover. Where major differences in working procedures are known to exist between different models, they will be mentioned.

Hints, tips and equipment

Next to the necessary drive and

enthusiasm for seeing the job through, the most important factor which will enable a successful restoration to be carried out is a good set of tools. Like experience, a set of tools is not generally obtained overnight but over a much longer period. However, regarding bodywork repairs, some tools are more useful than others so below is given a general guide to the options available.

As the majority of us are not blessed with the unlimited funds required to have someone else do the work and because in the end, we really enjoy the satisfaction of doing the job ourselves, the first major item on the shopping list should be to obtain suitable welding equipment if chassis repairs have to be carried out. It need not be that expensive and even after only a few jobs, plus perhaps carrying out some work for friends, the equipment will pay for itself. Nowadays the customer is spoilt for choice. For the amateur, there is now a wide range of semi-professional welding gear available at affordable prices covering electric arc/brazing, spot welding and gas welding techniques. Each technique offers its own set of advantages.

Excellent machines for all three options are available from manufacturers such as Clarke, who are said to be the UK's largest supplier.
Welding Note: On models fitted with an alternator, *always* disconnect the alternator in order to prevent damage to it from the electric current which has to pass through the vehicle when MIG or arc welding is carried out.

Moving away from welding and into more general body work repair hand tools, top of the list must surely come one of the smaller 4 or 4½ in angle grinders, such as the type made by Black & Decker. Once used for cutting out rust areas,

grinding back welds, or sanding off paintwork with the sander attachment, you'll wonder how you managed without one! Wire brush attachments can also be obtained, although of course a standard electric drill will also do this job, but perhaps not as well.

A good quality pair of tin snips or an electric nibbler are also useful – blades on cheap items tend to blunt quite quickly. A range of panel beating hammers and dollies can be invaluable but rather than buy a full, cheap set, it may be more effective in the long term to buy a couple of good quality hammers and a single dolly. Further specialist tools the author has found useful include a pair of door skinner pliers obtained from Sykes-Pickavant and a joddler (for putting an indented edge in repair panels for flush fitting) with hole punch head (useful for preparing panels for MIG plug welding). Sykes-Pickavant in particular also market an excellent range of bench tools including sheet metal cutters and bending tools.

Technical Advice

The fact that the Land-Rover was originally designed with ease of construction high on the list of priorities is now much to the advantage of any owner or potential restorer. If the vehicle was fairly quick and easy to build in the first place, the same may well be true when it comes to restoring one many years later.

Allied to this simple construction is the Land-Rover's resistance to rust. With the exception of the radiator grille panel, dashboard panel, door frames and tailboard frame, which are made of steel, the body of the Land-Rover is made from a special light magnesium-

aluminium alloy known as "Birmabright", with steel cappings and corner brackets. *All* steel body parts were galvanised from new.

"Birmabright" was originally developed for aircraft use and was claimed to be much stronger than pure aluminium. It also melts at a much lower temperature and will neither rust nor corrode under normal circumstances. "Birmabright" is work-hardening, becoming hard and brittle when hammered, although it is easily annealed. Exposed to the atmosphere, a hard oxide skin will form on the surface of it.

Panel Beating "Birmabright"

"Birmabright" panels and wings can be beaten out after accidental damage in much the same way as sheet steel. As mentioned above though, this will lead to a hardening of the material, cured by applying heat to the metal followed by slow air-cooling (a process known as annealing). As the melting point of "Birmabright" is low however, it must be heated slowly and carefully; a rough but useful temperature control is to apply oil to the *cleaned* surface to be annealed. Play the welding torch on the underside of the cleaned surface and watch for the oil to clear, which it should do quite quickly, leaving the surface clean and unmarked. Then allow to cool naturally in the air, when the area being worked on should again be soft and workable. Do *not* cool quickly with water or oil!

Another method is to clean the surface to be annealed and then rub it with a piece of soap. Apply heat *beneath* the area, as described above, and watch for the soap stain to clear, then allow it to cool naturally.

When applying heat for annealing, always hold the torch some distance away from the metal and move it about to avoid any localised melting. You must practice each of these techniques on a scrap Land-Rover panel, or risk damaging one of your vehicle's panels irreversibly.

Riveting Panels

Three types of rivet are used on the body:
1) Aluminium pop or 'blind' rivets are used only on box sections or where it is difficult or impossible to use any other type because of limited working space; these rivets are 'snapped-up' from one side only. The setting is controlled by the breaking of a headed steel mandrel which passes through the tubular rivet; the mandrel break occurs only when the thickness being riveted has been pulled together tightly and the rivet head on the blind side fully formed. The mandrels are either of the break stem or break head type, the latter being used in positions where the mandrel head is free to fall away after the rivet head is set. Where it is required to retain the broken off portion of the mandrel within the headed-up part of the rivet, as for example in box sections (where a loose mandrel head would rattle), or for sealing the rivet with filler or stopper, the break stem type is used. Either a mechanical or pneumatic hand tool can be used for fixing pop rivets.
2) Bifurcated or 'split' rivets are used for securing rubber and canvas together or to metal. The rivet is passed through the materials to be joined, a boss cap is placed over the tongues of the rivet, and these tongues then spread with a suitable drift.
3) Various sizes and lengths of round head rivets are used, and for these a suitably indented dolly is needed for the rivet head, while the tail of the rivet is peened over with a hammer, operated manually, electrically, or by compressed air and the finished shape of the rivet is finished with a 'set'; a special punch made for use in conjunction with the dolly.

Gas welding

Thanks to the growth in the home restoration market of the last few years, suppliers of gas welding gear are now selling some excellent equipment, obtainable from national companies like BOC who market the 'Portapack' range of equipment by Murex.

Two types of gas welding equipment are available. The type supplied by BOC uses mini oxy-acetylene bottles hired for a period of a few years at a time and refilled at quite low cost as and when necessary. Cheaper systems use refillable oxygen bottles but with discardable gas canisters. Both types are effective although the latter is more difficult to use and *far* more expensive in terms of running costs. Gas welding remains the most versatile technique of all, but has a few drawbacks in that a higher level of skill is required (why not enrol in one of the many welding classes run by local authorities?) and that, if using acetylene, the gas bottles are less safe to store and use. (Also, check local by-laws regarding gas bottle storage.) Moreover, novice gas welded panels are almost certain to buckle and distort and will take a lot more work to be made to fit properly and to allow a smooth and ripple-free paint finish.

The Land-Rover workshop manual states that "Birmabright" can be gas welded without major problems, although in practice, the welding of aluminium and aluminium alloy is extremely difficult for all but the most experienced welder. The principle difficulty is that, unlike steel, which goes through red and yellow to white heat when it is melted, aluminium

displays no perceptible colour change before suddenly melting and 'flushing' away from the weld area before welding rod can be added. Don't practice on your Land-Rover's bodywork: buy a scrap panel from a breaker and practise on that.

If you really want to have a go, the following guidelines should be adhered to.

A small jet must be used, one or two sizes smaller than would be used for welding sheet steel of comparable thickness. For example, use a No.2 nozzle for welding 18swg (.048 in) sheet, and a No.3 for 16swg (.064 in) sheet. The flame should be smooth, quiet and neutral, although a slightly reducing flame may be used – in other words, there may be a *slight* excess of acetylene.

Use only 5% magnesium/aluminium welding rod, Sifalumin No.27 (use Sifbronze Special flux with this rod), or a thin strip cut from an old piece of "Birmabright"; do not use too wide or thick a strip though, as trouble may be experienced in making it melt before the material which is being welded!

Clean the surface of the panel being worked on to ensure it is free of all grease and paint, dry thoroughly and then clean the edges to be welded, plus an area at least half an inch either side of the weld, with a stiff wire brush or wire wool. Cleanliness is essential! Also clean the welding rod or strip with wire wool.

An acid flux must be used when welding "Birmabright", and you should follow the instructions *exactly* for whichever make of flux you decide upon (some flux is used in powder form, while some is mixed into a paste).

As we said earlier, one of the problems of welding aluminium and its alloys is that it doesn't go "red hot" before melting, and so there is nothing about the appearance of the

metal to show that it has reached welding temperature. With some experience, you will be able to gauge this point instinctively, but a useful guide initially is to sprinkle a little sawdust over the work; this will sparkle and char when the right temperature is approached.

As the flux you should use is highly acid, it is essential to wash it off thoroughly immediately after a weld is completed. The hottest possible water should be used, with wire wool or a stiff brush. Very hot, soapy water is ideal because of the alkaline nature of the soap, which will tend to "kill the acid". Wear protective rubber gloves and goggles.

Once again, we strongly recommend that you make a few welds on scrap "Birmabright" before an actual repair is undertaken if you are not already experienced in welding aluminium and its alloys.

The heat of welding will have softened the metal in the area of the repair, and it may be hardened again by peening with a light hammer. Many light blows are preferable to fewer heavy ones. Use a "dolly" or anvil behind the metal to prevent denting and to make the hammering more effective. If you overdo it, however, the metal will stretch and buckle. Filing off surplus metal from the weld will also help to harden the work again.

Welding Tears and Patching Metal

Although aluminium alloy will not rust, it is still prone to damage from general wear and tear, particularly if your Land-Rover has been subjected to a great deal of off-road use during its life.

If one of the body panels is "torn" and the tear extends to the edge of the panel, start the

weld from the end *away* from the edge; also at this point, drill a small hole to prevent the crack spreading.

When welding a long tear or making a long welded joint, tack the edges to be welded at intervals of 2-4ins (50-100mm) with "spots". This is done by melting the metal at the starting end and fusing into it a small amount of the filler rod, repeating the process at the suggested intervals. After this, weld continuously along the joint from right to left, increasing the speed of the weld as the material heats up. After the work has cooled, wash off all traces of flux as described earlier, and file off any excess of build-up metal.

When patching a hole in a panel for any reason, cut the patch to the correct shape for the hole to be filled, but of such size as to leave a gap of $\frac{1}{32}$ins between it and the panel all round. Clean the patch and the panel, and then weld in the manner already covered. *Never* apply an "overlay" patch as this will look awful! Once the patch is welded in place, a skim of body filler can be applied over the top and rubbed down smooth to give an even, level surface (this procedure is covered later in this section).

Electric Welding

When your Land-Rover was originally built, electric welding was used in some of its construction. As far as home restoration is concerned, electric arc welding equipment comes under two main headings, these being arc/rod welding and MIG (metal inert gas) welding equipment.

The first technique is ideal for welding a chassis but tends to be rather too fierce for welding thin steel body panels. Panel welding *can* be achieved but only with an awful lot of care, and even then the job can

look rather messy. Special arc rod holders which operate in a pulse current delivery mode are available; carbon arc attachments can also be obtained quite cheaply to enable brazing work to be carried out, ideal for repairing and even replacing *unstressed* panels. The brazing attachment can also be used as a source of heat to help shift stubborn bolts and to bend exhaust pipes and so on. A further advantage of this equipment compared with other welding gear is that it is the most inexpensive while being quite versatile. On the other hand, brazed joints are not strong enough for major structural areas, a fact recognised by MoT test examiners in the UK who are instructed to fail any car that has been so repaired.

The type of welding that should probably be placed top of the list is MIG welding. Up until a few years ago, this welding option was only available as professional equipment well out of reach of the home restorer's pocket. Nowadays, cheaper models (though no less effective) have been developed for the amateur market. These machines are ideal for welding thin body panels, as well as chassis rails, and unlike gas welding requires relatively little initial skill before good workmanship can be achieved. Usually only a few hours practise is required before you start work with confidence on your Land-Rover. The disadvantage with this type of equipment is that, on its own, it cannot generally be used as a source of heat for bending pipe and so on.

It is worth pointing out that MIG welder models aimed at the non-professional tend to be supplied with disposable canisters of inert gas (Argon, Carbon Dioxide or a mixture of the two), which tend to work out rather expensive. However, the good news is that mini

professional gas cylinders may be hired and refilled from BOC Cylinder Centres in the UK (and their equivalents in other countries) which reduces the running costs significantly. (To use these, relatively inexpensive gas cylinder valves also need to be purchased – well worth buying if you start welding regularly.)

Spot Welding

To complete the electric welding theme is the technique of spot welding, used quite extensively in the original manufacture of your Land-Rover's body. Like the techniques described above, equipment is now available for "domestic" use. While spot welding is extremely useful in the initial manufacture of a vehicle, the Land-Rover being no exception, its use in restoring old vehicles is more limited due to needing a full range of spot welding arms to reach into awkward corners (the length of which affects the welding performance) and which may cost nearly as much as the original tool. Panels to be welded also need to be really bright and shiny on both sides.

Aluminium and its alloys are very good conductors of heat and electricity, and it is therefore most important to maintain the right conditions for successful spot-welding.

Safety

At the start of many sections is a 'Safety' note. Naturally safety is the responsibility of each individual restorer or repairer and no responsibility for the effectiveness or otherwise of advice given here, nor for any omissions, can be accepted by the author or publisher. After all, the jobs you will be carrying out will be *your* responsibility, so do take care to familiarise yourself with safety information available from the suppliers or manufacturers of the materials or equipment which you use. 'Safety' notes are intended to supplement this information with useful tips, as is the additional information on workshop safety and workshop practise in the appendix – you are strongly advised to read the appendix before commencing any of the tasks detailed in this book.

Take note of information in the text on safety hazards. NEVER drain petrol over a pit nor anywhere where a spark could ignite the vapour, eg. near a central heater boiler – outdoors is best. For obvious reasons, attempting to weld a fuel tank can be lethal and should be left to a specialist. Never use a flame near the fuel tank or lines. Drain fuel only into suitable containers. Do not use plastic containers which are attacked by petrol. The battery should be taken out prior to fuel tank removal, to prevent accidental shorting in the presence of fuel vapour. When storing the battery, take care to ensure that no object will fall unnoticed across the terminals and potentially cause a fire. Paint stripper is damaging to the skin and eyes – read instructions before use and wear gloves, goggles and protective overalls. Ensure that the vehicle is firmly supported when lifted off the ground – a jack is NOT safe enough. Wear goggles when probing beneath the car and beware of rusty, jagged edges. Never work beneath a car supported on a jack: use axle stands, ramps or a roll-over cage (see Suppliers Section) and, in the former case, securely chock the wheels that remain on the ground.

HTE1. The Clarke power washer can be used a great deal in the early stages of cleaning body panels, chassis and mechanical components prior to stripping down.

HTE2. An electric drill is an ► absolute 'must' and will be used a thousand and one times. Bosch make what is probably the best quality range of drills available, and include cordless drills-cum-power screwdrivers in their line-up. Cordless tools are safer and far simpler to use, while the power screwdriver feature can save a great deal of time when it comes to removing screws, nuts and bolts.

HTE3. You'll need a good range of hand tools as well. A suitable range is that made by Sykes-Pickavant, including the Speedline trade mark. Socket spanners have the superb 'surface drive' feature whereby force is applied to the flats of nuts rather than their corners, making it virtually impossible to round them off.

HTE4. Power grinding, cutting, sanding and even filing are all catered for by the extensive range of Black & Decker tools.

HTE5. This trolley jack, available from Machine Mart, has a 2-ton capacity and a high lift – ideal for the Land-Rover, in fact.

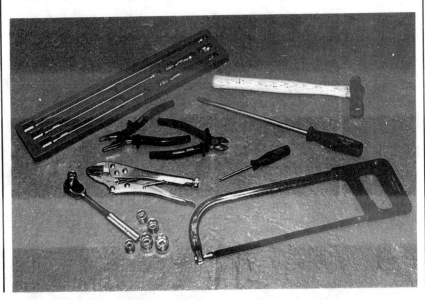

HTE6. For 'factory finish' distortion-free welding of steel panels a spot welder is essential. However, its limitation is that access has to be good before it can be used.

HTE7. If you have any more than a tiny amount of welding to do, it is not worth considering anything but a MIG. Clarke now claim to be the UK's largest supplier of MIGs suitable for home and garage use and the cost of buying a small MIG unit is considerably less than equipping yourself with a BOC gas welding set-up.

HTE8. Clarke are also suppliers of a whole range of workshop equipment including bench and hand tools, compressors in all shapes and sizes and the arc welder shown here – ideal for Land-Rover chassis welding.

HTE9. Fibre glass repairs have gained themselves a bad name in some quarters through being carried out incorrectly. Plastic Padding resin and mat are good for temporary repairs if you're carrying out a 'rolling restoration', but you'll find Plastic Padding Elastic filler an absolute boon when it comes to smoothing out ripples in panels and filling over welded joints. Plastic Padding filler is smoother and easier to top sand than most and its flexibility allows it to resist cracking exceptionally well. The same makers 'Stonechip Protect', available in black and white, is for spraying a smooth coat onto sills, valances and other vulnerable areas before painting the car, preferably. It gives a tough, chip resistant finish.

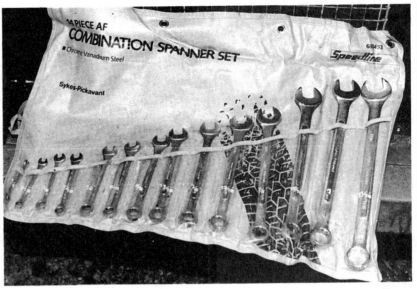

HTE10. You'll want to preserve the car once you have finished restoring it and for that purpose, Corroless anti-rust fluids and paint come very highly recommended indeed. The cavity wax has a rust killer in it so that it finishes off any rusting that has begun as well as sealing out any further rust-inducing moisture. Uniquely, Corroless body filler and primer also contains rust killer, while the Corroless 'High Performance Finish' contains microscopic glass beads, making the paint incredibly tough and absolutely perfect for using on the undersides of panels, chassis and other areas where you'll want the finish to be as hard wearing as possible.

HTE11. If you've ever seen ancient cars running around in Malta, the Canary Islands or Southern USA, you'll appreciate that where there's little humidity, there's little rust. Machine Mart stock a selection of de-humidifiers one of which can be used to keep your stored vehicle in a low humidity environment. You make a plastic sheet or canvas 'tent' over the car and place the de-humidifier at a gap at one end. Turn it on for an hour or so every day or set the machines 'humidity stat.' to the level you want and leave it on. You'll be amazed at the amount of moisture the de-humidifier will extract from the air surrounding your car and deposit in its collection tray. Alternatively, an adequately draught-proofed garage will be beneficial.

HTE12. For dismantling a Land-Rover of the older variety, you will need a set of AF (across flats) and BA spanners. Sykes-Pickavant sell the AF variety; contact Dunsfold Land-Rover for the more specialist size. More modern Land-Rovers also use some metric size spanners. Trial and error is called for, since Land-Rover's own records don't appear to indicate exactly which were used and where.

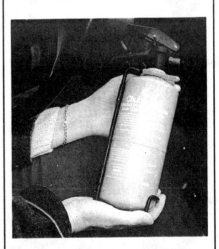

HTE13. Chubb have produced what they claim to be the first non-ozone damaging extinguishers for vehicles and workshops. This handsome beast can be mounted inside the vehicle and there is a larger workshop version. Not just recommended, but essential!

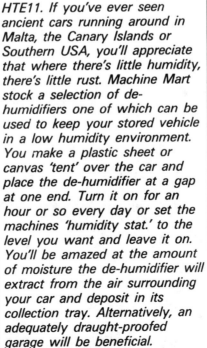

Fuel Tank Removal

Safety:

First, disconnect and remove the battery from the vehicle. Never drain a fuel tank indoors or where the highly flammable vapours can gather, such as over a pit. Store petrol drained from the tank in safe, closed, approved containers. If the empty tank is to be stored, have it steam cleaned to remove the petrol vapours. Place a damp rag in any openings and keep the tank outdoors for very short term storage. Keep all sparks and flames away from the fuel system whilst working on it.

Before carrying out any major body repairs, it makes good sense to drain and remove the fuel tank to a place of safety.

Removing a side-mounted fuel tank (Petrol and diesel models):

Tools needed: spanners (2 BA, $\frac{7}{16}$in AF, $\frac{1}{2}$in AF open-end), medium size screwdriver.

FT1. The side-mounted fuel tank, seen clearly with body removed. The filler pipe and breather are at the rear, the fuel supply pipe in the centre and the gauge sender unit at the front.

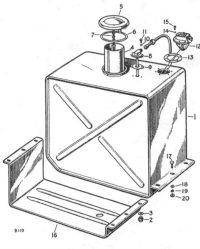

FT2. The Series I fuel tank assembly. Some models were fitted with an undertray which must first be removed. (Courtesy Land-Rover)

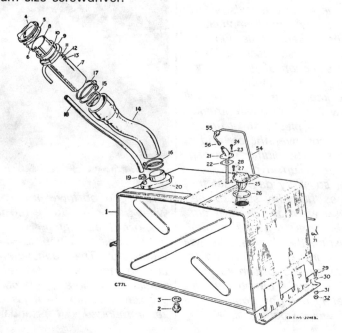

FT3. Components of the side-mounted fuel tank, Series II – on. (Courtesy Land-Rover).

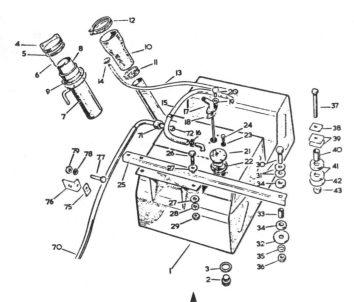

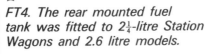

FT4. The rear mounted fuel tank was fitted to 2¼-litre Station Wagons and 2.6 litre models.

FT5. After removing the right-hand seat cushion and folding the seat squab forward, you can carefully disconnect the hoses, the tank-to-filler tube and the breather hose. Remove the cover panel for the fuel tank. Disconnect the wires at the gauge unit; disconnect the fuel supply pipe and, for diesel models, the spill return pipes.

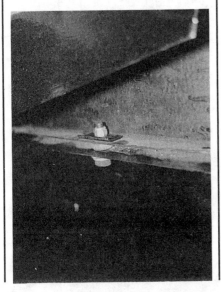

FT6. Support the tank and, while doing so, remove the tank securing bolts. Lower the tank and remove it from under the vehicle. After the tank has been repaired or you've bought a new one, or even if the tank is OK and you've removed it to enable you to proceed with a full vehicle restoration, when the time comes you can replace the fuel tank simply by reversing the above procedure.

FT7. Use the correct Land-Rover bolts and rubber insulating rubbers when reassembling, along with lock nuts or nuts and spring washers. The tank is not bolted direct to the chassis.

FT8. New pipe clips help prevent an unpleasant and potentially dangerous ingress of fumes into the cab. Check hoses for perishing.

"Care should be taken to prevent the entry of water."

FT9. Lighthearted advice from the original Series I Operation Manual – but vital, especially to those with diesel Land-Rovers! (Courtesy Land-Rover)

Removing a rear-mounted fuel tank (Petrol or diesel):

Tools needed: spanners ($\frac{7}{16}$in AF, $\frac{9}{16}$in AF open-end), medium-size screwdriver.

1). After disconnecting and removing the battery and having drained the fuel into a clean container (as above), release the clip securing the filler tube hose to the tank.

2). While supporting the tank, remove the tank securing bolts and lower the tank ONLY ENOUGH TO GIVE ACCESS TO THE PIPES AND LEADS ON THE TOP OF THE TANK.

3). Carefully disconnect the breather and air balance pipes, and disconnect the wires at the gauge unit.

4). Disconnect the fuel supply pipe and, for diesel models, the spill return pipe.

5). Lower the tank fully now and remove from under the vehicle.

6). As above, refitting the tank or fitting a new one is a case of reversing this whole procedure.

Bonnet removal and replacement

Tools needed: Medium-size screwdriver, pliers.

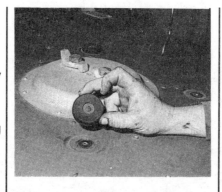

BR1. If your Land-Rover's bonnet is fitted with a spare wheel, unbolt and remove it, needless to say! If you're planning to strip the bonnet, remove the spare wheel buffers. Dunsfold fitted replacements later on, for those that were missing from the project Land-Rover.

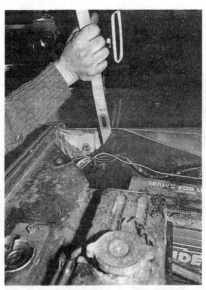

BR2. Remove the fixings at the end of prop rod...

BR3. ...and the similar split-pin and washer arrangement from the hinge pins.

"Re-fit all washers and split pins from whence they came, for safe keeping," advises Dunsfold's Philip Bashall. Carefully remove the bonnet, making sure you don't damage the front wings.

BR4. Lift the bonnet right back and slide the bonnet pins out to the left of the vehicle, working the bonnet back-and-forwards a little as you go. If you don't intend to replace or repaint them, it is advisable to cover the wings with a cloth to prevent scratches. It all depends how fussy you are!

As with most of the Land-Rover's body panels, the bonnet is made of aluminium alloy and as such cannot rust. If it is severely dented, you can make smooth once it has been removed using the hammer and dolly mentioned earlier, remembering that it will become work-hardened and may need annealing during this process. Once the dents are virtually level again, a few skims of body filler will help to get an even finish prior to painting. Remember though, that if your Land-Rover leads a hard life (with much off-road work, for instance), body filler may eventually crack. If possible, buy a replacement bonnet (you may be able to get hold of a secondhand one in better condition than yours).

Series I Bonnet

Should you be lucky enough to find a brand new, unused Series I bonnet, note that the hinges will not be fitted to it. You'll have to place the new bonnet panel in position on the vehicle and the hinges in position in the brackets on the dash. Then, using the hinges as templates,

drill the eight holes in the panel and bolt the bonnet panel to the hinges.

Pre 1950 bonnets are removed by lifting the bonnet back as far as it will go and sliding it out to the left, from its hinges. No split pins are fitted on 1954-1958 models. Exactly the same procedure applies, but the earlier type of bonnet prop-rod is replaced by a folding bonnet stay which must be detached from the bonnet before it can be folded back.

Grille Panel Removal

GR1. Unscrew the nameplate, which also releases the top of the grille.

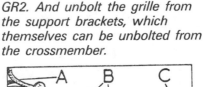

GR2. And unbolt the grille from the support brackets, which themselves can be unbolted from the crossmember.

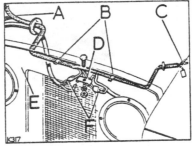

GR3. This drawing (Courtesy Land-Rover) shows the manner in which the front lamps are connected up.

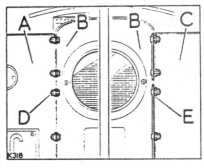

GR4. The grille panel is held to the front wings by four nuts and stub plates as shown in the Wing Repair section.

Front Wing Removal And Replacement

Tools needed: spanners (sizes 2 BA, $\frac{7}{16}$ in AF, $\frac{1}{2}$ in AF open-end and socket).

FWR1. The first stage in removing a front wing from your Land-Rover is to remove the bonnet (see previous section). Then disconnect the side-lamp and, if applicable, the flasher lamp and headlamp harness at the snap connectors in the engine compartment. Take care not to break any of these connectors – they will doubtless be very stiff to work after all these years.

FWR2. Remove the securing bolts and lift the mudshield out from under the wing. The splash plate under the front wing on the steering box side can be seen here. Once rusted through, mud will build up and cause rapid deterioration of the bulkhead. These are the four awkward bolts along the bottom and there are three more along the top to undo on the underside of the wing before the plate can be removed.

FWR3. Another angle showing the fragility of the rotten splash plate . . .

FWR5. One of the three fixing bolts for the steering box cover assembly, which is attached to the splash plate.

FWR7. A new Land-Rover Parts splash plate for the non-steering box side.

FWR4. . . . and a shot of the three nuts and bolts along the top edge of the panel.

FWR6. A new splash plate and a new steering box cover, both genuine factory items ready and waiting to be fitted at a later date.

FWR8. Using a socket or ring spanner, remove the bolts securing the wing to the scuttle pillar.

FWR9. The screwdriver points to the bolt holding the wing to the wing stay and the front of the sill panel. Clean off the mud, soak in releasing fluid and use a pair of spanners.

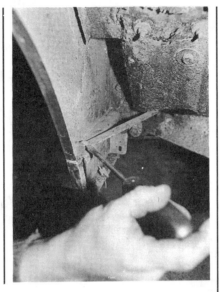

FWR10. Locate and remove the bolts that hold the wing to the rear wing upper mounting bracket. (Part Nos 44 & 45) (Courtesy Land-Rover)

FWR11. The view beneath the wing of the upper mounting bracket, less mud covering!

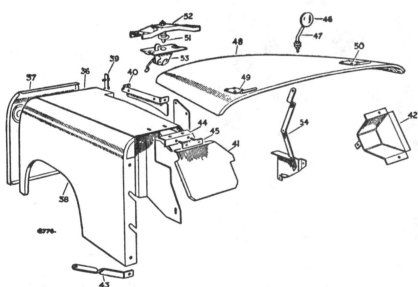

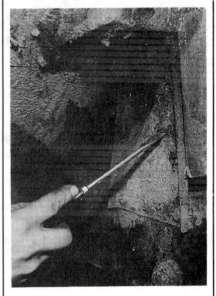

FWR12. A bolt that tends to get overlooked in all the mud! This one holds the inside of the wing to the steering box steady-plate. You may have to search hard for it!

FWR13. Wings are held to the scuttle with a pair of stud plates; one with two studs and one with three, the three stud plate fitting at the top; two stud plate beneath it. New galvanised parts from Land-Rover Parts to be used here by Dunsfold. Series III lower plates are shorter but still with two studs.

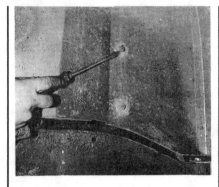

FWR14. *This is the view of the nuts from inside the front wing.*

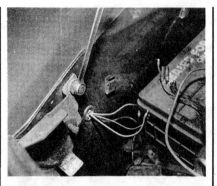

FWR15. *The bonnet stay support bracket must also be removed.*

FWR16. *When it comes to the rear ends of the front wings, there are four bolts going through into the bulkhead. The bottom one and top one are easy to get at, unlike the middle two. In their wisdom, Rover made angled slots for these middle two so you can start the bolts before fitting the wing or you loosen the middle two and leave them in place. Remove the top and bottom bolts complete but lift the wing up and slot it off the middle ones. Note that they are BSF head Acme bolts, screwing into spiral nuts.*

FWR17. *Don't forget to remove ancillary fittings, such as the wiring loom clip shown here.*

FWR18. *Lift away carefully at first, ensuring that the wing really is free of all wiring...*

FWR19. . . . after which the wing can be lifted completely away for careful storage. The project vehicle's wing panel was in excellent shape. The inner panel was not so good!

FWR20. This shows how the mud has built up between the wing and the footwell, leading to a lot of corrosion. This rot must be thoroughly dealt with before even thinking about fitting a new wing, and is described in a later section.

FWR21. When refitting, replace all bolts lightly, to allow for adjustment and alignment, before tightening and checking wing gaps as you go along.

FWR22. Series IIA and III front wing components (Courtesy Land-Rover).

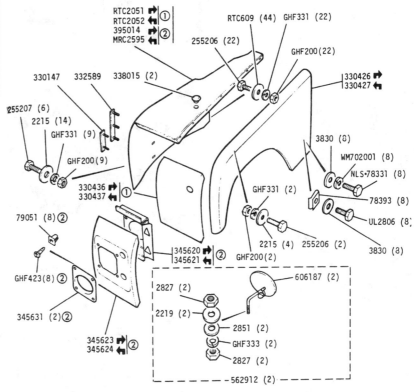

RTC2051 ➡ ①
RTC2052 ⬅
395014 ➡ ②
MRC2595 ⬅

RTC609 (44) GHF331 (22)
255206 (22)
GHF200 (22)

330147 332589 338015 (2)
330426 ➡
330427 ⬅

255207 (6)
2215 (14)
GHF331 (9)
GHF200 (9)
330436 ➡ ①
330437 ⬅

3830 (8)
WM702001 (8)
NLS•78331 (8)
78393 (8)
UL2806 (8)

GHF331 (2)
GHF200 (2)
2215 (4) 255206 (2)
3830 (8)

79051 (8) ②
GHF423 (8) ②
345631 (2) ②
345620 ➡ ②
345621 ⬅

345623 ➡ ②
345624 ⬅

2827 (2)
2219 (2)
606187 (2)
2851 (2)
GHF333 (2)
2827 (2)
562912 (2)

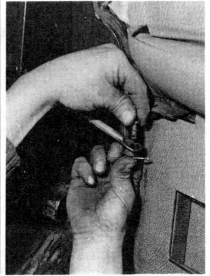

Side door removal

DR1 Disconnect the door stay by taking out the split pin which holds the clevis pin at the door end of the door stay. So that you don't loose the parts, re-assemble the clevis pin, washers and split pin onto the door stay itself.

DR2. If you're working by yourself, close the door so that it is held securely and take out the bolts holding the door hinge to the door pillar. There are captive nuts inside the door pillar. If you're carrying out a restoration, don't be tempted to disconnect the bolts from the door itself in the hope that you won't disturb the captive nuts in the door pillar because you will invariably have to carry out some restoration work to the bottom of the steel door pillars themselves.

DR3. Philip Bashall undoes the identical bolts in the top door hinge . . .

DR4. . . . and then lifts the door away from the vehicle.

DR5. When the door hinges have been unbolted, you may well find evidence of corrosion in the steel A-post behind the lower hinge. Welded repairs needed here!

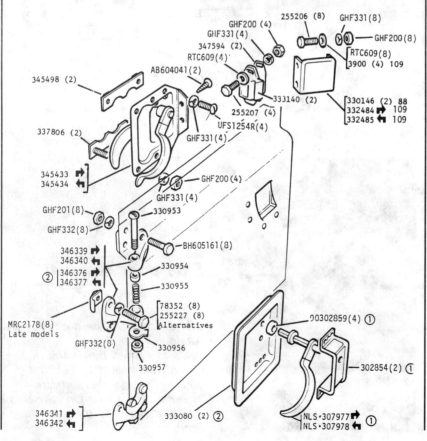

DR6. The layout of the door locks and hinges is self-explanatory. Note that if you disconnect the hinges in the way already shown for the rear doors you may find that the tab washers (Part No. 330956) break off and now is a good time to make a note to order new ones. A layout of the complete door will be found in the section showing how to replace door tops.

DR7. The Series I door does not have a door stay. Instead, there is a rubber buffer on each front wing against which the door can be folded flat. To remove the door, swing the door panel forward until parallel with the front wing and simply lift it from its hinges. Note that when you refit the doors, you may well wish to replace the door seals. The rubber seals are still available from Land-Rover for later models but the shape of the rubber means that the rubber sealing lip may not take exactly the right shape where the front seal has to curve around the front door aperture about level with the bonnet. You may find the seal sticks out when the door is closed and is not held down by the door. A simple trick is to hold this part of the seal down with masking tape for a few weeks after which time it 'remembers' its new shape and is always held into place by the door itself thereafter.
(Courtesy Land-Rover)

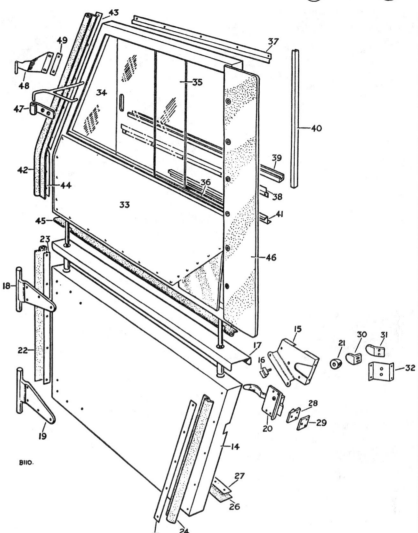

DR8. Shown here (with the sidescreen removed), the Series I door is being lifted off the hinges after being swung forward, parallel with the front wing.
(Courtesy Land-Rover)

Re-fitting side doors

To keep door hinges in good working order it is a good idea to strip them down and replace worn components. Lubricate thoroughly during reassembly.

(See diagram DR5 in the previous section). When refitting the door you can adjust the hinge by increasing or lessening the load on the spring (Part No. 330955) by tightening or slackening the special nut (Part No. 330957), after bending back the lock tab (Part No. 330956). These lock tabs frequently break and require replacement.

Door, trim and locks

TLH1. Station Wagons and some other specially equipped vehicles have interior trim in them. Typically, trim around the door lock is held in place with a threaded screw.

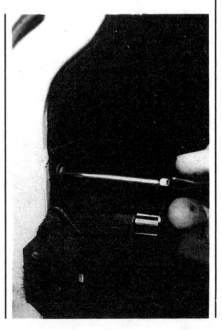

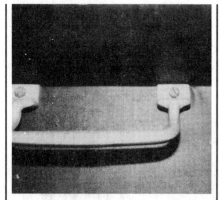

TLH2. . . . whilst similar screws hold the door pull handle in place

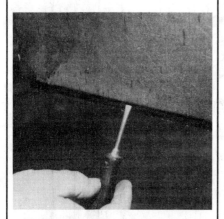

TLH3. With all retaining screws removed the door trim can be prised away from the door by carefully inserting a screwdriver . . .

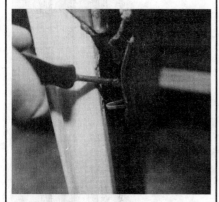

TLH4. . . . and ensuring that the screwdriver is close to one of the spring clips whilst levering the trim away from the door.

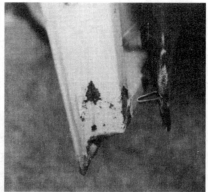

TLH5. Spring clips are very prone to pulling out of the hardboard trim panel and you may find evidence of corrosion behind there.

The drawing in DR5 in the previous section shows the layout of the Series IIA lock and hinge arrangement and is typical of most Land-Rover door locks. Parts ringed with a "1" are for the early type of lock with the detachable inner handle. Parts ringed with a "2" indicate the hinges which incorporate a bracket for an exterior mirror: an optional extra. This Series IIA lock and hinge arrangement is typical of most Land-Rover doors.

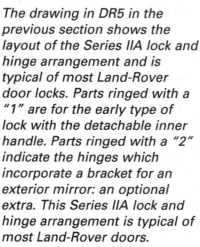

TLH6. The door lock is held to the door frame with two self-tapping screws.

TLH7. It is also held to the door panel by means of an upper plate with weld-on nuts and a lower threaded stud plate.

TLH8. Two cross head screws hold the top of the door lock . . .

TLH9. . . . while two nuts are fitted to the lower stud plate.

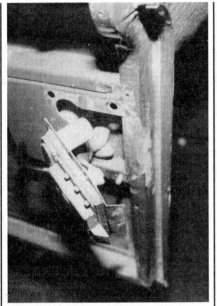

TLH10. With all screws out of the way the lock is simply removed.

TLH11. The door lock aperture can now be cleaned up for repainting. You may wish to treat some of the lock aperture with Waxoyl before re-assembling but try to avoid those parts where your hand might come into contact with it when opening the door from the outside.

TLH12. The nut and stud plates should be rubbed down and sprayed with a zinc-rich paint such as Wurth which comes in aerosol cans and has a high concentration of zinc. Obtain it from your local motor factors.

Door tops (Replacing glass and channels)

The supply of Land-Rover parts from Land-Rover Parts (who else?) is so good that Dunsfold's Peter Bashall was able to show how to construct an entire new door top – not bad for a 30 year old vehicle! Philip's father, Brian, took the photographs, and dictated the captions, showing what versatile chaps they are!

DT1. A diagram of what's involved in the making of a Land-Rover door top. Note that glass with ringed "1" is the clear glass part no. while "2" is the Sundym glass part no. Note also that Series IIA parts are identical. (Courtesy Land-Rover).

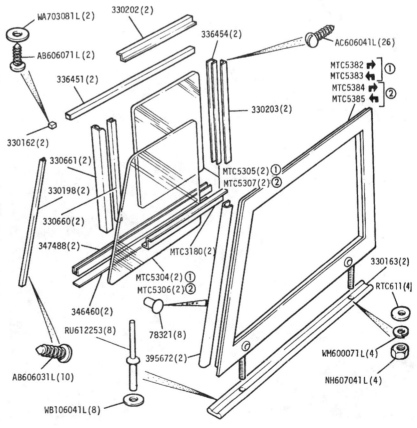

DT2. *And in the flesh the frame, the glass, the channels, the filler strips, the screws and a roll of glazing strip.*

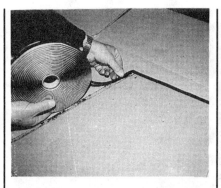

DT3. *The glazing strip is applied to the fixed pane of glass...*

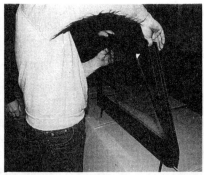

DT4. *... and this glass is then fitted to the frame, the glazing strip making a seal between the two.*

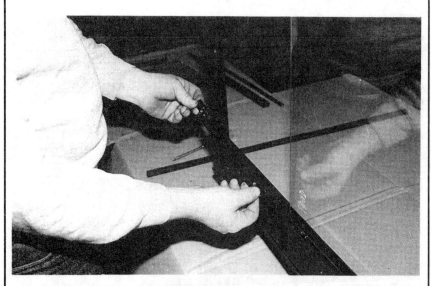

DT5. *The front glazing strip is fitted, held tightly in place by four screws.* ▲

◄

DT6. *The door top should have two spacer strips; the bottom one has cut-outs on the lower edge (shown here next to the thumb!) while the top one is plain. These spacer strips can now be fitted.*

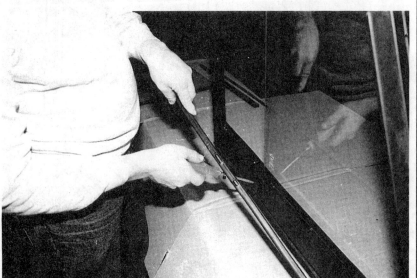

DT7. *The bottom glazing bar now goes into place. On this Series III example, there are two slots – one is a drain slot, while the longer slot coincides with the aperture where the door glass locker goes. Make sure the strip is the right way round before fitting!*

DT8. Put the strip in place, holding it tight against the glass (with a screwdriver) as well as right up to the front of the door top (with your finger!).

DT9. The screws that hold the strip in place MUST be fitted below the level of the felt; when drilling make sure the holes are at an angle so that the felt is properly held down by the screws. Also take care not to let the drill 'nibble' the glass.

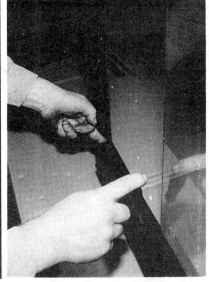

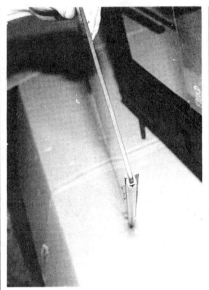

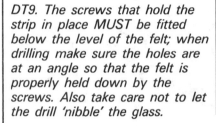

DT12. Shown here is the sliding section of glass. Make sure this is fitted the right way round. There is a draught excluder strip inside an aluminium capping – the long side should be facing OUT of the vehicle so that it is tight against the glass.

DT10. The drilling done, simply fit the five screws that hold this bottom strip in place.

DT11. The rear filler strip can now be fitted.

DT13. At this stage of fitting the sliding glass, make sure it rides freely in the felt channel and doesn't catch on any of the screws.

DT14. *The top elements can now be fitted. Shown here are the short filler strip, a plain strip (a spacer) and the top rail.*

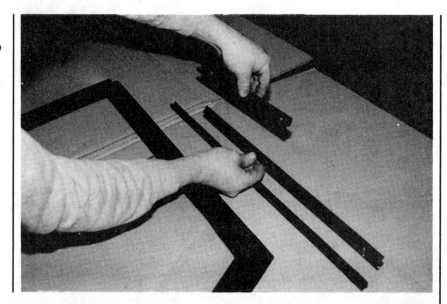

DT15. *The plain strip should be placed in first...* ▼

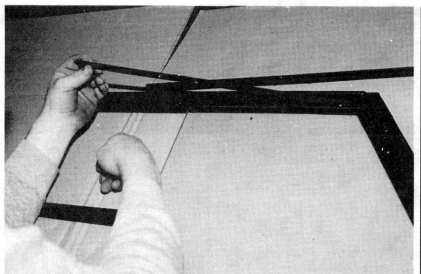

DT18. *The holes should be drilled at angles again...*

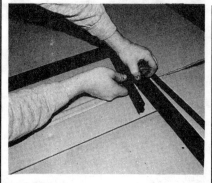

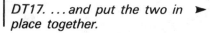

DT16. *...followed by the filler* ▲ *strip. At this stage, put the top felt onto the glass...*

DT17. *...and put the two in* ▶ *place together.*

DT19. ... taking care to hold the components firmly in place. ➤

DT20. A vital (but often overlooked) component of the door top is this small rubber buffer fitted to the front top corner. If it's not fitted, when you slide the window forward with any vigour the glass will catch on the door frame and may even break.

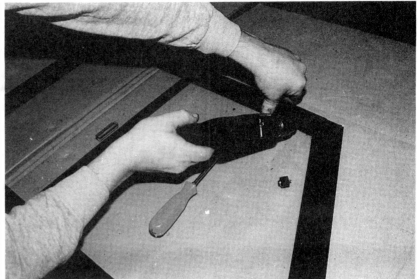

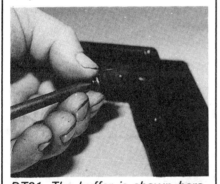

DT21. The buffer is shown here just about to be screwed into ▲ place ...

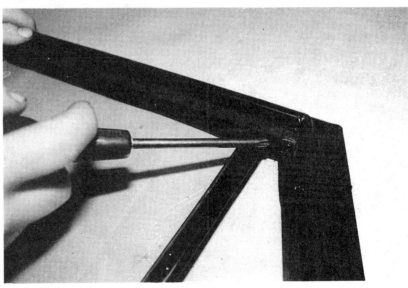

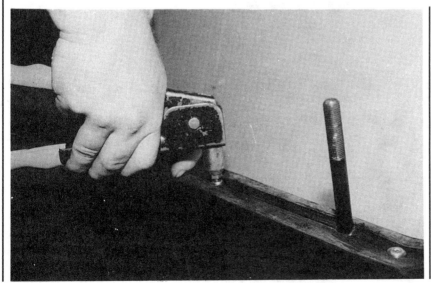

DT22. ... and this is what it ▲ should look like when fitted.

DT23. On the underside of the door top is a rubber sealing strip between the door top and the top 'capping' of the door itself. Without this, water leaks are inevitable. It is shown here being riveted into place. ◄

Shown in Side Door Removal, DR6 is an 80 in door top. Despite obvious differences, there are still filler strips and aluminium felt-lined channels holding the perspex or glass in place. Removal and replacement procedure on these early models is much the same in principle.

Window security modification

A Land-Rover parked in the Summer sun can become rather hot inside and Dunsfold Land-Rover carried out one of their ventilation modifications to the author's vehicle whilst ensuring that the vehicle remained secure. (You can leave the front vents open, especially if you have the optional wire mesh fitted inside them.)

SM1. Open the sliding glass as far as you can without being able to get your hand fully through the aperture. ►

SM2. Place a supplementary window glass lock in such a position that the glass will be prevented from sliding any further open. ▲

SM3. After having drilled a hole for a pop-rivet, rivet one end of the catch in place...

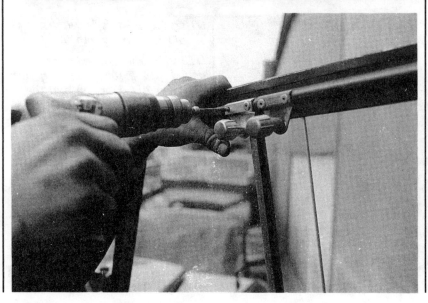

SM4. ...then drill the other hole and rivet the other end of the catch in place. (If you drill both holes before fitting the first rivet, there is a risk of their not lining up correctly.) You can now leave the original catch open while closing the supplementary catch and prevent the window from being opened any further than you want it to be. Very useful if you want to leave your dogs in the car but don't want them to be able to get out!

Station Wagon – Rear door removal

Workshop Hand Tools: Spanner sizes: 2BA $\frac{7}{16}$ in. AF, $\frac{1}{2}$ in. AF, $\frac{3}{4}$ in. AF. Screwdriver, pliers.

RD1. After FVJ's arrival at Dunsfold Land-Rover, and once a thorough inspection had been carried out, one of the first jobs had been to take off the rear door.

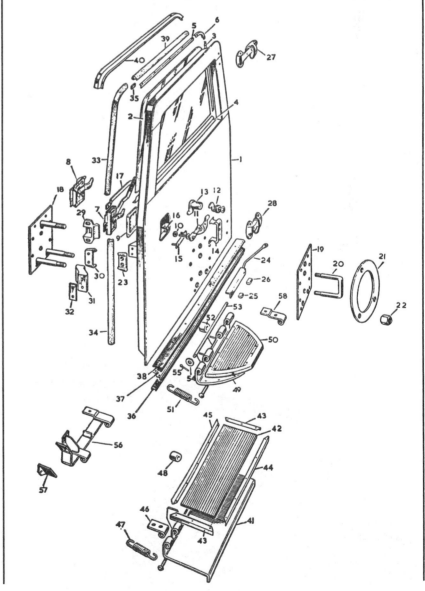

RD2. The Series II and IIA rear door components are clearly shown here along with the two optional rear steps. The rear door glass is held in place by self-tapping screws. New seals are available from your Land-Rover dealer.
(Courtesy Land-Rover)

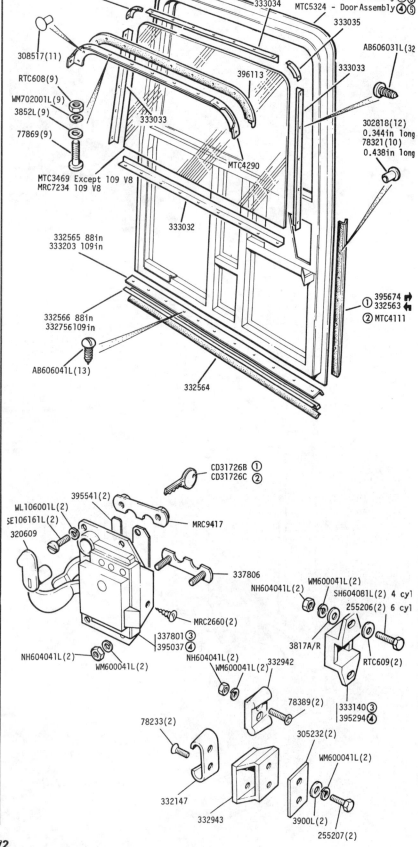

MTC6902 - Frame and Panel Assembly ③⑥
336890 - Door Panel Assembly ④⑥
RTC7275 - Door Assembly ③⑥
MTC5324 - Door Assembly ④⑤

333035

333034

333035

308517(11)

396113

333033

AB606031L(32

RTC608(9)

WM702001L(9)

302818(12)
0.344in long
78321(10)
0.438in long

3852L(9)

77869(9)

333033

MTC3469 Except 109 V8
MRC7234 109 V8

MTC4290

333032

332565 88in
333203 109in

395674
332563
②MTC4111

332566 88in
332756109in

AB606041L(13)

332564

CD31726B ①
CD31726C ②

395541(2)

WL106001L(2)

SE106161L(2)

MRC9417

320609

337806

WM600041L(2)

NH604041L(2)

SH604081L(2) 4 cyl
255206(2) 6 cyl

MRC2660(2)

337801③
395037④

3817A/R

NH604041L(2)
WM600041L(2)

NH604041L(2)
WM600041L(2)

332942

RTC609(2)

78389(2)

333140③
395294④

78233(2)

305232(2)

WM600041L(2)

332147

332943

3900L(2)

255207(2)

RD3. The Series III Safari rear door is essentially the same but a mixture of nuts and screws, self-tapping screws and rivets hold the rear glass in place. (Courtesy Land-Rover)

RD4. The fixings for the lock assembly are clearly shown in the drawing from the Land-Rover Parts Book and assembly is self-explanatory. When re-fitting the door and door lock, remember to adjust the striker plate, also shown in this drawing, so that the door draft excluders are slightly compressed when the door is shut. Those models of Land-Rover which are fully equipped with trim will have to have the trim panels snapped away before the door locks can be accessed. (Courtesy Land-Rover)

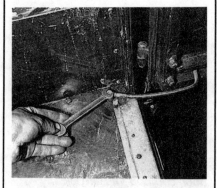

RD5. Start by unbolting the rear door stay from the rear body (there is a nut beneath the floor) . . .

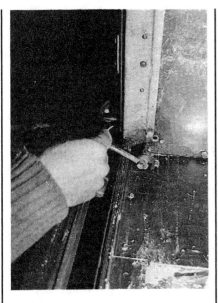

RD6. ... and lifting the door stay and the bolt plus washers that allow it to swivel away from the body. Keep everything together!

RD7. Philip Bashall at Dunsfold Land-Rover demonstrates the way in which the door hinges can be unbolted from the body – a socket spanner used inside the rear wheel arch undoes the fixing nut while the ring spanner held in Philip's left hand prevents the bolt from turning. They are invariably seized solid, in which case ...

RD8. ... ease back the tap washer on the hinge swivel pin securing nut ...

RD9. ... remove the nut and the spring and washer behind it ...

RD10. ... and Philip demonstrates that the rear door can now be simply lifted away.

RD11. Try to lift the door upwards as you take it away which leaves the hinge balls sitting in the lower cup of the rear hinge. Take each of the balls out and put them together with the swivel pins, the springs, tap-washers and nuts.

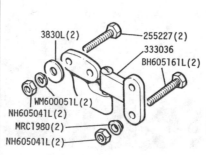

3830L(2)
255227(2)
333036
BH605161L(2)
WM600051L(2)
NH605041L(2)
MRC1980(2)
NH605041L(2)

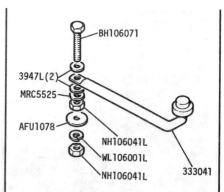

BH106071
3947L(2)
MRC5525
AFU1078
NH106041L
WL106001L
NH106041L
333041

RD12. And now, as Philip demonstrates, it's a relatively simple matter to saw the heads off the recalcitrant bolts. Do take care not to damage the bodywork or the hinge with the hacksaw. You may chose to grind or drill the head off – it's entirely up to you!

RD13. This shows the layout of the rear door hinge assembly. Note that the bolts into the rear body have a large flat washer on their rear surface.
(Courtesy Land-Rover)

RD14. The rear door check strap assembly. Note the order of the fixing washers and also note that you'll have to lock the bolt Part No. BH106071 as shown in RD6. while undoing the fixing nut from underneath the vehicle.
(Courtesy Land-Rover)

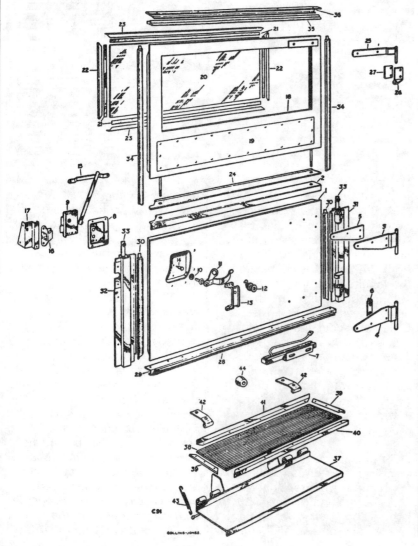

RD15. The rear door on the Series I Station Wagon is removed by removing the check strap and anchor bolt, and then opening the door as far as it will go and lifting clear of the hinges. To dismantle the door, you unscrew the nuts securing the door upper half to the lower half and remove the door lock, mounting plate and handles, it will be necessary to first remove the inner retainer for the door lock handle and then to partly unscrew the ring nut securing the lock and catch. The Land-Rover manual specifies the use of a special 'C' spanner but it should be possible to drift it round. After slackening the ring nut the lock mounting plate and handles can be removed complete. The door glass is held in place with retainers, secured by self-tapping screws.
(Courtesy Land-Rover)

Tailgate Removal

TR1. This is the Land-Rover ➤ *Parts Book drawing of the Series I tailgate but removal for all models is virtually the same. Lower the tailboard and unhook the tailboard chains. Remove the plain washer, spring washer and split pin from the right hand hinge pin and slide out the tailboard to the left. Land-Rover Parts are able to supply tailboards for later models but Series I tailboards are not available at the time of writing. (Courtesy Land-Rover)*

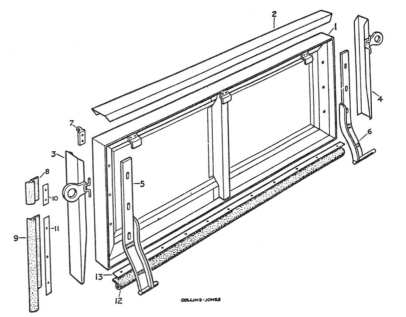

TR2. To remove later tailgates, take out the split pin, plain and spring washers from each side ...

TR3. ... and replace them on the hinge pins for safe keeping.

Bulkhead (or Dash Panel) Removal

See also page 89

Note – The following instructions are generally applicable to all models, but individual models may vary slightly, particularly with regard to equipment attached to the dash panel.

1). Once the bonnet, front wings, windscreen, doors and front floor and gearbox tunnel have been removed, the dash panel can then be taken out! Start by removing the fixings from the ball joint connecting the longitudinal arm to the steering box drop arm; then, using special tool Part No. 600590, extract the ball joint to release the longitudinal arm.

2). On petrol-engined models, disconnect the starter motor lead from the terminal on the switch. (On diesel models, disconnect the starter/heater plug switch leads from the switch.)

3). If your Land-Rover has a petrol engine, disconnect:

A) The high tension wire and the distributor wire from the coil.

B) The oil warning light wire from the oil pressure switch.

C) The mixture warning light wire from the switch on the cylinder head.

D) The fluid outlet pipes from the clutch and brake master cylinders.

E) The clutch flexible hose at the bracket on the dash.

F) The accelerator linkage, by disconnecting the control rod at the carburettor or injection pump.

4). If your Land-Rover is diesel-engined OR has a 2¼-litre petrol engine, disconnect (where applicable):

A) The engine hand speed control rod at the cross-shaft by removing the retaining nut and locknut.

B) The heater unit and heater water pipe hoses, if fitted, and the leads to AND the complete heater unit itself.

C) The dynamo leads.

D) The speedometer drive from the transfer box; release the cable from the clips on the transfer box, the chassis and the flywheel housing.

E) The headlamp and horn wires on the junction box on the dash.

F) The frame and dash section of the main harness at the snap connectors.

5). Check that all fuel and brake

pipes, electrical leads, controls, etc., are disconnected from the dash panel.

6). Remove the bolts securing the steering box support bracket to the chassis; remove the two tie-bolts, plain washer and nuts fixing the dash to the chassis; remove the nuts and bolts fixing the extremities of the sill panels to the dash. Lift off the dash panel complete.

7). Strip the dash panel by removing *all* fixings, from the junction box to the steering wheel; instrument panel to accelerator linkage. Most of these items are simple and self-explanatory when it comes to removal.

8). When refitting the dash panel, be sure to connect the wiring in accordance with the appropriate wiring diagram; adjust the accelerator, mixture or cut-off control and throttle linkage; set the road wheels straight ahead and the steering wheel in the mid-way position between full lock in each direction before securing the longitudinal arm to the steering box drop arm; bleed the clutch and brake systems, as detailed in your Haynes Owner's Workshop Manual.

Removing and replacing the rear hardtop

Tools needed: 2 BA, $\frac{7}{16}$ in AF and $\frac{1}{2}$ in AF open end spanner; medium-sized screwdriver.

HT1. Although it's rather a large part of a Land-Rover's bodywork the rear hardtop it quite easily moved by two people – being made of aluminium; it's lighter than it looks.

HT2. Before starting work, you'll have to remove the rear door and the upper trim where fitted.

HT4. The hardtop is held to the hood sockets just behind the door pillars and at the rear of the hood.

HT3. The hardtop is held to the windscreen with a line of nuts, bolts and washers. On 109 in models with four side doors, remove the bolts securing the hardtop to the door pillar.

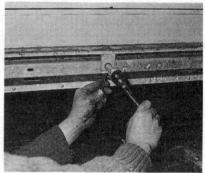

HT5. Remove the nuts, bolts and washers securing the hardtop to the centre mounting brackets and to those either side of the rear door.

HT6. Then it's back to strong arm tactics and the hardtop can be lifted away. Note that the set bolts fixing the hardtop to the hood sticks have to be lifted clear of the body when the hardtop is lifted away.

HT7. Also note the rubber washer at the top of the set screw between the hardtop and the body.

Fitting glass to a hardtop

There are two types of glass panel that you can fit to a hard top: a sliding glass arrangement or a fixed glass panel. In addition there are glasses that fit to the rear panel and to the roof panel on some models. The components supplied by Land-

Rover Parts for the sliding glass assembly are rather expensive although it must be said that the non-original sliding glass alternatives are not of the best quality. It was for that reason that we decided to fit correct and original fixed rear glass panels to our project car at Dunsfold Land-Rover. In addition, glasses were fitted to the roof section – simply because we all very much liked the look of them!

GH1. Philip Bashall carefully ▶ marked out the position for the hard top glasses after taking measurements from another original vehicle. He placed masking tape along the hardtop panel, and then made a card template from the glass to be fitted later. To the dimensions of the glass he added the depth of glass that needs to go into the glazing rubber. This was marked onto the hardtop sides, a hole drilled in order to start off and a jigsaw used to carefully cut the hole required all the way round.

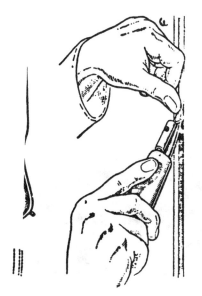

GH2. Land-Rover recommend the use of a special tool Part No. 262771 for inserting the filler strip into the glazing rubber.

They also recommend working with the panel to be glazed in a horizontal position wherever possible and you should, at the very least, have at least one, or preferably two people, to help you fit the glass, otherwise there is a very strong risk of the whole thing dropping onto the floor before you have got it fitted into place. Start by cutting one end of the glazing rubber so that it's perfectly square – use a sharp craft knife dipped into soapy water to help the knife blade slice easily through the rubber. Push the strip well into the aperture corners until it overlaps at the point where you first started, which Land-Rover recommend as the bottom centre, although it would seem less likely to cause a leak if you were to start at the top centre. Do note that the strip has a narrow groove and a broader groove and that the narrow one is the side that pushes over the aluminium aperture in the hardtop. Check again that the glazing strip is pushed well down all the way around and then cut it off to length PLUS one inch – in other words allow the sealing rubber to overlap by one inch. Now pull the sealing rubber back off again for a little way in both directions from the overlap. Refit it, this time easing it back so that the one inch

overlap turns in to a tight butt-joint. Push the excess down so that it is 'lost' around the opening. Now, with the aid of friends and flat bladed screwdrivers, ease the glass into the glazing rubber. Then start

fitting the filler strip after first squaring one end off with the craft knife. Commence fitting from the side opposite that from where you started the glazing rubber. This time, allow about a $\frac{1}{4}$ in. overlap and cut the filler

strip off square before pushing it home. If you can get hold of the special tool mentioned above, all well and good; if not, revert to the use of screwdrivers.

Hood and hood sticks

The hood arrangements vary from model to model but are essentially as shown in the accompanying diagrams. Note that there is one type of hood which is a full length affair, covering the cab, while a different type fits the pick-up type body with a fully enclosed cab.

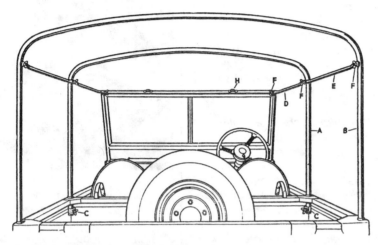

HA1. The early Series I hood sticks arrangements, showing the way in which the hood sticks are held to the body and to each other with a series of wing nuts. (Courtesy Land-Rover)

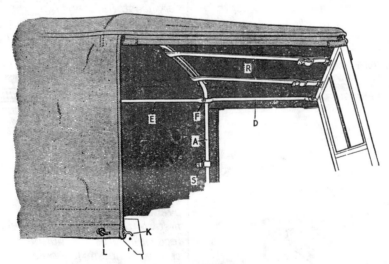

HA2. The front of the hood is held taught over the cab area with the straps shown as "R". (Courtesy Land-Rover)

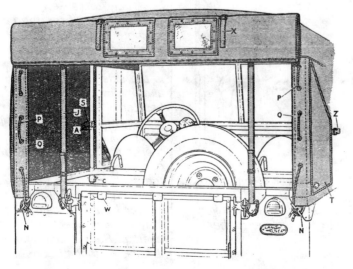

HA3. The Series I hood shown furled at the back with the straps marked "J" giving some shape to the full width rear curtain. (Courtesy Land-Rover)

HA4. Note that, to be perfectly original, the early hood should only have two very small rear windows as shown here. (Courtesy Land-Rover)

HA5. In all essential respects, this High Capacity Pick-up on the Series III is very similar. Note the different fixing arrangements. (Courtesy Land-Rover)

Truck cab removal

Tools required, see Hardtop Removal Section.

CAB1. Remove the nuts, bolts and washers holding the cab to the windscreen and those fitting it to the hood socket. On 88 in models, the cab is held to the cab mounting rail at the rear body with more nuts, bolts and washers while on 109 in models it is held in the same place with set bolts and washers. The cab can now be lifted away but note when replacing, that it is best to replace the sealing rubbers from the back rest panel capping and the front edge of the roof. (Courtesy Land-Rover)

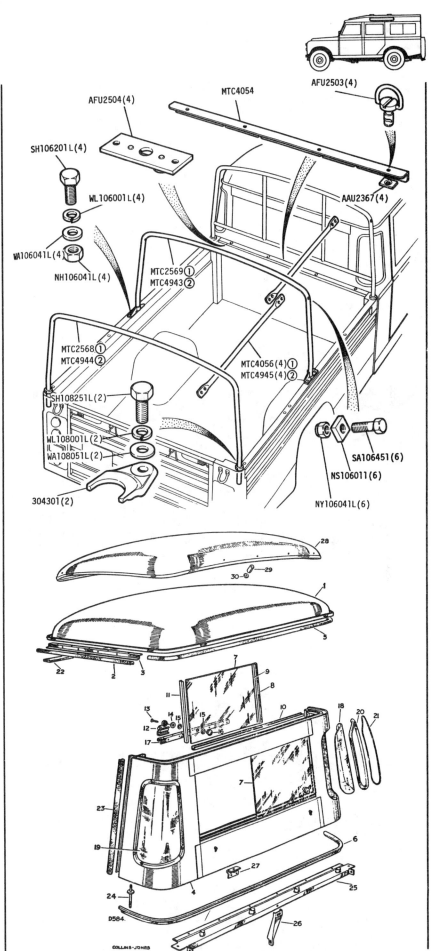

Windscreen removal

The windscreen itself is very easy to remove on all models and is simply a matter of slackening the nuts at the bottom corner of the windscreen and taking out the windscreen pivot bolts. Different types of windscreen wiper have been fitted over the years; check carefully that yours has been appropriately disconnected or moved out of the way so that no damage occurs.

Front apron removal

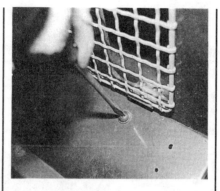

FA2. ...and the two screws at the crossmember brackets. Note that these screws, correctly in the case of our vehicle, should have plain washers beneath them.

FA1. Remove the two screws at the side members...

FA3. The apron can be lifted away.

Front floor removal

Tools required: $\frac{7}{16}$ in AF spanners and $\frac{7}{16}$ in BSF open ended spanner. Medium sized screwdriver.

The excellent Land-Rover Repair Operation Manual manages to dispose of this section in nine lines – which is fine if you're a trained Land-Rover mechanic and especially fine if the vehicle is new and the bolts are uncorroded. In practise, you'll find that most of the bolts and screws holding the floor in place will be rusted in and you would be best advised to soak each of them with releasing fluid, after scraping off the dirt beneath the vehicle, on several occasions before attempting to remove them.

Please also note that the sequence of photographs accompanying this section were taken, as were all of the photographs in this book, at Dunsfold Land-Rover and that the mechanics there are used to working an order that suits them rather than that set out in the manual. Therefore, don't be surprised if the photographs shown here appear to be out of sequence! They have been re-arranged to make it easier for the home enthusiast to work.

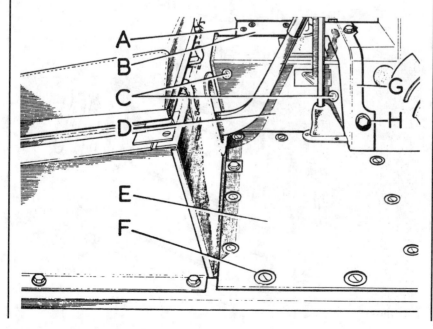

FF1. This diagram, (Courtesy Land-Rover Parts), is a view of the front floor from the right hand side on a right hand drive model. It will be referred to in the captions that follow.

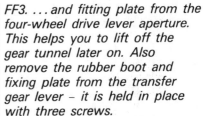

FF3. ... and fitting plate from the four-wheel drive lever aperture. This helps you to lift off the gear tunnel later on. Also remove the rubber boot and fixing plate from the transfer gear lever – it is held in place with three screws.

FF4. The manual says, "Remove both halves of the front floor boards." And that's it! Some screws will come out with a screwdriver; others will benefit from the use of an impact screwdriver – a tool that cannot be too highly recommended. You may get away with being able to hit the end of your screwdriver handle with a hammer whilst attempting to turn it, but a) it's not particularly good practice, b) it doesn't work nearly as well.
◄

FF5. Some screws are meant to be fitted with bolt heads; others may have been incorrectly fitted with them in the past. Our project vehicle's screws came out incredibly well, but Philip Bashall found that one or two of the bolt heads had to be ground off with the angle grinder. (Always wear goggles when using a grinder of any sort and follow the maker's instructions to the letter. Also, do not let the sparks fall on glass otherwise it will be permanently marked.) You have to be particularly careful when doing this, otherwise the grinder can easily slip and gouge the aluminium floor panels quite badly. You will have to use a sharp drill to remove the countersunk screw heads and then to drill out the screw from the seized thread beneath. It may well be best to drill off the seized bolt heads as well.

FF2. Take off the knob and lock nut from the transfer gear and four wheel drive levers ...

FF6. Commence removing the floor panel by easing them past the foot pedals...

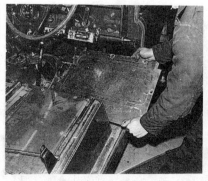

FF7. ...and then lifting the floor panels out of the vehicle.

FF8. The gearbox tunnel is ▲ held on with four bolts, two each side shown as letter C in FF1. You can lift it away after removing the gear knob and locknut or more easily if the gear stick gaiter has disintegrated, or simply by freeing the gaiter from the gear tunnel.

◄

FF9. The gearbox tunnel front panel, shown by letter G in FF1 is held with four bolts (letter H), one on either side...

FF10. ...and one on each ▲ side of the sloping section, this one being hidden beneath the heater.

◄

FF11. The gearbox tunnel front panel can now be lifted away.

Front floor removal – 2.6-litre models

The gearbox and front panel arrangement on the 2.6-litre models is still virtually identical, except that there are more and differently situated screws and bolts to be removed, before the gearbox tunnel cover and the front panel can be taken out of the vehicle.

Front floor re-fitting

When re-fitting the floor, gearbox tunnel and front panel, use a waterproof sealant between each of the joint flanges. Also remember to adjust the four-wheel drive lever. Take off the knob, fit the spring and lock nut and adjust the spring length until it is $2\frac{5}{16}$ in (58mm). Then, refit the knob and tighten the lock nut.

Seat base and handbrake lever removal

Tools required: $\frac{7}{16}$ in. and $\frac{9}{16}$ in. AF spanners. Before you can take out the seatbase, you have to remove the front floor as shown in the previous section.

SHB1. With Land-Rovers prior to 1954 you can lift out the seatbase over the short, horizontal handbrake lever without having to remove either the handbrake or the rubber grommet. From 1954-on, one or the other will have to be removed. The handbrake is held with the two nuts and spring washers, as shown. (Courtesy Land-Rover). ▶

SHB2. The Manual suggests that you might be able to ease the seatbase over the handbrake on later models without taking out the grommets. Dunsfold Land-Rover feel that it is best to take out the screws holding the grommet retaining plate in place... ▲

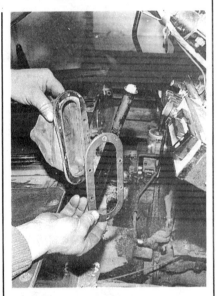

SHB3. ...and take off grommet and plate. ▶

SHB4. Although the pictures seem to have gone slightly out of sequence, you should now hold the lock nuts beneath the seatbase with a ring spanner and remove the bolts from above. ▶

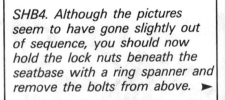

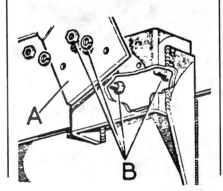

SHB5. It's now hunt the bolt time! Including those holding the seat belt mounting in place, there should be 23 of them altogether.

SHB6. Those behind the sills will require a socket spanner with and extension bar to lock the nut beneath the seatbase.

SHB7. The seatbase also bolts through to the rear body with a line of nuts, bolts and washers along the rear of the seatbase. You'll have to use a screwdriver to prise the two apart because they're bound to be held together with body sealer.

SHB8. Philip Bashall sets about releasing the seatbase from the floor side rail. Over the years, the sealant used to prevent the ingress of water will have caused the seatbase to glue itself firmly to the ground. Philip grabs hold of the seatbase at the front and the seat cushion mounting at the rear twists and pulls until the whole thing comes free.

SHB9. The seat base can be lifted up and over the handbrake lever, as shown, provided that it is pulled into the "on" position.

SHB10. *Philip and Guy lift the seatbase away from the Land-Rover body.*

Rear body removal and replacement

Tools required: 2BA and 4BA spanners; $\frac{7}{16}$ in AF and $\frac{1}{2}$ in AF open end and socket spanners; screwdriver.

It is quite possible to remove the rear body with the seatbase still in place. The rear bodies on all models of Series I, II and III Land-Rovers are essentially similar although there are detailed differences. The biggest differences come with the various models of Series III Land-Rovers although the basic removal principles remain exactly the same.

Before removing the rear body you must remove the rear door or tailgate, the hood and hood sticks or hardtop, the spare wheel, the seat cushions (on most models) while on 109 in. models it will only be necessary to tilt forward the seat squabs.

RB1. *This is a Series I 80 in* ▶ *body which differs in several important details from the later Series I bodies. They are more like the Series II & IIA bodies. (Courtesy Land-Rover)*

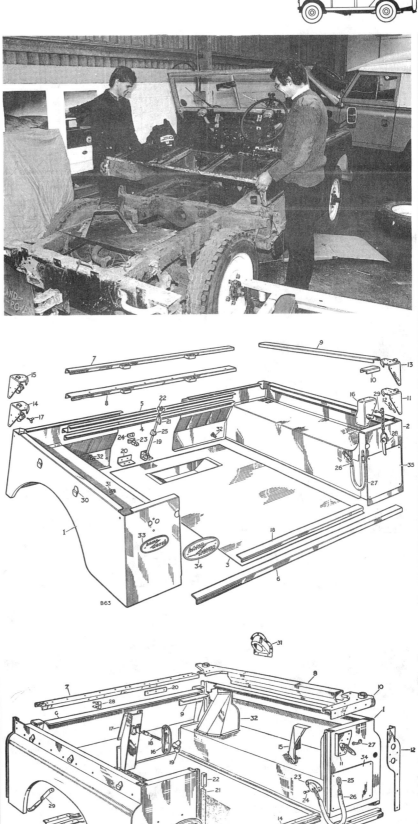

RB2. *This is the 88 in Series II and IIA rear body being removed in the following picture sequence. (Courtesy Land-Rover)*

RB3. One of the Series III rear bodies, showing the slightly different fixing system (note the captive nut plates at the rear of the body) but it is important to realise that there are several different types of body fitted to the rear of the Series III and that fixings are different. This is the 109 in body (except Station Wagon) up to vehicle suffix "B" inclusive.
(Courtesy Land-Rover)

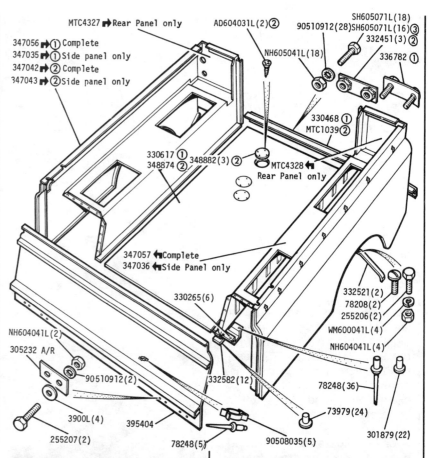

MTC4327 ➡ Rear Panel only
347056 ➡ ① Complete
347035 ➡ ① Side panel only
347042 ➡ ② Complete
347043 ➡ ② Side panel only
AD604031L(2) ②
90510912(28)
NH605041L(18)
SH605071L(18)
SH605071L(16) ③
332451(3) ②
336782 ①
330468 ①
MTC1039 ②
330617 ①
348874 ② 348882(3) ②
MTC4328 ◄
Rear Panel only
347057 ◄ Complete
347036 ◄ Side Panel only
330265(6)
332521(2)
78208(2)
255206(2)
WM600041L(4)
NH604041L(4)
NH604041L(2)
305232 A/R
90510912(2)
332582(12)
78248(36)
73979(24)
301879(22)
3900L(4)
395404
255207(2)
78248(5)
90508035(5)

RB4. Disconnect the battery ▲ and disconnect the wiring from the rear body rear lights. You will be able to pull apart the bullet connectors from the rear of the wiring loom on all models from 1954-on, while with earlier Series I models, it is best to disconnect the wiring from the rear lamps after first opening up the rear lamp bodies.

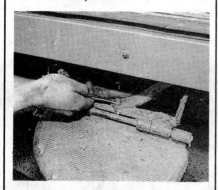

RB5. If a rear or side step is fitted you can unbolt it easily from the body.

RB6. Disconnect the fuel filler and breather hoses...

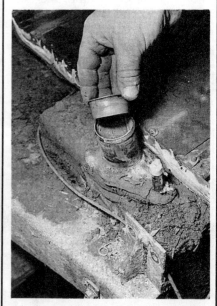

RB7. ...and ensure that the filler neck and breather neck leading to the fuel tank are completely sealed to avoid risk of explosion.

RB8. Remove the bolts, washers and nuts securing the rear body to the seat base (see previous section).

RB9. ...and remove the bolts securing the rear sill panel to the body...

RB10. ...and note that the body is held in place on the fuel tank side with this special plate fitted with weld-on threaded studs. This only applies to Series II – on and only on the 88 in models. (Where two fuel tanks are fitted to ex-military vehicles for instance, these special plates will be used on both sides.) On the non-fuel tank side, ordinary nuts and bolts are used.

RB11. Two more body mounting bolts behind the rear wing, looking towards the front of the car. This is the off-side centre body mount, just behind the fuel tank. If the nuts and bolts are not seized it's a simple procedure!

RB12. Philip Bashall removes the bolts holding the rear crossmember to the body – ten of them in all. Be careful not to damage the body when removing these nuts and bolts.

RB13. Philip eases the rear body away from the ubiquitous sealer. Be certain to use more sealer when re-fitting the body: it not only forms a weather proof seal, it also keeps aluminium and steel apart and prevents any electrolytic action from taking place between them – otherwise known as corrosion! ▶

RSB1. This is the rear body skin panel that can either be spot welded or pop riveted into place. Alternatively, if you wanted to recreate exactly the original dome-headed rivets, you could purchase the correct type of riveting set and attempt to form the rivets yourself. But be warned: creating dome-head rivets without blemishes of any sort is exceedingly difficult and unless you want to go to endless trouble to recreate originality, you would be best advised to use pop-rivets or spot welding. An alternative would be to use the Clarke MIG welder with the special wire for aluminium welding. You can theoretically gas weld aluminium but both gas and TIG welding of aluminium takes very considerable skill and practise and the later also requires expensive equipment.

RB14. FVJ now looking severely denuded with rear body completely removed.

Rear side body replacement

Land-Rover Parts produce two alternative rear side body panels. When fitting replacement panels to your Land-Rover, you are very strongly recommended to use components produced by Land-Rover Parts because then you can be absolutely sure that they will be original and that they will fit correctly.

RSB2. Land-Rover Parts also produce a rear side body replacement which incorporates the wheel arch/seat box assembly. One of the beauties of Land-Rover restoration is that Land-Rover Parts rank with only a tiny number of manufacturers in the world, such as Volkswagen and Porsche for example, in producing replacement parts for vehicles that go back a very long way indeed. In fact, there are many ways in which Land-Rover parts are superior to the German companies mentioned here because fewer component changes took place during the vehicle's production life.

Bulkhead removal

See also pages 75 and 76

The official Land-Rover name for the bulkhead is the dash panel, although everyone else seems to know it as the bulkhead! Tools required: 2BA spanners; $\frac{7}{16}$ in AF, $\frac{1}{2}$ in AF, $\frac{3}{4}$ in AF spanners, medium and small sized screwdrivers, pliers.

BWR1. This drawing of the Series III bulkhead (except 109 in V8) shows the general layout. All types of bulkhead are fitted in three places:
(Courtesy Land-Rover)

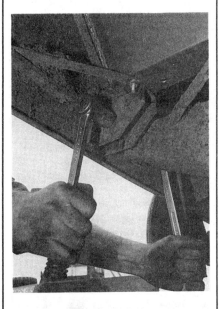

BWR2. A large bolt passes through each side of the bulkhead and connects it to the outrigger and there is also a steering box support bracket to be disconnected.

BWR3. The Series II & IIA bulkhead, shown with windscreen fittings. (Diagram Courtesy Land-Rover).

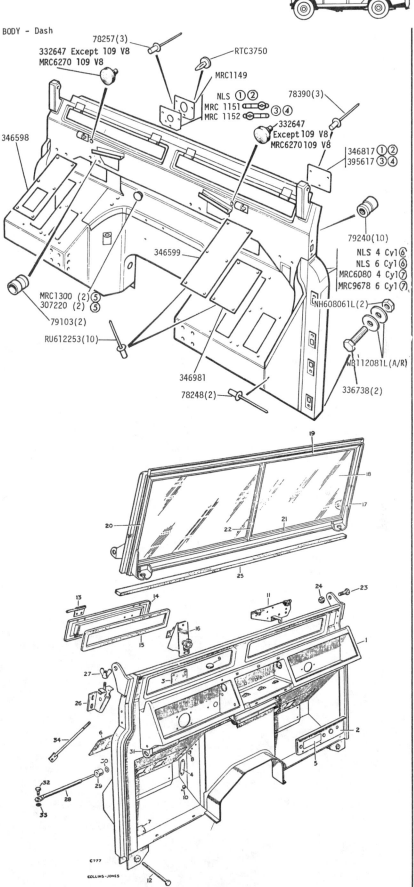

BODY - Dash

78257(3)
332647 Except 109 V8
MRC6270 109 V8
RTC3750
MRC1149
NLS ①②
MRC 1151 ③④
MRC 1152
78390(3)
332647
Except 109 V8
MRC6270 109 V8
346817 ①②
395617 ③④
346598
79240(10)
NLS 4 Cyl ⑥
NLS 6 Cyl ⑥
MRC6080 4 Cyl ⑦
MRC9678 6 Cyl ⑦
346599
NH608061L(2)
MRC1300 (2) ⑤
307220 (2) ⑤
79103(2)
RU612253(10)
WB112081L(A/R)
346981
78248(2)
336738(2)

COLLINS-JONES

89

BWR4. The vast majority of Series I bulkheads look like this one and are made of steel. When they corrode they can be very difficult to repair – see Series I Restoration Section. A very small number of late bulkheads were made of folded aluminium with a more angular appearance. Reproductions bulkheads, the only ones now available, are fabricated in this style, the original tooling having been scrapped. It had outlived is usefulness which is why Land-Rover went over to a fabricated bulkhead for the last few Series I models.
(Courtesy Land-Rover)

Although each bulkhead is only bolted into place in three positions, there are a large number of components to be removed before it can be taken from the vehicle.

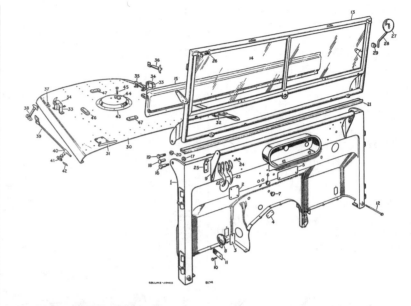

Bulkhead/Footwell repair

BFR1. With the front wing out of the way you can see clearly how corrosion has taken a hold on this part of the bulkhead.

BFR2. With the wing in place, the easiest way to spot such corrosion is from inside the vehicle and this is a view looking down inside the footwell on the left hand side.

BFR3. Dunsfold decided to cut away the entire corroded area on this side of the vehicle – the rust was much worst than appeared at first to be the case...

BFR4. ...and to replace the entire footwell area with a complete repair panel.

BFR5. On the other side of the vehicle the corrosion was more localised and it was possible to fabricate repairs to the bulkhead at this point. Here, a new side plate is being made out of a thick grade of steel. The exact shape was copied from what was left of the side plate on the vehicle.

BFR6. Once the new side plate had been fabricated, the old was cut away, the new one correctly positioned...

BFR7. ...and the new one tack welded into place using the Clarke No-Gas MIG Welder.

BFR8. The Clarke No-Gas leaves tack welds that are relatively clean, when compared with arc welds, but not as clean as those from an argon-arc MIG welder – but you avoid the hassle of having to purchase bottles of gas.

BFR9. The side plate was then MIG welded with longer runs back to the sound area of the bulkhead adjacent to the A-post.

BFR10. The Clarke welder was again called into play as another patch panel was fabricated, the old metal cut out on the new welded in at the end of the footwell panel.

BFR11. The repair was completed around the footwell and a new base fabricated for the bottom of the A-post. Before any welding could be carried out at the bottom of the A-post, it was necessary to remove the sill to avoid any risk of damage to the aluminium, although use of the Clarke MIG welder reduced the risk of damage through heat transference when compared with gas or arc welding. MIG has the distinct advantage that distortion is far less and heat stays in and around the area where it is put! ▶

Chassis repairs

The heart of any Land-Rover is its chassis. A bent wing can easily be replaced. A noisy gearbox is no problem (except

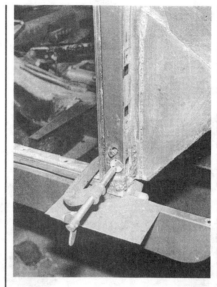

for the cost!) and in general, the Land-Rover is the ultimate in bolt-together vehicles.

However, if the chassis has gone, it's often time to scrap the vehicle – but with one or two provisos. If the components on the chassis are in very good condition, or if the vehicle is of special interest, you can relatively easily rebuild the vehicle around a new chassis, as an earlier Section shows. But what constitutes a scrap chassis and what simply indicates that repairs are needed? Brian Bashall dictated the notes for this section – information right from the horses's mouth!

CR1. A Land-Rover being built up by Dunsfold Land-Rover around a brand new chassis for an owner who wants to keep his vehicle going 'for ever'. You could opt for a non-Land-Rover galvanised chassis or stick with the all-original, brand-new item.

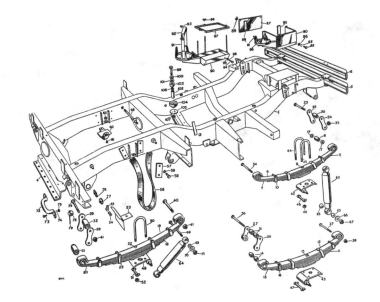

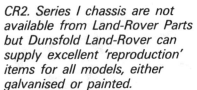

CR2. Series I chassis are not available from Land-Rover Parts but Dunsfold Land-Rover can supply excellent 'reproduction' items for all models, either galvanised or painted.

CR3. Ideal paint for the chassis, giving the appropriate degree of semi-gloss appearance and a hard-wearing finish, is Finnigan's Smoothrite. Finnigan's No. 1 makes an ideal rust-resistant primer. Strongly recommended!

Chassis inspection – (Series II – on)

◄

C1. An aerial view of FVJ's stripped down rolling chassis, albeit with the bulkhead still in place. Our project vehicle needed quite a few repairs to the rear crossmember and outriggers, so it was necessary to remove the body to allow access to the top of the chassis. Not all of the following photographs were taken from FVJ. It wasn't that bad!

C2. With the radiator front valance removed, rot can immediately be seen on the top of the chassis. This is obviously a structural point, with the spring mounted immediately below it, and is quite a common "rot spot".

C3. In the same area, the side of the chassis has also rotted, something which wasn't evident until the front valance had been removed.

C4. The same section is shown here in detail, with the severity of the rot even more obvious. It will be necessary to remove the front bumper in order to repair it.

C5. The checking of outriggers continues, this time the nearside body mount. The top of the section is again rotten, previously hidden by the seat box, and the screwdriver goes through the metal in several areas.

C6. The rear tank outrigger is being inspected, this usually rotting on the chassis side. Scrape away the "scale" and prod around with a screwdriver again to check the condition.

C7. Another favourite place for corrosion! The check strap brackets in which the mud builds up and sits quite happily eating away at the side of the chassis. Regular hosing down underneath your Land-Rover would go a long way towards curing many of these chassis problems...

C8. A close-up of the gusset plate on top of the crossmember, looking straight into the chassis. Rust has eaten through what is a fairly thin section of metal, allowing mud inside the chassis.

C9. It may not look too bad but a quick poke around with the trusty screwdriver will reveal extensive corrosion here on the gearbox outrigger and the main chassis. The chassis on this particular example was scrapped, but illustrates well the sort of areas to look at when inspecting a Land-Rover. ▼

C11. At the end of the chassis,▲ where it slopes downwards, water gathers inside with inevitable consequences... unless someone has had the good sense to remove the rubber bungs that were fitted at the factory! Fortunately, in this instance, they have been removed and the area is solid.

C10. If, when you scrape ▲ away the mud, you find black paint underneath (as shown here on FVJ), you're doing well!

C12. Check, check and check again! At the back of this chassis, near the spring hanger, there is rotten metal, while just a little further to the right of the photograph can be seen black paint and no corrosion problems. The moral of the story is to be extremely *thorough*.

C13. From the outside, this crossmember looked superb. With the body removed it was obvious it had been badly repaired with body filler. The consequences are that the crossmember has very little strength, making this vehicle a danger to drive... particularly if it was used for towing.

C14. The spring hanger itself is a crucial area of any Land-Rover, so be particularly observant when checking around here. ▼

C15. Rot like this around a ▲ shock absorber is very worrying, this being a structural chassis section and the only support for the "shocker".

C16. This rear crossmember, taken from Dunsfold Land-Rover's rubbish tip, is a disgraceful example of a 'repair' carried out with filler in order to fool the ministry testing station, but with no strength to speak of. It's a dangerous and irresponsible thing to do. If buying, check with a magnet; it won't stick to filler!

C17. The Series III chassis, complete with various fixtures, fittings and Land-Rover parts numbers, Note that not all the parts shown fit all vehicles. Part (1) – two required with two-piece axle casing; Part (2) – optional; Part (3) – Germany; Part (4) – up to May 1980; Part (5) – June 1980 – on; Part (6) – metric; Part (7) – 88 in and 109 in only; Part (8) – 109 in 1-ton; Part (9) – alternatives. (Courtesy Land-Rover)

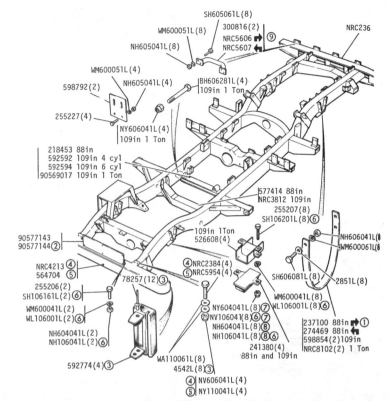

Outrigger replacement – Series II – on

This section deals with what to look for and how to deal with problems in the Land-Rover Series II – on outriggers; probably the most corrosion-prone parts of a Land-Rover's chassis. Note that, contrary to the actions of some garages and DIY-ers, the outriggers cannot be properly replaced with the floorpan in place because the top of the outrigger cannot then be welded to the chassis.

OR1. A bulkhead outrigger, showing a classic case of rot that you can't see until the floorpan is removed. The outrigger will invariably be full of mud and totally rotten.

OR2. The driver's side outrigger, again with the floor removed, shows a build-up of mud on top of the outrigger, which never dries out and therefore rots quite badly. Prod around with a screwdriver and remove the scaly rust; tap the outrigger and if there is a "ring" the outrigger is usually dry and clear, whereas a dull, hollow thud indicates a problem. Series I vehicles are different in this area – see the end of this Section.

OR3. Another very tatty crossmember! The mud is still there and the metal virtually disintegrated when it was prodded with a screwdriver. This is again on the offside of the vehicle; outriggers and crossmembers on the nearside usually last a little longer as the heat from the exhaust tends to dry them out more. ➤

OR4. A completely corroded outrigger, this one supporting the bulkhead and the door pillars. If this is insecure, you can expect an MoT failure certificate, all this being attached and connected to the steering.

OR5. The bulkhead bolt should➤ be removed, in this case not a problem as its mounting had simply rotted away! This is the big bolt that traps the bulkhead and the outrigger together, and is obviously of great importance.

OR6. Shown here are an outrigger and bulkhead, with the bolt being undone (it's usually rusty!). The nut and bolt rust themselves into the socket and removal is far from easy...

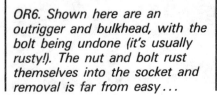

OR7. ...so much so that you may need to apply heat or, as in this instance, even drift out the bolt.

OR10. When encountering rusty nuts and bolts, you can always resort to a hand-grinder or a hacksaw. Hard work but often the only way to deal with these stubborn fellows!

OR11. A bolt is shown here ▲ being drifted out, while the bracket is still on the outrigger...

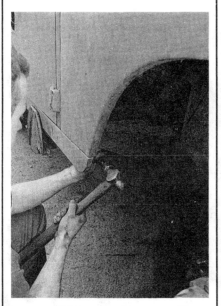

OR8. Here we see a wider view of the same bolt being drifted out backwards, giving an idea of the best stance to take.

OR9. The stay that holds the ➤ bulkhead outrigger to the chassis (an important "steadying influence" on each of these parts!) is cut away; as the stay is going to be replaced at a later stage, it is easiest just to saw through it, particularly as it's a very simple, easy-to-replace component.

◄ OR12. ...but this can often lead to the bracket simply falling away due to extensive corrosion!

OR13. This crossmember has ▲ to be chiselled off, but a hacksaw is needed to get a starting point for the air-chisel.

OR14. An air-chisel is shown here actually cutting away the original weld. If you don't have access to an air-chisel, you can hacksaw down as far as possible and finish off the process with a hand chisel; one of the problems with an air-chisel (even if you do have one) is that it can sometimes cut away some good metal that you intended keeping!

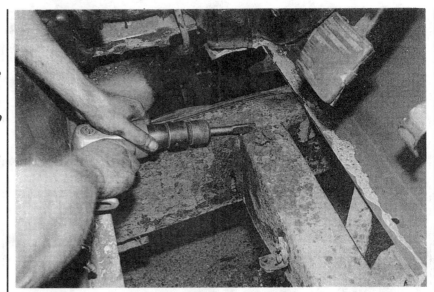

OR15. Another method of removing an outrigger is to carefully cut away the old weld with oxy-acetylene equipment. The beauty of this method is that it avoids the risk of "tearing" the chassis, something to watch out for when chiselling, but all the safety points connected with oxy-acetylene must be remembered during this process.

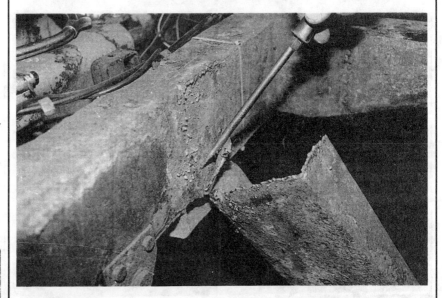

OR16. Both of these outriggers have been removed using oxy-acetylene, achieved without damaging the main chassis section in any way.

OR17. One of the outriggers is actually lifted away...

OR18. ... and can be compared here with a (reproduction) brand new one, complete with base plate for going on to the chassis. This does in fact put the outrigger eye-bolt about $\frac{3}{16}$ in further out, so do be careful when fitting this that you don't position the bulkhead socket wrong in relation to the bulkhead. You may be able to surface-mount this new outrigger or you may have to cut out the side of the chassis and sink it in.

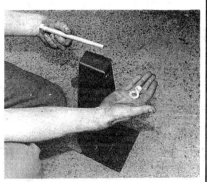

OR19. The bulkhead bolt ▲ described earlier is seen here (a long, thin bolt through the socket, with a washer and lock nut) prior to assembly.

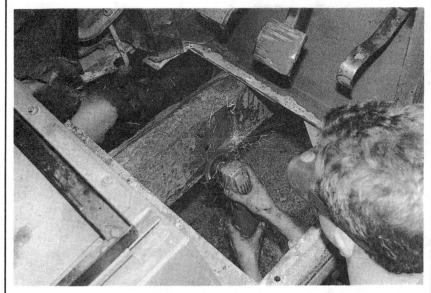

◄
OR20. The chassis side must be cleaned up before attempting to fit a new outrigger. The side is being "scurfed" here with a grinder to ensure the weld will be successful. Do invest in an angle grinder if you don't already have one, as it will save a tremendous amount of sanding and filing in an instance like this. Do wear goggles (essential, as shown here) and heavy industrial gloves whenever working with old, jagged edges of metal and/or grinding stones (important, as not shown here!)

OR21. There's no point welding over rusty areas – you'll simply be hiding the damage rather than repairing it, only to experience even greater problems later. An angle grinder can be used to cut out rust and to get rid of all the bad metal.

OR22. The main chassis section to which you intend welding a new outrigger should be thoroughly prepared. Clean it off carefully . . .

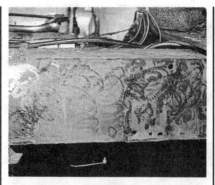

OR23. . . . and then "scurf" it with a grinder to give the weld a good "key". Obviously, all paint and surface rust should be removed from the area before welding begins.

OR24. A new bulkhead outrigger is offered up (although the old one has yet to be removed at this point). You can see clearly how the mounting back-plate on this reproduction outrigger could affect the position of the hole for the bulkhead bolt.

OR25. The main chassis section will need measuring and scribing prior to fitting the bulkhead outrigger, to ensure correct location. On this particular example, the chassis has not been cleaned and de-rusted properly, something which will doubtless be regretted in future years! Needless to say, the work was not carried out by Dunsfold Land-Rover.

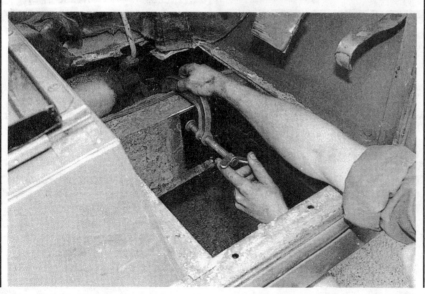

OR26. Still on the same vehicle, the outrigger is clamped in place before initial tacking and final welding.

OR27. The DIY welder can use a Clarke or other top-line make of MIG welder but only if it is one of the more powerful models, or alternatively a Clarke (or similar) medium to heavy-duty arc welder can be used (with extreme care!). With any welding, the secret is first to ensure everything is firmly clamped...

OR28. ...before going on to the stage of tack-welding, at which point you must double-check for correct alignment. Once the outrigger has been tacked, the clamps can be removed. ▶

OR29. Once the outrigger has ▲ been tacked and the bulkhead bolt is in position, the whole section can be seam-welded. Don't be tempted to cut corners at this stage as it is essential to retain the vehicle's original strength.

OR30. Once the welding has been completed, a bracket can be fitted for the side-step. The holes are marked, being careful to ensure their correct position beforehand.

OR31. Moving on to the petrol tank front outrigger (another favourite rusting place), the same system of replacing applies. The outrigger is shown here being offered up after removal of the old one. ►

OR32. It should be clamped in ▲ place...

OR33. ...and then welded on in much the same way as already described. Incidentally, don't be surprised if, when refitted, your fuel tank springs a leak; this often happens after being removed and refitted on to new outriggers.

Outrigger replacement – Series I

OR34. Series I outriggers are not available as Land-Rover original parts, and the repro. parts do not have the relevant mountings for the master cylinder. You have to cut the bottom out of the outrigger, transfer the holding plate from the old outrigger (cut and grind it off after measuring its exact location; weld on to the new), then cut a hole for the linkage in the opposite side. The bottom of the outrigger can then be welded back up with a new plate. The mounting flange has also to be modified to accept the footbrake lever attachments. You will also have to transfer the old brake lever stop to the new outrigger or, as is more likely, fabricate a new one. The whole thing is rather time-consuming!

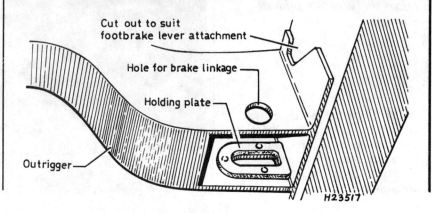

Cut out to suit footbrake lever attachment

Hole for brake linkage

Holding plate

Outrigger

H23517

Rear crossmember replacement

CM1. A tidy looking rear crossmember to begin with, but scraping away the paint revealed a repair patch and body filler. The latter is inexcusable in any part of a Land-Rover chassis, particularly the rear crossmember which takes so much strain when towing.

CM2. A closer look at the rear end of the chassis, the crossmember still looking quite sound here!

CM3. When replacing a crossmember, it is essential that the new one fits exactly. It is a good idea to make a very simple angle-iron jig before cutting off the crossmember.

CM4. A different view of the angle-iron, showing how the simple skeleton frame has been made...

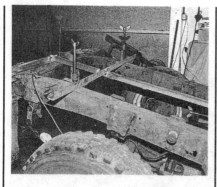

CM5. ...and welded for extra rigidity and accuracy. The frame or jig needs to be carefully clamped to the chassis before work begins and...

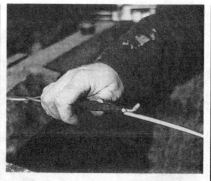

CM6. ...before you even think about cutting off the rear crossmember the wiring has to be rescued that runs inside the chassis.

CM7. The cutting is about to start! In this instance, oxy-acetylene is to be used.

CM8. The first cut has been made, taking care at all times to ensure that not too much chassis is cut away unnecessarily. It's best to cut away a little at a time than to make one cut too far!

CM9. Here we see the outside of the chassis rail, the operator getting rid of the crossmember body outrigger. In the home workshop, you really must ensure that rear mud flaps and anything else that is flammable is removed first.

CM10. Work is now started on the far side of the chassis rail and here we see the crossmember very close to removal.

CM11. The crossmember on the floor, with some of the previous repairs now visible.

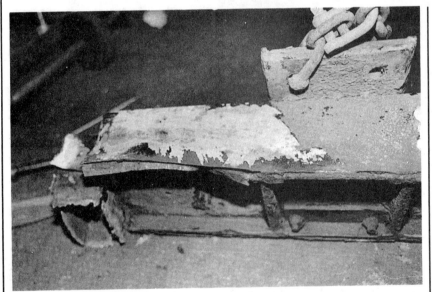

CM12. A new crossmember ► (with extensions) that has been slipped over the rusty chassis as a makeshift repair. Absolutely no welding has been carried out on top of the chassis, and this is a potentially dangerous vehicle. It looks good but the crossmember isn't really attached to much.

CM13. Back on the subject of ▲ how to do it properly, the first of the plated repairs can be seen here. When plating, make sure you use substantial steel or else a great deal of strength will be lost.

CM14. Seen here is the plate ▲ that's been cut and will be put in adjacent to the rear spring hanger. The bottom of the chassis has been cut out ahead of the spring hanger.

CM15. Chassis extensions are welded in position. They overlap onto the bottom of the chassis by about six inches to ensure adequate strength.

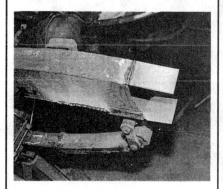

CM16. Another view of the extensions, all ready to accept the new rear crossmember.

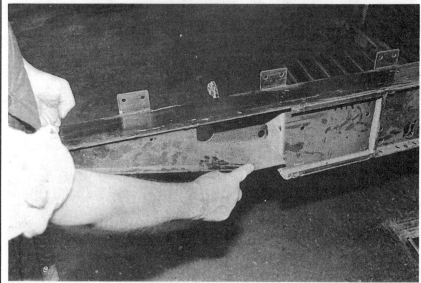

CM17. New Land-Rover Parts crossmembers require the aforesaid extension plates to be fitted because, as shown here, they are 'bare' in the area in which the chassis rails are to be fitted, just as on the production line. Some non-Land-Rover crossmembers come with extensions built in.

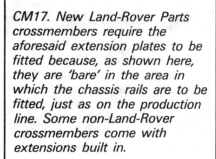

CM18. This is the rear of a new Land-Rover (original) chassis, illustrating the way it was originally joined together. You will have cut right through the ends of the original chassis rail ends in order to have removed the rear crossmember.

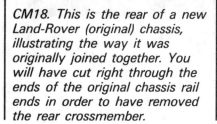

CM19. Philip and Brian Bashall hold up a Land-Rover 'Genuine Part' crossmember, for illustration purposes...

CM20. ...the crossmember can now be slid into place, but don't forget to keep cross-checking with the jig for accuracy and positioning.

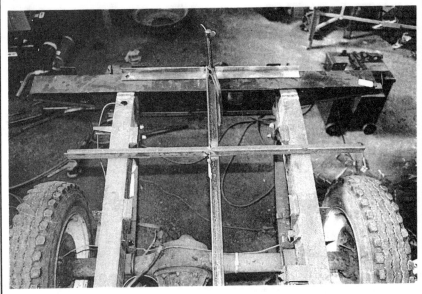

CM21. These gusset plates repair the side of the chassis and weld into the crossmember.

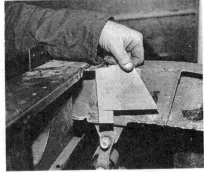

CM22. Shown here is the inner gusset plate. Cut and weld at an angle rather than vertically as this will again provide greater strength.

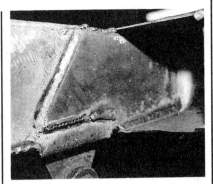

CM23. The plate is now in position with the seam-welding completed. Note the angle of cut and weld.

CM24. *The top of the repaired chassis section should be welded to the crossmember...*

CM25. *...and another gusset plate should be made as a strengthener in this area.*

CM26. *This can now be welded in place. Note in this picture the piece of wire in the chassis which was attached to the five-core cable before cutting began. The cable can now be retrieved through the back section again.*

CM27. *Not wishing to appear pessimistic, but it is also possible to purchase a full, rear half-chassis if things have gone too far. But if things are really so bad, you would probably be better off with a full chassis replacement, especially when you consider the extreme difficulty of correctly aligning a half-chassis when welding it into place.*

Finally, all the way through this process, it is advisable to put the angle-iron jig in position regularly, just to check the positioning of the new crossmember... before it's too

late! Once the repairs are completed, prevent corrosion setting in again by treating the chassis with a rust-inhibiting primer followed by grey primer and chassis-black on top, then spray Waxoyl into the inner faces and enclosed box sections. Underseal is not necessarily the best thing as it can crack and trap water behind it. Always remember to hose down the underside of your Land-Rover at regular intervals – it saves a lot of work *and* expense in the long run!

Body removal

A section featuring various tips about removing a Land-Rover body:

Start by removing the nuts and bolts holding the rear body onto the crossmember. Be careful not to damage the body when doing this.

Split the seat box and the rear body. As with all the floor panels, gearbox tunnels and so on, there is an adhesive sealer between the two surfaces (partly to keep the steel and aluminium sections separate and prevent a metal-to-metal reaction).

110

If your Land-Rover is fitted with an optional side-step, this is a fairly easy piece to unbolt and remove.

A hardtop mounting bolt which goes through the hood tube; a special bolt with a built-on washer on top; the large washer, spring washer and nut go underneath.

Removal of the valance between the radiator surround panel and the bumper. There are two bolts along the radiator panel and two self-tapping screws through the chassis at the front. This panel can now be removed. Check for corrosion on top of the chassis underneath the valance.

The offside centre body, just behind the fuel tank, is now removed. If the nuts and bolts aren't seized, it's a simple procedure!

The rear body is then completely removed and the fuel tank exposed. You *must* blank off the filler tube, in this case using a plastic bung. When removing the fuel tank, be careful not to strain the flanges or the tank may spring a leak.

The bonnet stay needs to be removed before the front wing can be taken off. Again, there should be no great problem to undo the bolts holding it in place.

You may have to search hard for the bolt that holds the inside of the wing to the steering box steady plate.

Footnote – It is essential to remove the fuel tank connections before taking off the body. For details, see the Fuel Tank Removal section.

Fitting a complete body to a galvanised chassis

Land-Rover chassis are very strongly built and very long lasting as a consequence. If left untreated, even the strongest chassis will deteriorate over a period of time and owners are well advised to treat all the enclosed sections with Waxoyl whilst the outsides would benefit from being painted with Hammerite or Smoothrite, the latter giving a more original appearance. If treated on a regular basis, a sound Land-Rover chassis should last almost indefinitely. However, if your vehicle has a completely rusted out chassis and the vehicle is still worth saving, you may wish to consider fitting one of Dunsfold's galvanised chassis frames, whose life time should measure many decades rather than years.

GC1. A Dunsfold mechanic takes this opportunity to service the mechanical components before the body is fitted.

GC2. The completely built up rolling chassis which has been fitted with a new fuel tank at the same time.

GC3. The truck cab body is ▲ attached to the Dunsfold hoist (actually a very large ex-military fork lift truck, used especially for this particular job!) in such a way that no damage can be caused.

GC4. The complete body is ▲ lifted well into the air, right over the Land-Rover's mechanical components. It is considered possible for six able bodied men to carry out this part of the work, although it would probably be as well to have another well informed person on hand to ensure that the body is correctly fitted to the chassis as it is lowered – see following captions.

◄

GC5. Very slowly, the body is lowered over the mechanical components. The body itself is not perfect, but now that the chassis has been replaced, the body can be ungraded over a long period of time – an instance of a "rolling restoration, carried out in an intelligent way." You do the structural, non-cosmetic stuff first, then the essential electrical and mechanical components, and only then the least important cosmetic aspects.

GC6. This is where the informed observer will be essential – checking that nothing is fouling on the way down.

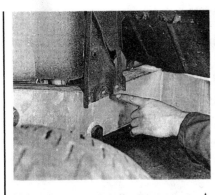

GC7. It is especially important ▲ to ensure that the body to chassis mountings fit the correct side of the chassis rails rather than sit on top of them.

GC8. While that weight is off ▲ the body shell, another pair of hands can relatively easily pull the body forwards or push it back while the observer checks that all is well.

GC9. The body fits neatly into place on the chassis.

◄

GC10. The new fuel tank is ▲ connected up to the filler and breather hoses. If an existing fuel tank had been used, it would have been bunged for safety.

GC11. At the front of the vehicle, before any of the mounting bolts are fitted, it is important to fit the rubber buffer between the body and the chassis mounting plate as shown.

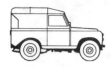

GC12. You can now fit the mounting bolts to the chassis mounting near the front wheels...

GC14 ... and bolt the rear of the body to the rear crossmember. For other mounting points see the relevant sections on piece meal body removal in earlier parts of this Chapter.

Fitting a tow bracket

The simplest way of fitting a tow bracket to a Land-Rover is to bolt a towing pin or tow ball to the holes provided in the rear crossmember. The only problem is that the holes are too high for most non-agricultural trailers.

FTB1. Dunsfold Land-Rover fitted a Dixon-Bate adjustable tow coupling to the project Land-Rover. This component is available from all Land-Rover Parts outlets. Also fitted was the Dixon-Bate combined tow ball and towing pin to enable towing of either type of trailer hitch. When coupled with the ability to lower and raise the tow hitch level at will this is the most flexible system available. The only major disadvantage is that the spare wheel can no longer be carried on the rear door wheel carrier on models so equipped. The model that succeeded the Series III, the 110 overcame this problem. ▼

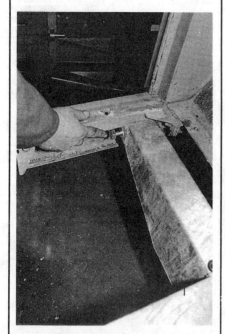

GC13. ... and fit new bolts to ▲ the outrigger-to-bulkhead mounting points...

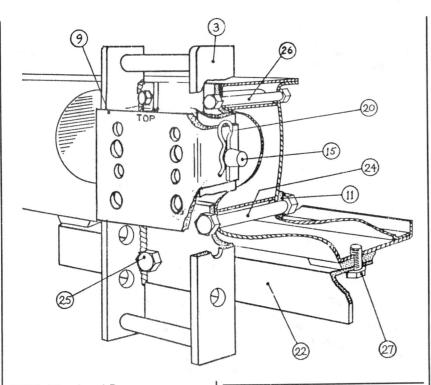

FTB2. The Land-Rover Parts/Dixon-Bate adjustable tow bracket is fitted by bolting the adjustable bracket through the holes in the Land-Rover crossmember (see bolt Nos 26 & 24) and the bottom of the bracket is reinforced by fitting part No. 22 – all fairly straightforward! (Courtesy Dixon-Bate)

Land-Rover Parts also supply towing electrics kits allowing either a single seven pin plug and socket for normal trailer use or dual sockets for caravan use, the second socket providing auxiliary power for equipment such as caravan refrigerators and interior lights. Another Land-Rover Parts accessory is the split-charge unit which allows the Land-Rover's electrical system to charge both the vehicle and auxiliary batteries as you are driving along. You will note from FTB1. that Dunsfold Land-Rover like to fit the single trailer wiring socket into the power takeoff hole in the rear crossmember because there it is perfectly protected from accidental damage.

Painting – Preparation and Safety

The importance of getting the paintwork right on a restored Land-Rover can't be over-stressed! You may have spent weeks of your life making your vehicle as sound as the day the makers conceived it, but unless the paintwork is right, the whole effect will be spoiled. It's a big mistake to believe that a vehicle designed as a workhorse won't benefit from being made to look its best. Re-painting a car is actually a major subject in itself, but provided you keep things simple, there will be enough information here to enable you to have a go at doing it yourself. If you feel you need to know more this author has written another book with Haynes called *The Car Bodywork Repair Manual* which is about the same size as this book, but which does nothing but give information on how to fix car bodywork. So there is a very large amount of information in there on all aspects of paint

spraying for the home sprayer.

But back to the specifics of the Land-Rover: Your first decision must be to pick the type of paint you wish to use. The very best is not at all suitable for the home sprayer unless you possess well above average levels of equipment. It's known generally as 'two-pack' paint because the paint is mixed with a hardener before spraying and it then sets rather like an adhesive. The finish from the gun is superb, the paint film is much harder than anything else on offer and it doesn't need polishing for many years, a wash and leather down restoring its shine. The snag is that the air-borne particles of paint are toxic, containing iso-cyanate; the family connection with the word 'cyanide' not being coincidental! Professionals use an air-fed mask when spraying with this type of paint, but the home sprayer would also have to be certain that the spray mist would not cause anyone else potential harm. This clearly is impossible in most domestic circumstances, such as where the garage is attached to the house or where children or other inquisitive souls could be in the vicinity.

The author's Land-Rover is shown being sprayed in this section by GM Accident Repairs, near Godalming, using Glasurit paint in a professional booth, and that may be another option open to you; to go as far as you can in preparing the car then take it to a specialist (who will invariably criticise your preparation and want to do more – if he doesn't, ask yourself why!) and have the paint put on. This is actually quite a cost-effective thing to do because the most time-consuming part of the job is the preparation. Glasurit paints are supplied to Land-Rover as 'original' equipment, by the way, so its use for refinishing is perfectly appropriate here!

The only other type of paint

that I could possibly recommend is Cellulose Enamel paint. Cellulose isn't and hasn't been used by any of the vehicle manufacturers for many years, but it is more suitable for DIY use. If a face mask of the correct type is used and the spray area kept ventilated, the fumes are not especially dangerous (but read carefully the Safety Section of the Appendix to this book) and the finish will be quite durable. It also has two advantages for the home restorer. Any home paint job is almost certain to have bits of dust of kamikaze flies land in it and these can be most easily polished out from cellulose, and so can any runs that the unskilled sprayer might have incurred. Also, if cellulose is 'cut & polished' (rubbed down with extremely fine abrasive paper then with polishing compound) it is possible to obtain the sort of 'mirror' finish that no other paint will give. Trouble is, it doesn't last, and you have to polish the shine back again, in the end polishing right through the paint over a period of years.

Safety
Cellulose paint:

The spray is volatile – keep away from all flames or sparks – and so are the fumes from paint and thinners while thinner dampened rags are also a fire hazard. The spray can cause you to lose consciousness if inhaled in a confined area. Always use a suitable face mask (see your supplier) and ventilate the work area. Protect hands with a barrier cream or wear protective gloves when handling paint. Keep well away from eyes.
'2-pack' paint:
Spray from this type of paint is toxic to the degree that it can be lethal! (The hardened paint on the car is not

dangerous, of course!) Only use with an air-fed mask from a clean compressed air source (i.e. not from within the spray area) and never use this type of paint where the spray could affect others. It can also cause eye irritation and eye protection should be worn. Protective gloves should be worn when mixing and handling paint. Those who suffer from asthma or other respiratory illness should have nothing to do with this type of paint spraying! There is also a fire risk with peroxide catalysts.
General:
Don't eat, drink or smoke near the work area, clean hands after the work is complete, but never use thinners to wash paint from hands. Always wear an efficient particle mask when sanding down.
OBTAIN AND THOROUGHLY READ THE MANUFACTURER'S DATA AND SAFETY SHEETS BEFORE USE.

For best results the old paint should be removed. (If spraying over old paint, you may have to apply a separate layer of a special isolating paint as different paints can show disastrous reactions if sprayed on top of one another. Check for this effect first by wiping over a small area of old paintwork with the new paint thinners. If wrinkling occurs the two paint systems are incompatible and an isolator will be required. Check repaired and pre-primered areas too. Make sure that the areas where you don't want stripper are adequately masked over. Old newspaper is acceptable, but since newsprint 'leaching' out into new paintwork is not unheard of, strong brown wrapping paper is better. Ensure that you wear gloves (and wear safety glasses) in case of spills etc. Stripper, as you might expect, is very corrosive and will damage eyes and skin if

splashed on to them. Read the safety notes that come with the stripper before use. Let the old paint wrinkle up and then remove with a metal scraper, still wearing gloves and goggles! But take *great* care not to scratch or scrape the aluminium with the scraper blade.

It is far from unknown for Land-Rovers to be painted by brush or spray-on oil-based paints, more suitable for goods vehicles. Any attempt to spray 2-pack or cellulose paint on top will involve a severe reaction taking place. There are two solutions, if you don't wish to respray with the same type of inferior, slow-drying paint again. One is to strip all of the old paint off; another is to completely prepare the surface, then spray it with an isolator paint, such as that produced by Glasurit, which has a water base and thus will neither react with what is beneath nor the paint to be sprayed on top.

PS1. The Glasurit range covers the highly commended 2-pack paints shown here and also a full range of the more DIY – friendly cellulose paints.

PS2. The Clarke 'Ranger' is a very popular 'first time buyer' compressor, just capable of completing a full respray, and fine for smaller jobs including use for other purposes such as tyre inflating, etc.

PS3. Going further up the scale, the Clarke 'Rebel' Air 50 is probably as large as the average DIY user will buy but it will cope easily with a full paint job or for powering most air tools. There are many other first class compressors in the huge Clarke range.

PS4. This is the compressor-operated Clarke random orbit sander which does an excellent job of quickly sanding filler, paintwork and primer without leaving scuff marks (virtue of the 'random orbit' feature), saving hours of hand-work. Highly recommended! Before carrying out any preparatory work on your Land-Rover, you should wipe down all of the paintwork with wax-and-grease remover, such as that made by Glasurit shown in R19 and R20, in the section to follow. This will get rid of grease and silicone deposits that will otherwise be integrated into the bodywork when you sand down – it won't just be sanded away!

The Respray

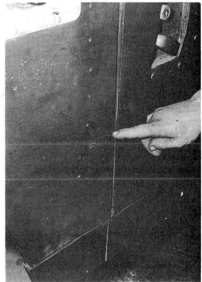

R1. One of the great attractions of the author's Land-Rover, FVJ, was that the bodywork was in such sound and original condition. Although aluminium does not easily corrode, it does dent more easily than steel and this ding, just behind the driver's door, was the worst scar that FVJ had suffered.

R2. FVJ was still equipped ▲ with her original paint, and so it was decided to respray on top. The first job was to use a power sander just to take off the paint from the area of the dent and the area that surrounded it, but taking care not to go deeply into the aluminium nor to damage any of the rivet heads.

R3. Gerald Perrett of GM Accident Repairs who carried out the preparation and painting on FVJ, mixed Glasurit 2-Pack filler on a piece of card. First job was to use the spatula to scoop sufficient filler onto the card...▶

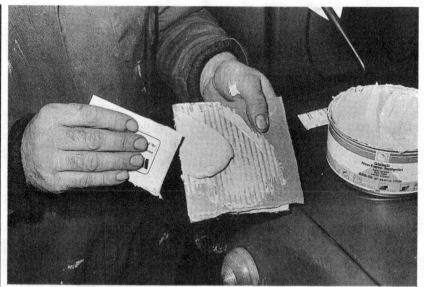

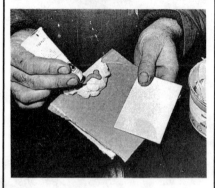

R4. ... followed by the amount of hardener recommended in the instructions. ▲

R5. Filler and hardener have to be mixed until they form a uniform colour. NOTE THAT GLASURIT STRONGLY RECOMMEND, FOR SAFETY REASONS, THAT YOU ALWAYS WEAR RUBBER GLOVES WHEN WORKING WITH 2-PACK FILLER OR STOPPER OF ANY KIND. FOLLOW THE SAFETY NOTES WITH THE PACKAGING AND ASK YOUR SUPPLIER FOR APPLICATION NOTES AND FOLLOW THEM. ▶

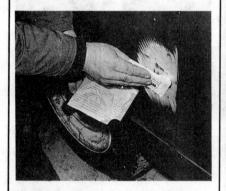

R6. Gerald applied filler to the dent...

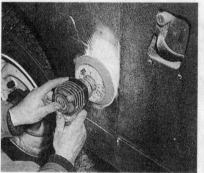

R7. ... a random orbit sander was used for sanding down the filler (for DIY preparation mentioned earlier, the Clarke sander would be ideal)...

R8. ... and the filler was left flush with the surrounding panel. Note that Gerald is wearing goggles and this is essential for safety reasons.

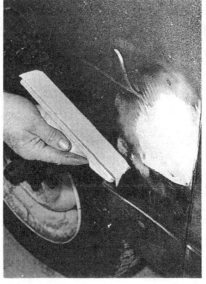

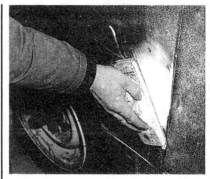

R11. The coarse sand paper is used to reduce the filler down to the final level required . . .

R9. As ever, it was necessary to apply more filler, although this time it could be applied in a very thin coat. When the level of the filler is built up sufficiently, Glasurit 2-Pack stopper can be used to take out any minor blemishes (Stopper is a much smoother and finer version of filler. Cellulose stopper is not recommended because as it dries it shrinks.)

R10. GM Accident Repairs have a full range of sanding blocks to suit each length of sand paper required. You would be well advised not to support the sand paper with your fingers, but to make up a wooden block to do the same job.

R12. . . . . and then the aforementioned stopper applied in a very thin coat.

R13. Here the author applies body filler to light accident damage to his Series I Land-Rover. Note that the correct type of filler must always be used – Glasurit fillers are specially formulated so that they will "stick" to aluminium (this was so that they could also be used over zinc-plated panels such as those used by Audi and Porsche) but some are not. Check before you use! If you have to use a filler that is not formulated for use on zinc and aluminium, ensure that you spray or brush paint the area being worked on with 'etch' primer before applying the filler.

R14. An electric orbital sander is here used for sanding down – fine where there is only a small area to work with and where you are confident of covering up the subsequent sanding marks with a high-build primer or by more hand sanding. But DON'T use electrical equipment with water from wet-or-dry rubbing down lying on the floor or on the panel.

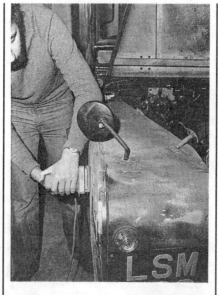

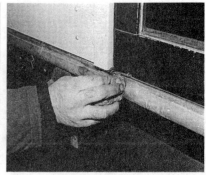

R17. Gerald used a pad of wire wool to buff them...

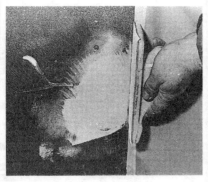

R15. Back to FVJ, Gerald dealt with the front edge of the filled area using a sanding block once again so as to ensure that he ended up with a straight edge of the corner of the panel.

R16. We discussed with GM Accident Repairs the condition of the zinc plated strips on the Land-Rover, some of which were becoming discoloured.

R18. ... and restored them to their former condition and colour. If the galvanising has completely gone, you will either have to replace the strips with better ones, have them re-galvanised, or paint them with something like Wurth zinc-rich primer followed by a coat of clear lacquer. This will give an approximate colour match and an extremely high level of protection although the strips will not look perfectly original.

R19. Before going any further Gerald wiped the entire bodywork of the Land-Rover down once again with Glasurit wax and grease remover...

R20. ... using a brand new clean rag and turning it regularly. It was now time to begin final flatting.

R21. The old fashioned way is with a rubber sanding block, wet-or-dry paper and water with a spot of washing up liquid in it.

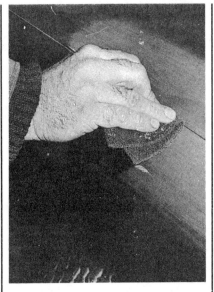

R22. For some of the trickiest little places, GM Accident Repairs favour the use of an abrasive cloth, rather like a washing up pad but specially produced for the job and available from your local motor factors.

R23. For the larger flat panels it was back to the random orbit sander...
◄

R24. ... which is held flat on ▲ the panel and moved carefully across it avoiding any raised areas, and avoiding corners and curved surfaces.

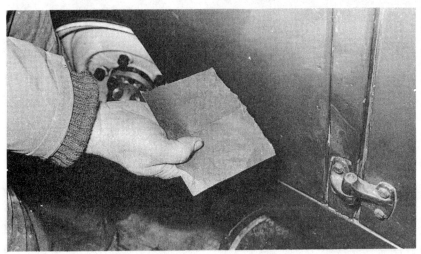

R25. For the small areas around the hinges and the curved part of the wing top, Gerald went back to wet-or-dry paper...

R26 ... and because he was not sanding large areas, the fingers were the best tool for the job.

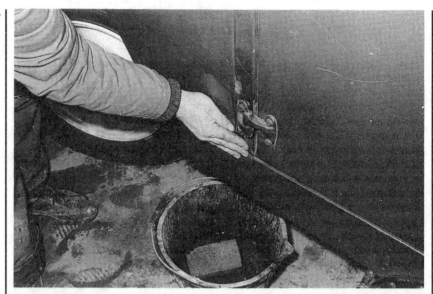

R27. FVJ was by now looking rather denuded with patches of bare aluminium where the paint had been sanded through. Some of the masking off had, by this time, been carried out ... ►

R28. ... and Gerald continued by putting a line of masking tape along the edge of the galvanised strip. ▲

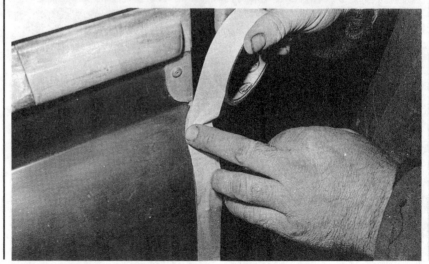

R29. Around the twiddly bits on the corners, Gerald eased the tape so that, as far as possible, it followed the shape of the galvanised strip but where necessary over-lapped it ...

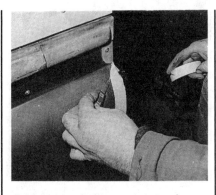

R30. ... and then using a sharp knife, he cut the tape to the shape of the galvanised strip, tucking the edge of the tape over the edge of the strip.

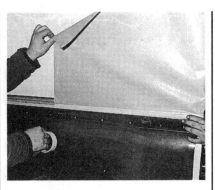

R31. Brown paper with more masking tape was used to cover the hardtop and the large areas such as the engine bay which were not to be painted.

R32. The Series I restoration covered elsewhere in this book and carried out on behalf of John Fletcher in Worcestershire, involved the vehicle's paintwork being applied whilst the body was in component form.

R33. Here you can see that several coats of primer have been applied and flatted down to remove all traces of blemish. John's restoration shop uses an airline which is invaluable when it comes to blowing sanding dust away from the work area, especially if you're using dry sanding paper – another option. Note that, even with a full strip down, the galvanised strips are left in place because of the difficulty of replacing the rivets satisfactorily.

R34. Back at GM Accident Repairs, Gerald's painter moves into the paint store to select the appropriate Glasurit primer...

R35. ...while FVJ was pushed into the spray booth and there heated for a while until all traces of moisture had been driven from the bodywork.

R36. Starting at the far right hand corner the Glasurit 2-Pack primer has been applied, working forwards towards the front of the vehicle.

R37. Gerald's painter is working in vertical strips, having moved around the front of the vehicle and now working down one side.

R38. He can here be seen moving the gun from top to bottom as he sprays the front left hand wing. Just in the foreground, you can catch a glimpse of the bonnet which is sitting on a trestle ready to be sprayed separately.

R39. FVJ, resplendent in her first coat of etch primer. Note how, in the earlier views, the painter wore the sorts of protective equipment that you might think would be suitable for walking on the moon! This indicates the potential hazards of 2-pack and its unsuitability for DIY spraying.

Applying the top coat

Before the top coat can be applied, a further coat of Glasurit primer was sprayed onto the vehicle giving sufficient depth to sand out any of the tiniest blemishes which would have appeared. The rest of this section details how a DIY sprayer might apply cellulose paint as a top coat, even though FVJ was painted in the superior 2-pack Glasurit paint used by GM Accident Repairs. In one or two of the succeeding shots, you may notice cans labelled 'Valentine'. The Valentine range of cellulose paints has since been superseded by Glasurit's own range of cellulose paint. If you use Glasurit paint at home, be sure to specify to your supplier that you want Glasurit cellulose. After the final coat of primer had been sprayed and rubbed down, a very thin coat of black paint was sprayed as a mist, hardly covering the primer beneath. In a moment you'll see why!

Tools required:
The same Clarke equipment and other 'hardware' as was used previously. Top coat paint must be strained through a paper filter obtainable from your paint suppliers. After painting, be prepared to use P1200 wet-or-dry paper and polishing compound for polishing out any dirt particles that may get into the final coat.

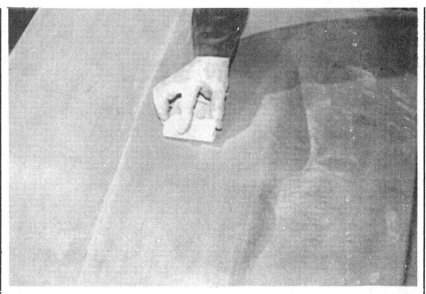

TC1. When the primer is 'blocked' down with fine paper, the thin 'guide' coat which was sprayed on with the Clarke gun (although you could have used aerosol for greater speed), is sanded off as the primer filler coat is made smooth. It remains visible in the low spots, however, picking them out.

TC3. Use an airline to blow any dust from around the top of the tin. Clarke produced a trigger operated 'Blowgun', if you prefer.

TC2. Before spraying the top coat, wet the floor to lay the dust. Take great care to avoid electrical connections and to not use electrical appliances anywhere near the wet floor.

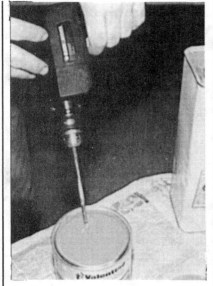

TC4. A cordless drill is used for several minutes with a paint stirrer to mix the entire contents of the cellulose paint – an essential step.

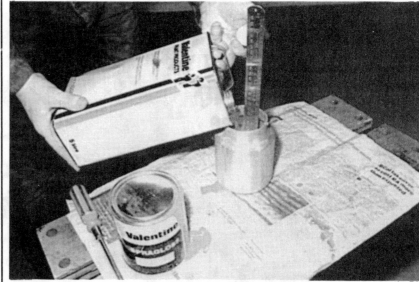

TC6. Pour in an equal amount of thinner. Note: The supply of copious amounts of newspaper is essential!

TC7. After using the Clarke Air ▶ airline to blow off the panel once more, wipe it down yet again with spirit wipe...

TC5. Use a steel rule, if you haven't got the correct painter's measuring stick, to measure the correct amount of paint and thinners.

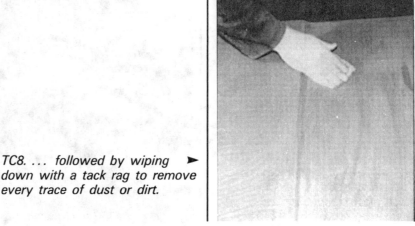

TC8. ... followed by wiping ▶ down with a tack rag to remove every trace of dust or dirt.

TC9. An accepted way of checking that the Clarke gun is held the correct distance away is to use a hand span as a measure.

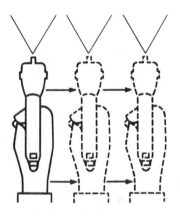

TC10. Keep your wrists stiff and avoid swinging the gun in an arc from your elbow, to ensure even spraying. Always spray at a steady, even pace. (Diagram Courtesy of Glasurit).

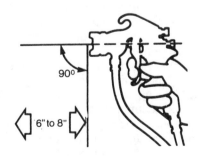

TC11. Always hold the spray gun at right angles to the surface you are painting, keeping it between six and eight inches from the car. (Diagram Courtesy of Glasurit)

Fitting a radiator muff

Back in 1930-something Kingsbury radiator muffs were all the rage. They are still made today to the original high specification with chromium plated brass fittings and leather tabs by Latex Cushion Ltd in Birmingham. It is possible to purchase a radiator muff for every single model of Land-Rover from Latex Cushion or through retailers.

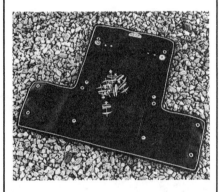

RM1. A Kingsbury radiator muff with all its fittings for a Series II and IIA Land-Rover.

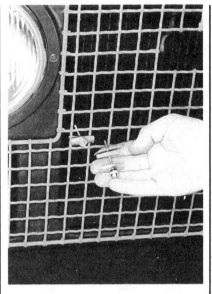

RM2. The muff mounting clips ▲ are screwed to the radiator using the muff itself as a guide as to where they go. When the muff is removed in the summer, the clips can be left in place.

RM3. The centre panel of the muff can be rolled down, and in a temperate climate, the flow of air through the radiator will probably be sufficient all the year round. If in doubt, however, remove the muff during the summer months and fit a temperature gauge to be certain.

4 Series I Restoration

RN1. The original Series I, the way Land-Rover conceived it.

We spoke to Dunsfold Land-Rover's Brian Bashall, a true expert on the marque, to gain an insight into the prospect of restoring a Series I Land-Rover and exactly what's involved. He supplied a lot of useful and interesting information during our time with him.

Restoration can be divided into four sections, but whatever your methods it is going to cost money and a lot of time!

At the outset, you should perhaps decide which of these four paths you intend following with your own particular Land-

Rover: 1). The best Land-Rover in the world with new parts all round – something of a fool's paradise really in Brian's view! 2). A concours level, being the highest standards to which you can possibly get your Land-Rover (within reason), not altering the original specification... but, of course, you won't use the vehicle because it won't necessarily comply with all of today's regulations. 3). Concours but with concessions to today's traffic conditions and regulations, ensuring it can be used both safely and legally on the road... though not taking it out in the rain of course! 4). And finally, a very tidy example with essentials like windscreen washers and flashers fitted as a

matter of course; a high enough standard to attract admirers and onlookers, but useful enough to use every day if required.

Most Land-Rover restorations end up based on the latter principle – real eye-catchers but with up-to-date improvements.

In Brian's opinion, the idea of a restoration is to get a vehicle up to the condition in which it left the factory (with obvious concessions, as already mentioned); so many concours Land-Rovers now boast highly polished and burnished parts (from the radiator brass to the brake pipes), none of which were like that when the vehicles left the factory and, Brian feels, actually detract from the appeal of a restored vehicle.

SO1. LYC 187, a 1950 80 in Land-Rover, looked a little the worse for wear before its restoration began! It was obvious right from the start that this particular Series I, owned by John Fletcher in Worcestershire, had led a hard life during its four decades both on and off the road.

SO2. The beauty of this example was the fact that it was complete, albeit badly corroded in places. The chassis was in poor shape, the lights were rusted out and it was typical of any Land-Rover that had spent most of its life as a farm vehicle!

SO3. An aerial shot of the 1.5-litre engine, which again was remarkably complete. Even the old fashioned coil was there, as were the regulator and fuse box. Even if nothing is savable in such a case, at least it's clear where everything goes – a great help to any would-be restorer.

SO4. The car-number plate fitted at the factory (the number beginning with 'R' for right-hand-drive), attached by screws to the left-hand side of the engine bay. It is important when buying a Land-Rover for restoration to check that it has its identifying plates, as well as (if possible) the old-style logbook and the latest V5 Registration Document.

SO5. Another small plate, this time proclaiming "Manufactured By The Rover Co. Ltd, Birmingham, England"; this can be found on the Series I alongside the dashboard. There should be another plate in the form of a lubrication chart on the radiator surround panel. ▶

SO6. The big strip-down is well under way! The bulkhead, body and seat box are all removed, leaving the bare running gear. This is a major undertaking that should not be embarked upon lightly. Remember that when stripping a vehicle, you'll need the space for about five vehicles once everything is spread out around you. You'll need to keep everything where you can easily find it again and it's a good idea to take lots of photographs at each stage of the strip-down/rebuild to help you remember where different parts go. The instructions we have given for body removal for the Series IIA elsewhere in the book are essentially the same as for the Series I shown here.

SO7. An indication of the state of the chassis, with lots of really thick rust! You can also see the fairly solid looking fuel tank, and the brake reservoir attached to it. The handbrake mechanism looks equally the worse for wear!

SO8. A close-up of the gearbox. This particular one is of the freewheel variety, despite having the "yellow knob" rather than the chain-through-the-floor system usually associated with early Land-Rovers. You could be forgiven for thinking you'd got a later gearbox with a cut-out, but in fact that didn't come in until 1952.

SO9. The square plate on the right-hand side of the instrument panel carries instructions for High and Low range settings, plus a warning underneath about four-wheel-drive on hard surfaces. The steering box was later modified as it used to break away from the bulkhead – that rusty plate under the steering column is an angle plate intended to strengthen the bulkhead at that point and prevent the steering box from "fretting".

SO10. The nearside outer front wing was in very good condition. There was virtually no corrosion and even the rear edge of the wing (where there are two bolt holes and two slots) was intact and remarkably corrosion-free. Fibreglass or aluminium replica front wings for the Series I are now available, as supplies of originals have virtually dried up.

SO11. A common (but not too ▲ serious) problem on old Land-Rovers is the "arc" of corrosion that sets in where the tailgate chains swing against the bodywork. The D-shape light on this example is one of the originals with the divided glass (now very hard to come by), and the old Land-Rover plates are also difficult to obtain and can corrode quite badly.

SO12. Still at the back but on the opposite side, the number-plate is attached – note the larger letters on these early models' number-plates compared with those of today. At this time, all Land-Rovers left the factory with blank, black plates front and rear so that, wherever in the world they ended up, the letters and numbers simply had to be painted on!

SO13. One of the problems on the 80 in Land-Rovers was that they had no capping on the vertical of the rear body and this invariably got bent and cracked – as can be seen. This one has received a patch sometime in its life.

◄ SO14. This shot shows the "Threepenny Bit" windscreen wiper motor, a correct feature on a Land-Rover of this age. Also visible is the trafficator switch mounted in the centre of the windscreen frame, and the windscreen heater can also be seen. Being a civilian Land-Rover, the panel at the bottom of the windscreen is non-opening.

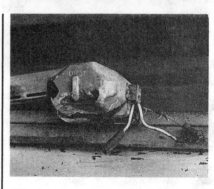

SO15. A close-up of the wiper motor which should have a black "crackle" finish. The plastic sleeve connectors are incorrect (they should be black rubber).

SO16. An alternative view of ▲
the wiper motor.

SO17. The bulkhead ▲
reinforcement plate (which is
badly rusted) can be seen clearly
here. Decay in this area is a real
problem on 80 in models. The
pressed part of the bulkhead and
the footwell have rusted out on
the door pillar – not an unusual
problem!

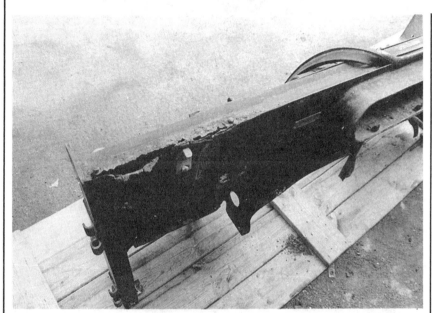

SO18. Higher up, where the
horizontal and vertical sections
join under the windscreen, these
can break away. This is an MoT
failure point as, on the driver's
side, the steering box is mounted
on the rear face of the bulkhead
and is therefore quite loose. The
answer is to rebuild the vertical
rear side of the bulkhead and the
horizontal under the windscreen.

SO19. Another view of the
driver's side, rotted away. The
rubber seal that mounts on this
surface under the windscreen
always traps the water and
never dries out fully, hence the
problem with rot. Also shown
are the two bolts for the steering
box mounting.

SO20. Corrosion can be seen here on the passenger-side door pillar, as well as round the clip at the top of this panel (in the top-left of the photograph) – this is quite a high loading area and the clip could simply break away due to the extent of decay.

SO21. A similar shot to above, this time from the driver's side. Again, there are corrosion problems round the footwell, the door pillar, steering box mounting and the top edge of the panel. The main body of the bulkhead is pressed out in one piece, including the footwells; this is then welded to fairly substantial door pillars. Later on, modified aluminium bulkheads were fabricated for the Series I, with all the advantages of no corrosion – these are now very rare though. The replica bulkheads you can now buy are a copy of the aluminium item, and it is a credit to the owner of this Series I that the original, steel bulkhead was retained during the restoration.

SO22. A different angle of a rotten door pillar prior to repairs. The extent of the corrosion is clearly visible here and would severely weaken the whole structure.

SO23. The repairs to the door pillar get under way! A piece of right-angle steel is cut and the first bout of welding begins; when cutting out a rotten section, take the metal back a lot further than the spot where you think the rot extends to. There's always *more rot than you first thought!*

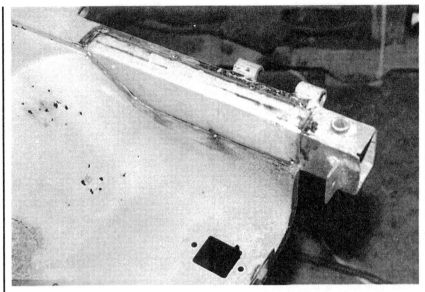

SO24. The welding to the door pillar is completed and...

SO25. ... is ground down and smoothed off. To give a perfect finish, small amounts of filler are used...

SO26. ... followed by primer-filler for the final touch prior to painting. As you can see, the end result is a very professional looking repair and an indication that even major structural panels can be restored rather than replaced.

SO27. These brackets are fitted between the two "skins" of the bulkhead. They carry cage nuts which in turn carry the steering box top mounting bracket, as well as the windscreen toggle bracket. These brackets should be saved, although new ones can *be* obtained.

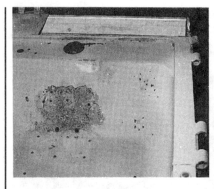

SO28. The area round the steering box mounting, with more rust and corrosion clearly visible. Repairs had already started to the double skin of the bulkhead (top of photo) and were completed in much the same way as the door pillar repairs.

SO29. A front view of the completed bulkhead, with all the repairs finished. A good-as-new body section that can justifiably be hailed as the original. Quite an achievement!

SO30. The bulkhead from a different angle. A rear-end shot with the door pillars looking remarkably straight and original and the whole bulkhead ripple-free.

SO31. As can be seen here, even the steering box carrier and the sidelight holders have been neatly repaired. At this stage, the wiring for the sidelights should be threaded through (while everything is so accessible) to prevent much cursing later!

SO32. The chassis was sandblasted and primed to reveal any problem areas. It is essential that the chassis is protected immediately after sandblasting as, on a damp day, surface rust can form within about ten minutes!

SO33. A close-up of some of the corrosion revealed by the sandblasting. At this point, rust had not got too much of a hold and, once blasted, simply left pockmarks that need some form of filler or lots of paint to hide. These marks make no difference to the strength of the chassis and you can rest assured that the sandblasting will have ◄ removed all traces of rust.

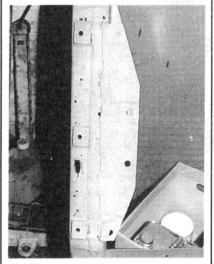

SO34. A view of the reinforced rear crossmember, showing how the bottom of this member has rotted (the three tapped holes are for the agricultural plate to be bolted through). The rust holes were revealed after a thorough investigation and much prodding around.

SO35. The battery box (this particular design was peculiar to the 80 in), the air cleaner carrier, the protection guard for the fuel tank and the radiator fan shroud, all of which have been sandblasted to reveal corrosion. The latter two items are often missing from old Land-Rovers.

SO36. The bonnet, having been stripped; again, this was remarkably "all there" compared with some examples, with the spare wheel carrier (different to the later models), the four support pads for the wheel and the windscreen support bracket and clip still fitted. The bonnet is shown here in naked aluminium.

SO37. A more detailed shot of the windscreen support and its location.

SO38. The underside of the bonnet, showing the reinforcing ribs and how the spare wheel carrier picks them up. The bracket on the right-hand side is for the bonnet support.

SO39. With the vehicle sprayed, the fitting-up process could begin. The chassis on a Series I of this age was finished in a deep bronze-green as opposed to just bronze-green for the vehicle itself. Incidentally, the first 50 Land-Rovers had galvanized chassis, the next 1,500 were painted silver (probably to make them look galvanized!) and the following models' chassis were finished in green. The radiator surround panel shown here was aluminium and was prone to breaking on its three bottom mounting bolts, requiring some specialised aluminium welding.

SO40. Here we see the radiator back in position, and behind it the engine and bulkhead are already refitted. The wiring is also in place; if required, new wiring harnesses are still available.

SO41. The bulkhead from inside the vehicle, with the instrument panel in place (all neatly restored). The hole to the bottom-left of the starter button (which is below the instrument panel) should have an oval plate on it, removable to allow you to pull the rocker shaft through backwards to avoid removing the engine or damaging the bulkhead.

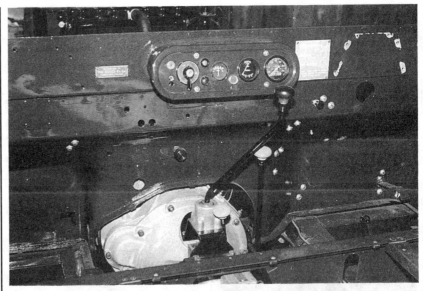

SO42. An illustration of what a superb restoration was carried out on this particular Land-Rover; the attention to detail was tremendous. The build-up process continued, with the gear levers, handbrake assembly and pedal arrangement now back in place. ▶

SO43. A close-up of the pedal ▲ arrangement, showing the brake and clutch cross-shafts going through the chassis. It is well worth plying them with grease before assembling them as they're very awkward to get at afterwards. The vehicle will soon be ready for having the floorpan refitted; the felts are already fitted to the pedal shafts in anticipation.

SO44. The general layout of the bulkhead, by now beginning to look extremely well finished and nicely detailed.

SO45. The floorpan is back in place at last, together with the seat box and the centre seat cover. BSF-thread cage nuts were originally used to hold the floorpan in place, which after all this time can be very difficult to remove during restoration.

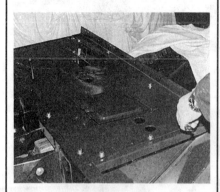

SO46. Here we see the seat ▲ box centre panel actually being installed; the four large holes locate rubber buffers in the seat base to prevent it sliding around. The little square flap in the centre is for access for the power take-off if fitted, also handy for adjusting the handbrake from above.

SO47. Another frontal view, now virtually complete (the only major missing panel being the bonnet). By this stage, the Series I is beginning to look a lot more "together".

◄ SO48. When carrying out a restoration, it must be remembered that each and every component will require a restoration in its own right. Here we see the air cleaner upon removal from the Land-Rover; it is imperative before dismantling something like this that you know exactly where everything goes and it is all properly assembled again afterwards. The "rock" filter on the right-hand side of the photo hangs over the battery terminal, and if the hose clip holding it in place is not tightened properly the filter could drop onto the battery and cause a fire.

SO49. Being full of oil "slopping" around inside, the air cleaner is usually not too badly rusted. This particular one was in good condition but obviously needed checking over and tidying.

SO50. The air cleaner was taken apart to reveal the matrix in the middle and the oil bath in the bottom. The very rare "Oil To This Level" transfer was missing, but there was a ridge on the lower container to which the oil should be filled. There are small rubber connectors on the inlet side to the carburettor and there is a pipe from the engine crankcase, which also joins there so that it "eats" its own fumes. Emission controls weren't envisaged forty years ago!

SO51. The air cleaner should be cleaned thoroughly and, purely for aesthetic reasons, sprayed if required before re-assembly. Shown here is the fully assembled air cleaner after work was completed.

SO52. The Lucas horn, another component that needs looking after! Inevitably, it will become full of water over the years and suffer from a rusty diaphragm. It will also be difficult to take apart – you might find that the screw heads shear off and the dome adjuster nut in the centre screws off. When dismantling the horn, leave it to soak for a long time in some diesel fuel (or similar) before trying to undo the screws. If your Land-Rover's horn is missing, a company called Holdens at Hartlebury, near Kidderminster, specialises in old Lucas components and does actually stock horns from time to time. See appendices.

SO53. The engine, now reassembled, was finished in the proper blue-grey colour. Any black components on it should have a satin rather than a gloss finish. It is up to the individual to decide how far to go with any particular engine; if it was running well before the restoration there are many who say "Leave well alone", while others believe in a policy of engine rebuilding as a matter of course during any restoration.

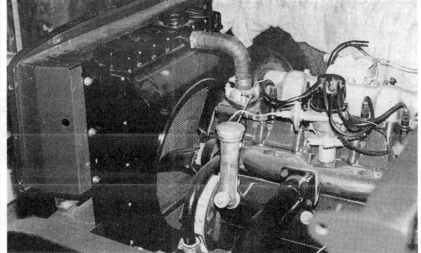

SO54. The oil filter clamp traps a ridge on the oil filter, holding it firmly in place. To be practical rather than totally original and correct however, mount the filter upwards from below so that the ridge is below the clamp, making future filter removal very easy as you've only got to slacken the clamp's securing bolts and the filter drops down. The filter needs to be removed to get the starter motor off, so it's as well to plan ahead at this stage.

SO55. The transfer box covers have been removed here, showing the input into the transfer box. The gears are all copper plated. The Series I gearbox and transfer box layout is broadly similar in concept to that in the Series II, IIA and III, with a main box feeding through to a transfer box which then takes the drive down to the offside of the vehicle, so the propshafts can have a clear run to the front and rear axles. The ratio is also reduced at this point. The Series II 'box is virtually the same as the Series I, with a dipstick filler; the Series IIA and III had side fillers, the latter gearbox being fully synchromesh. ▶

SO56. The exhaust down-pipe can be seen here, in position ready to come out through the front wing. Also shown are the engine mountings, plus a good view of the hoses and the back of the radiator. The original type of Bakolite ventilated plug caps with built-in suppressors are fitted to this example.

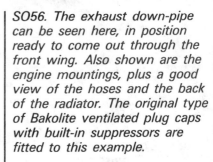

SO57. Here we can see the offside of the engine, together with the dynamo, fuel pump and, on the bulkhead, the petrol filter. The dipstick doesn't slide into a tube; a spring clip simply holds it in position, though it is not unknown for water to enter the engine via here when a Land-Rover goes "wading"! The plate on the side of this engine tells us that it is a works reconditioned unit.

SO58. *A detail shot showing the SU fuel pump and filter, and the throttle return spring system. The voltage regulator can also be seen at the top of the photograph. Fuel pumps are now quite expensive; it has been known for owners to fit an alternative fuel pump (such as that fitted to the Morris Minor), though this must always be seen as a compromise and ideally should be avoided.*

SO59. *The bulkhead with the sidelights in position, with a good view of the electrics. The regulator design was changed later, having two fuses on the front cover before going back to this type again. Just to the right of the radiator cap, on the radiator top itself, there is a small, circular disc; this gives the month and year of manufacture and is a nice, period touch. This radiator was reconditioned by Serck Marston, a company with radiator centres all over the UK, who are able to recore any Land-Rover radiator, complete with the correct radiator matrix.*

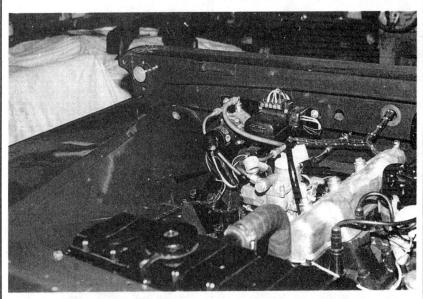

SO60. *From another angle, we can see that the original coil has been retained; a new coil would do its job well but the original one manages to look the part too. The terminal nuts on the coil should be black Bakolite knurled nuts rather than the brass ones used here. The distributor is non-original (simply because of availability); if you're lucky enough to have an original one on your Series I, Holdens of Hartlebury (mentioned earlier) will gladly recondition it for you.*

SO61. The Series I's semi-floating axle can be troublesome. There is a sealed bearing in the axle, which you need a press to get apart, located with a sleeve on which the oil seal runs. When the bearing starts to wear, oil will appear on the brake shoes (the seal will fail if the bearing is "sloppy"). The photograph shows a round drive flange on the differential, indicating an early ratio differential (later ones have a square drive flange, a sign that they are 4.7:1 ratio as opposed to the early 4.8:1 ratio). Series I and II axles are not directly interchangeable, the latter being physically larger.

SO62. A detailed study of the ▶ handbrake; the expander is on the near side and the adjuster on the far side. The centre nut has yet to be tightened in this photograph, vital to stop any play in the output shaft as well as trapping the speedo drive scroll. On this early model, the speedo cable fits into a brass holder on the right-hand side of the vehicle, going through a right-angle bend on the chassis. The cable used to break at this point, so later 80 in models had speedo cables running on the left-hand side and through a far more gentle curve.

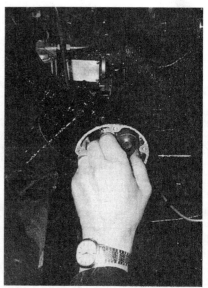

SO64. Proof that the steering ▲ box can be dismantled while still on the vehicle! The worm and nut system was criticised when it was new, so imagine how awful it seems nowadays! There is always "slop" in the sector shaft bushes and on the nut itself; oversize nuts can be obtained but the casing then needs reaming out to take them.

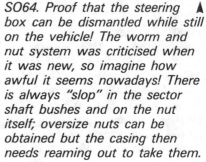

SO63. The refurbished axle is back in position. New copper brakes pipes (standard on the earlier 80 in anyway) can be seen; these have been led along the rear edge of the axle, whereas the originals ran across the front edge and often got crushed! Series II, IIA and III Land-Rovers had steel brake pipes originally, but surely copper replacements are a sensible precaution, albeit at the expense of originality?

SO65. Still on the subject of steering, where the steering column and the aluminium body of the steering box are riveted together, corrosion can set in and they can actually break away from the rivets, with dire consequences. Here the steering box is being reassembled. Aluminium-bodied steering boxes can also split below the collar, just below where the column enters the box. Unfortunately, nothing can be done to prevent it – but buy a replacement or replica 'off-the-shelf' if yours looks suspect.

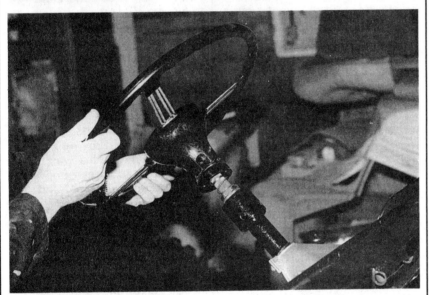

SO66. A finishing touch! The steering wheel goes on; these early versions were on splines and located by a pinch-bolt. There is a shroud on the back of the steering wheel which hides the two thin adjuster nuts which adjust the column. The sector shaft has no adjustment but on later (particularly military) vehicles there was a modification to stabilise it. These early steering boxes were not noted for their longevity!

SO67. After its total restoration at the hands of the conscientious 'Em.', John Fletcher's beautiful little Series One really does look superb.

In conclusion, Dunsfold Land-Rover felt that this Series I restoration was a credit to its owner. Much care and attention has gone into ensuring that this is a truly first class example of its type.

5 Mechanical restoration

Engine History

(Taken from comments dictated by Brian Bashall)

In April 1948, when the Land-Rover was first introduced, it inherited the 1.6-litre, overhead-inlet, side-exhaust, bypass-filtered Rover car engine. This was kept in production until September 1952 when the 2.0-litre (bored-out 1.6) engine was launched, again with a bypass-filter; boring out the engine left the spacing between 1 and 2, and 3 and 4, cylinders down to about $\frac{1}{4}$ in, which became a problem later on.

With the introduction of the 86 in Land-Rover in 1954 came the 2.0-litre full-flow engine – complete with full-flow filter and modified bearings, a great improvement but still suffering from a very small gap between the cylinder bores. In 1956, this was rectified when the engine received 'staggered bores' to increase the distance between the cylinders to $\frac{3}{8}$ in, overcoming much of the previous head gasket problems. At the same time, the wheelbase of the Land-Rover was increased to a choice of either 88 in or 109 in to accommodate the 2.0-litre diesel engine that was to be launched in 1957. Looking much

like the modern 2$\frac{1}{4}$-litre petrol engine, the diesel engine was a wet-linered unit of Rover design.

In 1958, Land-Rover's engine range was quite extensive. It comprised the 2.0-litre petrol or 2.0-litre diesel engines fitted to the last of the Series I models, plus the first of the Series IIs with the same two engines AND (later that year) the 2$\frac{1}{4}$-litre petrol unit.

1961 saw the Series IIA introduced, the 2$\frac{1}{4}$-litre petrol-engine receiving such modifications as a stronger crankshaft, altered water pump position (because of cylinder head cooling problems) and modified water pump and thermostat housings. This engine was extremely popular, continuing in production right through until early 1984, although a 5-bearing crankshaft was introduced in late 1980.

The 2.0-litre diesel was dropped in favour of a 2$\frac{1}{4}$-litre diesel in 1962, based on the petrol-engine block; the crankshaft was dimensionally the same as the petrol model's but made of a different material, plus different pistons, much larger conrods and so on.

The 2.6-litre six-cylinder engine joined the range in 1967, a de-tuned version of the Rover 110 car engine. Again, there were a number of modifications, such as the water pump and

carburettor, to suit the Land-Rover. By Land-Rover standards, this was quite a 'flier'; the engine was pleasantly smooth and these six-cylinder models made ideal towing vehicles. The alloy cylinder head was to be a source of trouble though.

Solex carburettors disappeared from the Land-Rover range in 1967, replaced by Zenith units. This was a better off-road carburettor, with a central float chamber and improved economy.

In 1981, Land-Rover introduced the 'Stage I' 109 in model for the home market, complete with a de-tuned 3528cc V8 engine from the Range Rover, plus the four-speed centre-differential gearbox.

The first of the One Ten models arrived in 1983 (the 'Stage II'), fitted with the 2$\frac{1}{4}$-litre petrol engine, albeit with major emission modifications that somewhat killed its performance. The V8 engine was available as an option, as was the 2$\frac{1}{4}$-litre diesel (rather underpowered in this bigger body shell).

In June 1984, the short-wheelbase Land-Rover 90 was introduced, finally replacing the Series III. It was fitted with a 2$\frac{1}{2}$-litre diesel engine with belt-driven camshaft and lots of other detail changes. This model boasted excellent performance, and its engine also became

available in the One Ten.

The 2½-litre turbo diesel arrived on the scene in 1986 (to replace the normally aspirated diesel engine), remaining an optional engine to the V8 up until the launch of the Defender in 1990, which was fitted with the inter cooled 2½-litre turbo diesel unit from the Land-Rover Discovery.

Engine problems!

The overhead-inlet, side-exhaust units (up until late 1958) often had camshaft problems, with the followers wearing prematurely; bear this in mind when dealing with pre-1958 Land-Rovers. Exhaust valves also tended not to last too long; head gaskets are prone to blowing; and this engine also had a rear main 'thrower' system on the back of the crankshaft which, after a lot of off-road use, could lead to oil getting onto the clutch, or a lot of 'wading' could lead to the scroll on the crankshaft pulling water in from outside, causing severe problems! Otherwise, these are excellent engines, with good performance, and they are easy to work on.

The 2.0-litre splayed-bore engine had a proper rear main seal, which succeeded in keeping the oil in. The early 2¼-litre Series II engines had a cooling problem, often causing cracked heads, and tended to suffer from crankshaft 'knock'; later IIA models, with stronger crankshafts, got rid of the engine noise and cylinder head problems.

The six-cylinder engines inherited the same problems as the early 1.6 and 2.0-litre units; it used to 'eat' exhaust valves, and corrosion or warping of the aluminium head was not uncommon.

By the time the V8 was fitted to the Land-Rover, it was already well proven in the Range Rover. A superb engine in every way, but it is imperative to keep the water level topped up to prevent overheating – once the head or block is distorted on the all-alloy V8, you're in trouble! Otherwise, this engine is easily capable of very high mileages with few problems.

The 2½-litre turbo diesel engine had a poor reputation initially, mainly due to heavy oil consumption, though much depended on how the engine was run-in and how the piston rings had bedded down. This engine is a lively unit and it was a great temptation not to run it in properly when new, leading to 'hot spots' on the piston rings and poor sealing. Modified pistons were fitted in late 1987 and overcame the oil blowing problem. The modified turbo diesel (with inter cooler) fitted to the Discovery and Defender models is reputed not to suffer the same troubles. This unit has a 25% increase in output but also a reduction in fuel consumption. Instant starting with this direct injection engine is a good feature.

2¼-litre petrol engine.

The cylinder block is of cast iron. Reboring is possible up to a maximum of 0.040in (1.0mm) oversize above the standard bore size of 3.562in (90.49mm). Further reclamation is obtained by fitting cylinder liners and boring out to standard bore size. Liners may be rebored up to 0.010in (0.25mm) oversize.

The crankshaft is supported by three bearings. The thrust is taken by the centre bearing. The bearings are white-metal lined steel shells.

The camshaft is supported by four bearings and actuates roller-type cam followers, operating valve rockers through push-rods, and lead/tin plated bronze slides. Adjustment is made on the adjusting screws on valve rockers. Again, the bearings are white-metal lined steel shells.

The camshaft is chain driven and a chain tensioner is fitted.

The engine is lubricated by a pressure fed oil system which incorporates a pump located in the crankcase sump and an external full flow oil filter.

Mechanical components

Safety Notes–
ALWAYS disconnect the battery before starting any other work.

NEVER work or stand beneath an engine suspended on a hoist, or have an arm or hand in a position where it could be crushed. Even the sturdiest of hoists could give way or ropes or chains could slip. When attaching to the engine, try to use mechanical lifting fixings rather than trying ropes. Always have someone with you to lend a hand.

With the engine out of the vehicle, ensure when working on it, that the block is securely chocked and that there's no danger of it falling over. Don't trust anything but the stoutest of benches; hire a purpose-built stand or work on the floor.

Remember that Land-Rover mechanical units are generally much heavier than those used in modern cars – so use appropriate lifting and supporting gear.

Cylinder head removal and overhaul

Tools needed: spanners (sizes $\frac{7}{16}$ in, $\frac{1}{2}$ in, $\frac{3}{8}$ in, $\frac{5}{8}$ in, $\frac{9}{16}$ in AF open end; $\frac{7}{16}$ in, $\frac{1}{2}$ in, $\frac{5}{8}$ in, $\frac{3}{4}$ in AF socket; $\frac{5}{16}$ in, $\frac{3}{8}$ in BSF open end; 2 BA open end; 14mm box spanner); medium-size

screwdriver; pliers; (SPECIAL TOOLS NEEDED – Torque wrench).

The cylinder head can easily be removed with the engine in the vehicle. Disconnect the bonnet prop and tie the bonnet back against the windscreen with suitable padding between bonnet and screen surround. Disconnect the battery and drain the water from the engine and radiator. Remove the air cleaner complete with the hose and elbow that connects it to the carburettor. The engine of the author's Series IIA Land-Rover, shown being stripped here, was converted to run on unleaded petrol following the manufacturer's instructions. This is a service that is offered to owners by Dunsfold Land-Rover.

►

ENGINE - Cylinder Head 2¼ Litre Petrol

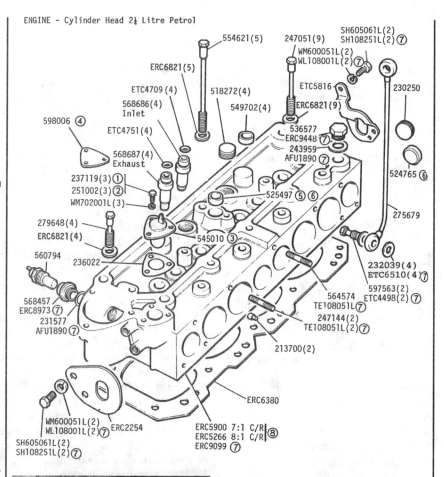

CY1. The 2¼-litre petrol cylinder head, which differs from the overhead-inlet, side-exhaust head fitted to earlier models. Note that the parts indicated with a number 7 are supplied as a kit when an exchange cylinder head is purchased from Land-Rover and when the original engine was fitted with imperial screw threads. The kit converts the external, imperially threaded components to the metric threaded cylinder head. (Courtesy Land-Rover).

◄

CY3. Next, the three rocker cover domed nuts were removed and any clamps and fittings placed carefully in a plastic bag for safe keeping.

CY2. Philip Bashall started by removing the breather cap after first unscrewing the retaining screw shown in his right hand. He also removed the rubber 'O' ring for safe keeping. As you can see, this engine is out of the car but the procedure for carrying out the work is exactly the same as when it is still in the vehicle.

CY4. It was then a simple matter to lift off the rocker cover. ►

CY5. Philip disconnected the coolant hose elbows at the thermostat housing ...

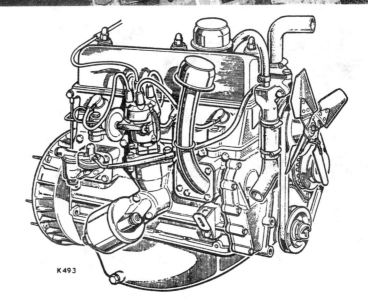

K 493

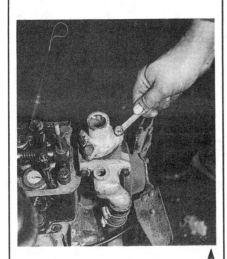

CY6. ... and disconnected and removed the top of the housing. The elbow still left in place and shown in CY5 also has to be removed.

CY7. Also remove from the right hand side of the engine: the vacuum pipe at the distributor; distributor leads; fan cowl shroud; the oil gallery pipe and the bypass hose shown at the bottom of the elbow in caption CY6. (Courtesy Land-Rover).

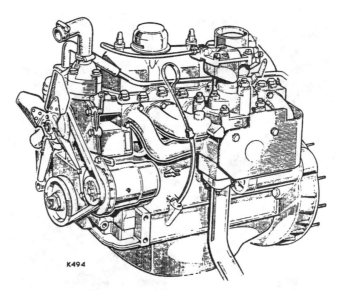

K 494

CY8. Disconnect the accelerator linkage at the ball joint at the carburettor (item D); take off the choke cable (item C); disconnect the fuel inlet pipe at the carburettor and release from the clip on the engine (item B); disconnect the front exhaust pipe at the manifold ... (Courtesy Land-Rover).

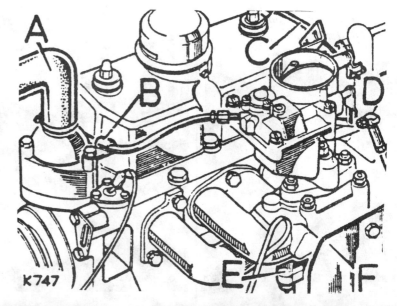

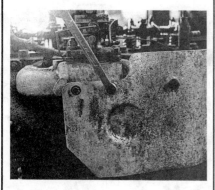

CY9. ...remove the heat shield ▲ if it helps to gain access to the exhaust manifold.

CY11. The manifolds bolt onto ▲ the side of the cylinder head, some of the retaining nuts being easily located...

CY10. Remove the spark plugs. ▲

CY12. ...while some will need the use of a socket on an extension probing between inlet and exhaust manifolds in order to remove some of the less accessible nuts and fittings.

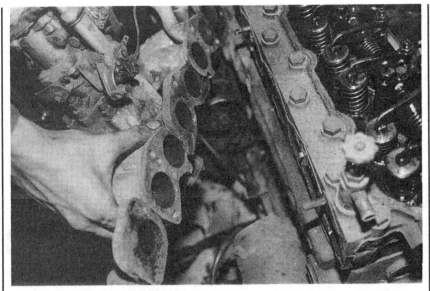

CY13. The manifolds and carburettor assembly can be lifted away complete.

CY14. The external oil gallery ▲ pipe is held on by this special nut.

CY15. Don't forget to unscrew the heater tap, using an appropriately sized spanner, from the top of the cylinder head. ◄

CY16. Take out the bolts ▲ holding the rocker assembly in place . . .

CY17. . . . and lift off the rocker shaft assembly as a complete unit.

CY18. Note that the rocker shaft pedestals are located with locating tubes, one of which is shown here in place while the other one is missing. ▶

CY19. Some will be found to ▲ have remained lodged in the cylinder head, in which case remove them now for safe keeping.

CY20. Undoing the cylinder head studs requires less finesse than tightening them up again later as Philip shows here, slackening the studs before having carried out the rocker gear removal described earlier. ▶

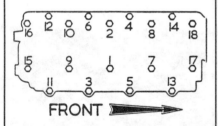

FRONT ⟫⟫⟫⟫⟫▶

CY21. Undo the cylinder head ▲ studs in the order shown here and follow the same order when tightening the head, as shown later. (Courtesy Land-Rover).

CY22. Before lifting off the cylinder head take out the push rods and, so that you can put them back exactly where they came from, take a piece of card, push eight holes in it, write the numbers 1 to 8 alongside the holes and push the push rods into the holes ready for cleaning up and refitting later.

CY23. With all the studs completely out, the head can now simply be lifted away.

CY24. Take this opportunity to examine the bore in the cylinder block for wear (see your Haynes Owner's Workshop Manual) and also for cracking between the cylinders and water jacket and for evidence of cylinder head gasket blow-by.

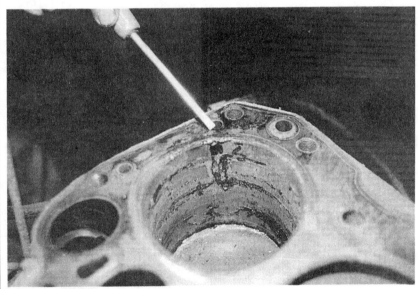

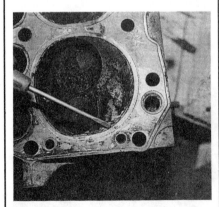

CY25. Also look for evidence of cylinder head gasket blow-by on the cylinder head itself and again for signs of cracking, especially around the exhaust valve.

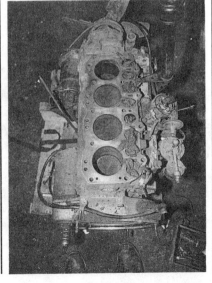

◄ CY26. You can now clean up the face of the block and also the piston crowns if they are very heavily encrusted with carbon, but before you do so, stuff rags into the push rod passages and also, preferably, into the oil ways. Do try to leave the carbon around the outer edge of the piston crown – it helps as an oil seal. Let an old piston ring into the top of the block, push down to the level of the piston and clean the piston inside the piston ring.

CY27. The cylinder head itself can now be overhauled as detailed in your Workshop Manual and new valves and guides fitted or, as shown here, the valves can be lapped in with a power operated lapping tool. Most people would do this by hand.

CY28. The cylinder head fitted to FVJ was, as previously described, adapted to run on unleaded fuel with appropriate valve seat inserts by Dunsfold Land-Rover. This is the converted and overhauled head ready for refitting.

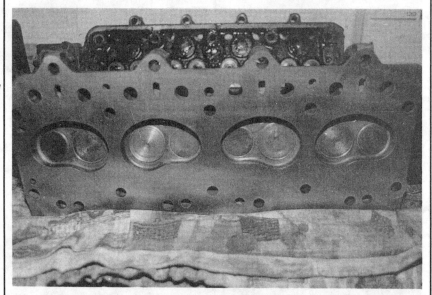

CY29. The new head gasket has been placed onto the block and a pair of old engine studs with their heads cut off have been screwed into two of the stud threads. Before getting this far, you would be well advised to ensure that all the stud threads are entirely clean and that the studs themselves are not binding as they are being fitted. The best way of cleaning them out would be to take an old stud, cut a slot about an inch along the length of the stud at the threaded end, and then screw the stud into the head. Any debris that has fallen into the threaded holes will be forced into the slot and, provided that the stud is unscrewed at regular intervals, and the slot cleaned out with a hacksaw blade, the threaded hole will be completely cleared of debris.

CY30. Philip Bashall lowers the modified head back onto the block.

CY31. Here you can see that Philip had had the foresight to put a screwdriver slot into the top of each stud so that each one can simply be screwed out with the head sitting in the correct position. You don't have to do it this way; it just makes life a little easier! You could just as well place the gasket and then the head onto the block, then insert a stud at a time, taking care to ensure that the first two pass cleanly through both head and gasket into the threaded block beneath without damaging the gasket. ▶

CY32. After placing the push rods back into position and ensuring that they bottom correctly into the spherical seats in the tappet slides, you can refit the rocker shaft assembly, engage the tubular fixings referred to earlier and tighten the cylinder head and rocker shaft fixings in the order shown earlier. ▼

CY33. The half inch UNF bolts ▲ should be tightened to a torque of 65 lb ft while the $\frac{5}{16}$ in UNF bolts should be tightened to 18 lb ft.

CY34. With the engine cold ▲ the tappet clearances can be set to 0.010 in (0.25 mm) for all valves. The tappet setting is most easily carried out in the following sequence with number one tappet being at the front of the engine: set number one tappet clearance with number eight valve fully open; set number two tappet clearance with number seven valve fully open; set number three tappet clearance with number six valve fully open; and so on. This is known in the 'trade' as the 'rule of nine'.

CY35. Some ancillaries are ▲ best replaced as a matter of course at this stage, such as the cold start sensor shown here, the thermostat housing and the distributor cap. Once again and as always, the best parts to fit are the genuine items supplied by Land-Rover Parts.

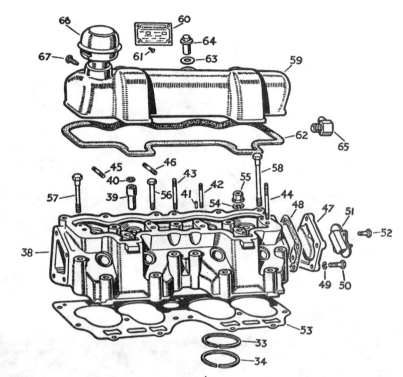

Cylinder head overhaul – Overhead-inlet, side-exhaust valve models

The Land-Rover overhead-inlet, side-exhaust valve engine was used in the first Series I models and ran right through to the introduction of the 2¼-litre all overhead valve engine, while the six-cylinder 2.6-litre engine continued the same tradition.

CYB1. This particular engine layout was that first seen in the Rover Company motor cars of the era. (Courtesy Land-Rover)

CYB2. The four-cylinder engine's side valve rocker cover can be tricky to get at with the manifolds in place, but unbolted from the engine and the exhaust pipe, the single retaining bolt is simple to remove with a spanner. The six-cylinder engine cover is held in place with a line of four finger nuts.

CYB3. Remove the cylinder head following a similar procedure to that outlined for the all-overhead valve models, but note that on the Series I engine, two of the cylinder head bolts are not bolts at all but studs threaded at each end. Remove them by taking both cylinder head nuts, tightening them hard against each other and then turning both spanners in an anti-clockwise direction (with most of the 'unscrewing force' on the bottom nut) so that the stud comes out of the block.

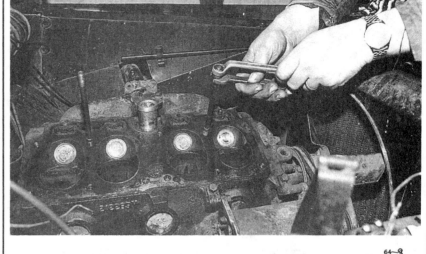

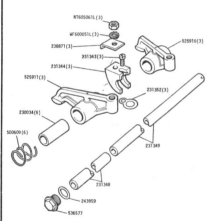

CYB4. The inlet valve gear in ▲ the cylinder head is similar to that of other models. Here are details of the inlet valve rockers for the 2.6 litre petrol engine. (Courtesy Land-Rover)

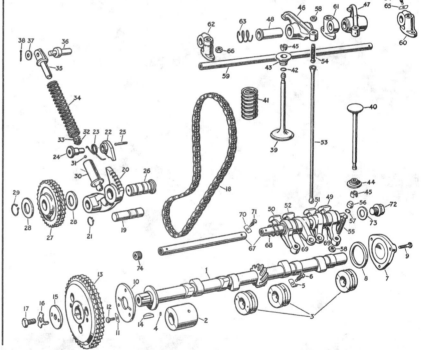

CYB5. This is the layout of the ▲ inlet and exhaust valve gear in the four-cylinder engine and the timing chain and tensioner arrangement. (Courtesy Land-Rover)

CYB6. To remove the exhaust valve, turn the engine over until the cam lobe is furthest away from the rocker ...

CYB7. ... so that you can insert a valve spring compressing tool ...

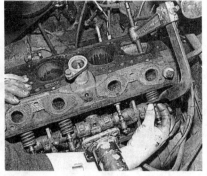

CYB8. ... compress the valve springs and remove the collets.

CYB9. And here are the collets, quite easily dropped when working in the lower confines of the engine bay.

CYB10. It's then an easy matter to withdraw the exhaust valve itself but take this opportunity to see whether there is any serious amount of lateral movement between exhaust valve and guide which is fitted into the block. If more extensive work is required, refer to the Series I Land-Rover Workshop Manual, available from Dunsfold Land-Rover.

CYB11. The double valve springs can also be lifted away at this stage but ensure that just as with the push rods for the overhead inlet valves, the exhaust valves and springs are saved in the correct order because the valves will have bedded into the place from whence they came and the valve springs are selected as matching pairs.

CYB12. It's not at all uncommon for exhaust valve seats to burn out and here we show one being chiselled away with a sharp cold chisel drifted between the bottom of the seat and its seating in the block. Land-Rover recommend that the seat itself, which is made of brittle metal, is deliberately shattered but we have found that this particular seat came out in this fashion.

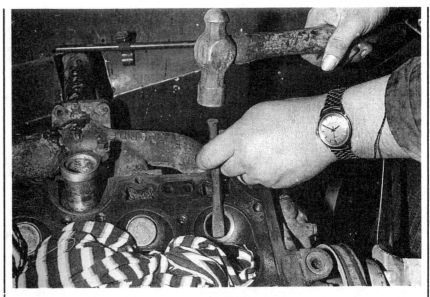

CYB13. After driving the chisel beneath the exhaust valve seat, we tapped the chisel sideways, levering it against the side of the cylinder head in order to lift the valve seat insert out of its position.

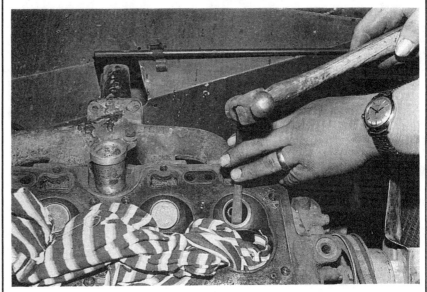

CYB14. A fragment of the old seat – it broke as it came out, is placed above the new one. It should be fitted with a special drift which is inserted into the cylinder head with the valve guide removed, but we found that the new insert could be tapped very carefully into place, making absolutely certain that it is properly aligned all the way until it seats fully into the cylinder head.

CYB15. Removing an exhaust valve seat.

Safety note: Land-Rover strongly recommend that when removing an exhaust valve seat, you fit a metal plate over the block similar to the one shown in this drawing, chiselling through the gap between plate and cylinder bore. Any gaps should be plugged with a heavy pad of cloth. Also note that when fitting the new valve seat, there is a risk of the seat shattering and flying around with consequent risk of damage to eyes. **WEAR GOGGLES AT ALL TIMES WHEN REMOVING AN OLD VALVE SEAT AND WHEN FITTING A NEW ONE.** (Courtesy Land-Rover)

CYB16. The valve can be ground into the new valve seat in the normal way, placing a smear of fine grinding paste around the valve seating area...

CYB17. ...and then grinding the valve into the valve seat in the normal way. Be sure not to use too much grinding paste so that none of it becomes transferred into the sump. It is difficult to imagine anything that could wear an engine more quickly than valve grinding paste circulating around it in the engine oil! Make doubly sure that you wipe all traces of it away with a rag dampened with paraffin but once again be careful not to wash the grinding paste into the sump.

CYB18. Inlet valve seats are less likely to become cracked or pitted than exhaust valve seats but pitting can and does take place and they will benefit from some attention with the grinding paste.

CYB19. The procedure for grinding in valves to the cylinder head is exactly the same, of course.

CYB20. Where a new valve seat has been fitted, it will probably be necessary to back off the adjuster screw quite extensively. In any case, it's a good idea to ensure that the adjuster screw and the lock nut are both free...

CYB21. ...before inserting a ▲ 0.012 in (3mm) feeler gauge and adjusting the tappets until the feeler gauge is an interference fit with the lock nut tightened.

CYB22. Now place the cylinder head gasket in position on the block with any writing that may be stamped on the gasket uppermost. We used the two cylinder head studs to align the gasket, although it may have been best to have placed them in the position where they will eventually be found.

CYB23. Make absolutely sure ▲ that the sealing ring that goes between water pump housing and cylinder head is renewed and replaced before refitting the cylinder head itself.

CYB24. The two cylinder head studs can now be fitted to the positions marked with an X in CYB25 (Spot the deliberate mistake in this photograph!) and the cylinder head lowered into position.

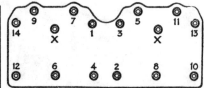

CYB25. This is the correct order for tightening the Series I cylinder head bolts. Those marked with an X also secure the rocker shaft. The $\frac{7}{16}$ in bolts should be tightened to 50 lb ft. and the $\frac{3}{8}$ in bolts to 30 lb ft. (Courtesy Land-Rover)

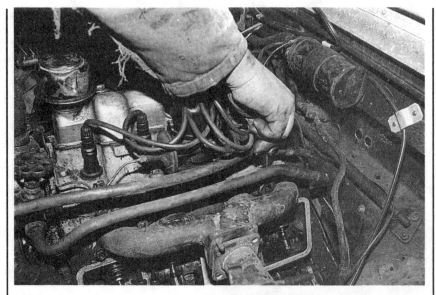

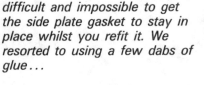

CYB27. We refitted the exhaust manifold whilst waiting for a new tappet chest gasket to arrive by post from Dunsfold Land-Rover.

CYB26. The tightening order for the 2.6-litre engine bolts. 'A' should be tightened to 50 lb ft.; bolts 'B' to 30 lb ft. (Courtesy Land-Rover)

CYB28. It is somewhere between difficult and impossible to get the side plate gasket to stay in place whilst you refit it. We resorted to using a few dabs of glue...

CYB29. ...before offering up the gasket to the side plate and leaving it in place long enough to dry...

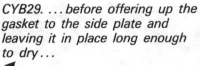

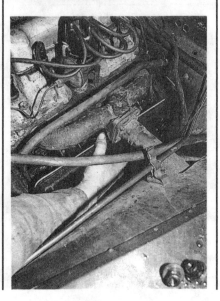

CYB30. ...before fitting the side plate on the engine.

CYB31. *Just as a footnote: we had previously used a block and wet-or-dry paper to sand every trace of gasket sealant from the exhaust manifold faces before refitting it to the engine. Unfortunately, these exhaust manifolds are rather prone to cracking, especially where they bolt to the exhaust pipe and you may well have to resort to having it built up by a specialist who is equipped to weld cast iron. Needless to say, these exhaust manifolds have not been available for a long time! Look in your edition of Yellow Pages for a suitable welding specialist. You certainly cannot weld cast iron satisfactorily at home.*

CYB32. *These are the valves and push rods for the 2.6-litre petrol engine. Ensure that you always replace the valve stem seals on all of the engines mentioned here when overhauling the valve gear. Seals that have split or gone hard with age will turn your engine into a heavy smoker! (Courtesy Land-Rover).*

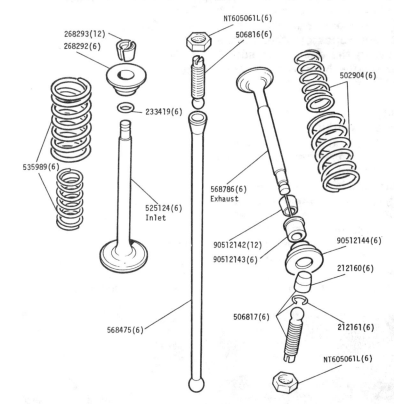

Engine removal

Hand tools needed: spanners ($\frac{7}{16}$ in x $\frac{1}{2}$ in AF (2 off) open end; $\frac{5}{8}$ in, $\frac{11}{16}$ in AF open end; $\frac{7}{16}$ in, $\frac{1}{2}$ in AF ring; $\frac{1}{2}$ in, $\frac{9}{16}$ in AF socket; $\frac{5}{16}$ in, $\frac{3}{8}$ in BSF open end; 2 BA open end); medium-size screwdriver; pliers.

This section shows two engines being removed in very different ways. Several years ago I went with a young friend and neighbour of mine, now tragically deceased, to buy a good second-hand Series I engine from a prominent Series I Club member. This is really the very best way to buy

second-hand components if you possibly can – from a trustworthy Club member and in a state in which you can hear it running or see it being used before you purchase. My good friend Nigel decided, in his usual practical way, that the best way of removing this engine was to take out the radiator and grille panel, allowing us to pull the engine out forwards. The other

engine in this sequence is shown being removed by Dunsfold Land-Rover. It's the engine that is fitted to FVJ and is shown being removed after the bodywork has been taken off – which you might think is cheating! However, it enabled us to illustrate the removal procedure quite well and the only difference is that Dunsfold Land-Rover, where they have

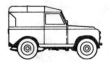

full hydraulic lifting gear, would take the engine out with the grille panels still on the vehicle. If you are doing a full restoration you may wish to leave removing the engine until the bodywork is off, just as we did; if you are taking the engine out and you have full lifting gear, there is no reason why you shouldn't lift it out with the grille panel still in place – but do remember that even the four-cylinder unit is a very heavy old lump which weighs around 450 lb – almost four and a half cwt.

Safety
Always use a proper block and tackle or a very strong hoist to get the engine out. Make sure that any ropes or other means of lifting the engine are sound and secure. NEVER allow any part of your body to get beneath the engine whilst it is being lifted and make sure that you are working in a clear working space so that there is no risk of tripping and causing an accident. There is a risk of petrol spillage when removing the engine, so make certain that there are no naked flames or sparks in the vicinity – such as from a central heating boiler. Ensure that any petrol pipes are securely plugged and that the battery has been

disconnected before starting work.

Start by taking off the bonnet or by tying it back to the windscreen.

Then remove the air cleaner and disconnect the following items on the left-hand side of the engine:
A) Front exhaust pipe.
B) Heater hoses (if heater is fitted).
C) Carburettor linkage at ball joint.
D) Cold-start inner and outer cables at carburettor.
E) Distributor leads at ignition coil.
F) Engine earth cable.
G) Engine mounting rubber upper fixing.

Disconnect the following items on the right-hand side of the engine:
A) Fuel inlet pipe at fuel pump.
B) Battery lead at clip adjacent to fuel pump.
C) Starter motor leads at dash panel.
D) Dynamo leads at voltage regulator.
E) Engine electrical leads at snap connectors adjacent to dash.
F) Release disconnected cables from retaining clips at dash panel.
G) Release speedometer drive cable from cable clip. If necessary, disconnect the

vacuum pipe from the distributor to free the drive cable during engine removal.
H) Engine mounting rubber upper fixing.

After fitting suitable lifting equipment as shown in the following photo sequence, take up the slack sufficient to support the weight of the engine. Remove the engine front mounting rubbers as follows:
A) On the left-hand side, remove the lower centre fixing from the suspension rubber.
B) On the right-hand side, remove the support bracket fixings as the lower centre fixing on the R-H suspension rubber is inaccessible when fitted.

Lift the engine sufficiently to withdraw the left-hand suspension rubber and the right-hand suspension rubber *and* bracket complete. Then lower the engine to its original position to maintain alignment with the gearbox.

Remove the fixings securing the bell housing to the flywheel housing.

Supporting the gearbox using a suitable packing block or a jack, pull the engine forward sufficient to disengage the drive from the gearbox. Ensure that all cables, pipes and so on are clear; then hoist the engine from the vehicle.
Note – If it is necessary to replace the engine mountings and you intend using spring washers in place of the previously used lock plates on the engine mounting feet to cylinder block fixings, torque load the fixings to 80 lb ft.

ERM1. With the Series I engine referred to earlier, we started by taking out the radiator shroud and the radiator itself...

ERM2. ... along with the ▲ grille, as shown in the bodywork section of this book...

ERM3. ... and the whole grille panel was lifted away.

ERM5. Back with the author's ▲ Series I, the engine was lowered into place with the radiator removed but with the grille panel still in place, proving that it really is a 'can do' job ! Also the bonnet was left on and tied back, well out of harm's way.

ERM6. From now on, Dunsfold Land-Rover give a brief resume of the main points when preparing an engine for removal, this one being the author's Series IIA. The throttle linkage was removed from the carburettor... ►

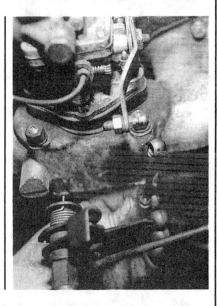

ERM4. Nigel used this engine ► hoist to lift the engine, carefully supported on a rope, and to draw it forwards from the Land-Rover. If you are working with a block and tackle, it's best to ensure that you have several feet of space clear behind the Land-Rover and, once the engine has been lifted, push the vehicle backwards leaving the engine clear to be lowered carefully to the floor. Ensure if you are working off a beam in a building that it has ample capacity for the great weight of the engine being lifted plus any shock loading that may occur.

ERM7. . . . and the carburettor cable similarly disconnected. Go carefully through the earlier paragraphs for full details of all the components that have to be removed before the engine can be taken out. ➤

ERM8. This is the engine mounting bolt to chassis on the right hand side . . . ▲

ERM9. . . . and the engine mounting to engine stud which also must be removed before the engine is lifted. ▲

ERM10. The layout of the ▲ *engine mounting nuts, bolts and stud. Unless the engine mountings have been replaced recently, it makes sense to remove them now.*

◄

ERM11. The exhaust down pipe being detached from the bottom of the exhaust manifold.

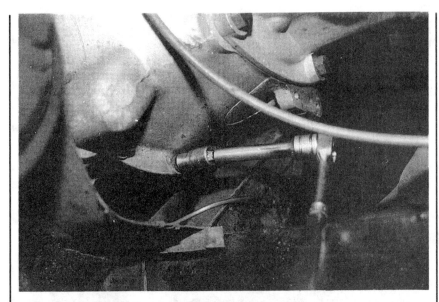

ERM12. Bell housing nuts and bolts are reasonably accessible and at least it's not difficult to get underneath a Land-Rover! The semi-universal joint between the ratchet extension and the socket on the Sykes-Pickavant socket set make access that much easier.

ERM13. Taking the weight of the engine on the lifting hoist as described in the earlier paragraphs.

◄

ERM14. The Dunsfold Land-Rover hoist shows how the engine can be slid forward off the gearbox and then lifted clear of the bodywork. Of course, there is no bodywork fitted to FVJ at this stage, so you'll just have to use your imagination! At least it shows that it can be done.

ERM15. You are strongly advised to lower the engine to the ground and work on it there rather than on a workbench. As pointed out earlier, the Land-Rover engine is exceptionally heavy and it's safest whilst on the ground, supported on wooden blocks to prevent it from toppling.

Engine stripping

Author's Note
There isn't room in this book to deal with every detail of stripping and rebuilding a Land-Rover's engine. Instead, we have tried to guide you through the process with the aid of the sorts of practical hints and tips picked up by a lifetime of Land-Rovers by Brian Bashall of Dunsfold Land-Rover.

The Haynes Manuals – one on the SII, IIA and III 4-cylinder petrol models and one on the diesels, are excellent value for money – while the 'official' Land-Rover manuals are incredibly detailed, if a little formal and 'starchy'. Naturally, perhaps, they assume that you are O.K. on some of the details – which is where we come in! The Land-Rover Parts Books are also gold mines of information – and have the added advantage that they give you the correct part numbers. *I firmly believe in sticking to Genuine Land-Rover Parts wherever possible* – their quality is second-to-none, or in buying 'obsolete' reproduction Series I parts from Dunsfold Land-Rover, a company soaked to the core in Land-Rover quality.

More notes from the horse's mouth: Brian Bashall of Dunsfold Land-Rover:

"Always clean the engine when it is out, so that you can see what you are dealing with. You also need lots of strong boxes to hold everything which comes off. Be methodical and make note of what nuts and bolts go where. Start with a nice clean engine and take all the auxiliaries off, take the flywheel off and then the fuel pump, distributor pump drive, distributor, water pump, manifold, and take the head off as shown in an earlier section."

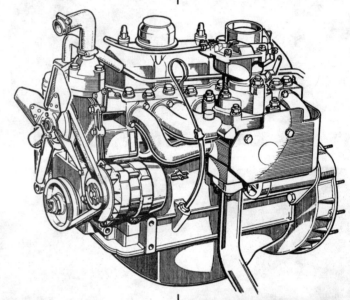

ES1. The engine shown being stripped down in this section is the 2¼-litre petrol engine. Notes on other engine types are added at the end. Further details can be found both in the Haynes Owner's Workshop Manual and in the official Land-Rover workshop manuals available from Dunsfold Land-Rover.

ES2. The glass bowl of the ▲ fuel pump being removed. It is probably best to remove this before taking out the engine.

ES3. Using a special tool loosen the crankshaft pulley nut, making sure the engine is safe and well supported. A deep ¾ in drive socket and a lump hammer will do it. You have got to shock the nut – it is no good pussy-footing around, because it won't come undone by gently pulling.

ES4. The fan needs to come off, after undoing the four bolts shown.

ES5. The water pump flange and the by-pass hose, the semi-circle of water pump retaining bolts clearly visible.

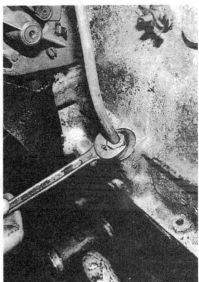

ES6. The dipstick tube – be ▲ careful not to bend when undoing the retaining nut in the block.

ES7. The oil pump feed at the block, leading to the cylinder head. It feeds all the rockers and is quite flimsy if unsupported.

ES8. The oil filter body being ▲
removed.

ES9. This is the sump filler ▲
tube. One bolt on the top
(pointed at here by the
screwdriver) . . .

ES10. . . . and six bolts in the side
plate.

ES11. Now we have a fairly
stripped engine we have to
remove the cam followers and
the tappets. Remove the lock
wiring, preventing the bolts from
unscrewing in typical Land-Rover
'belts-and-braces' fashion.

ES12. Remove the locating bolts. ►

ES13. The body of the cam ▲ follower has the hole to receive the locating bolt. You will have to sacrifice a screwdriver here unless you want to buy a special tool. Put a little right angle bend on it so that it hooks on to the hole and you can snatch them out.

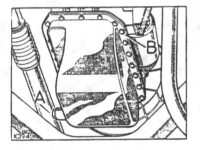

ES14. Turn the engine upside ▲ down to remove the sump, undoing the bolts 'B'. (Courtesy Land-Rover)

ES15. Now you can remove ▲ the oil pump which, being cast, breaks very easily if you knock it sideways. Unlock the lock tabs – and take care!

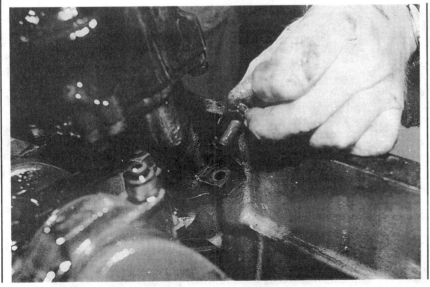

ES16. Remove the two bolts; but don't start knocking the body of the pump about with a hammer in order to loosen it!

ES17. *You must rotate and pull it a bit at a time. If you break the neck of the pump you're in for an expensive replacement!*

ES18. *The oil pump drive shaft can now be removed.*

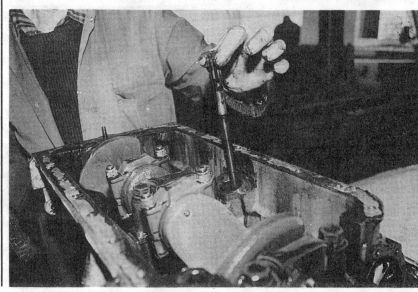

ES19. *The front of the engine. You can now see the timing cover exposed and the water pump has been removed. Look for corrosion in the pockets there. Remove the timing cover bolts in a systematic way.* ▼

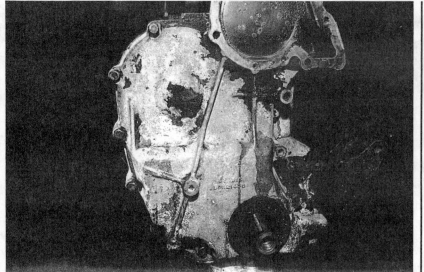

ES20. *Shows the three bolts that held the sump up into the timing cover. This is for reference in case you want to remove the timing cover with the sump still in place.*

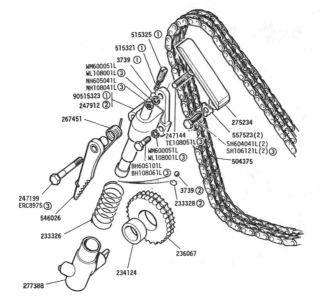

ES21. With the timing cover off you can see the timing chain, the slipper plate which is the anti-slap plate, and the timing chain tensioner, you can just about see the ridges of wear on this slipper plate and the first nut is coming off on the tensioner assembly.

ES22. The timing chain tensioner is removed, leaving the slipper plate still in place.

ES23. The timing chain and tensioner assembly, and the tensioner sprocket. (Part No.546026). (Courtesy Land-Rover).

ES24. Tensioner and timing chain. The latter, well worn, should not be capable of being bent like this – the acid test for a worn timing chain.

ES25. Start by scribing a timing mark across the camshaft, camshaft sprocket and cylinder block.

ES26. The camshaft lock plate sprocket being undone.

ES27. The sprocket being removed, after removing bolt and lock plate. Land-Rover recommend the use of a special puller with legs screwed into the threaded holes in the sprocket. Try levering carefully from behind with two large screwdrivers.

ES28. This is the camshaft thrust plate coming off. There are two lock tabs to knock back and bolts to remove and one set screw to take out.

ES29. Check the rear face of the thrust plate to make sure there is no excessive wear.

ES30. Before you can get the camshaft out, you have to remove the distributor screw gear, which is engaged on the camshaft. This is done by removing the filter head and the gasket and this exposes the grub screw which holds the bush for the screw gear.

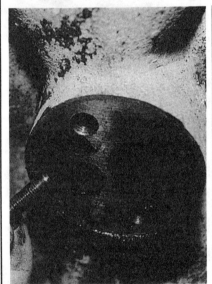

ES32. Be very careful when removing the camshaft! You must support it because it has five soft thin walled bushes in the block and if you just drag the camshaft out you will probably damage the bushes which will cause a drop in oil pressure when you next come to run the engine.

ES31. The screw gear removed. ▶

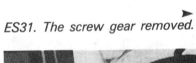

ES33. The camshaft out with ▲ screw gear and cam followers. Keep them in order, one to eight, because they must go back in the order in which they came out.

ES34. Back to the rear of the engine, with the flywheel housing still to come off. You can see a lot of black gunge which indicates that the rear main seal is leaking.

ES35. In addition to the bolts shown in the previous shot, there are also these two bolts at the top of the flywheel housing. Undo all bolts and remove the housing. Take note of the 'O' ring oil seal within the housing.

ES36. Now carefully turn the engine so that it is lying with the crankshaft exposed. Unbolt the locknuts from each big end in turn...

ES37. ... and lift off the big end caps. Look carefully for damage and look for scores on the crankshaft. Mark each big end cap and connecting rod – it is essential that they are kept as matching pairs.

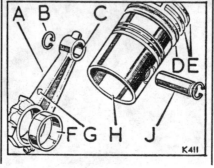

ES38. Get the pistons out and look out for broken rings and pistons. You are not going to use them again but you want to know where the broken bits are, rather than having them lying around in the engine. Tap each piston complete with con. rod upwards and out of the top of the bore, using the handle-end of a hammer, for instance.
(Courtesy Land-Rover)

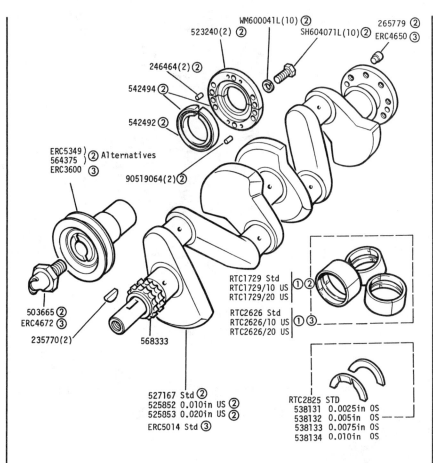

WM600041L(10) ②
523240(2) ②
SH604071L(10)② 265779 ②
ERC4650 ③

246464(2)② ②

542494 ②

542492 ②

ERC5349) ② Alternatives
564375
ERC3600 ③

90519064(2)②

503665 ②
ERC4672 ③

235770(2)

568333

RTC1729 Std
RTC1729/10 US ①②
RTC1729/20 US

RTC2626 Std
RTC2626/10 US ①③
RTC2626/20 US

527167 Std ②
525852 0.010in US ②
525853 0.020in US ②
ERC5014 Std ③

RTC2825 STD
538131 0.0025in OS
538132 0.005in OS
538133 0.0075in OS
538134 0.010in OS

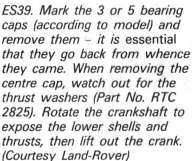

ES39. Mark the 3 or 5 bearing caps (according to model) and remove them – it is essential that they go back from whence they came. When removing the centre cap, watch out for the thrust washers (Part No. RTC 2825). Rotate the crankshaft to expose the lower shells and thrusts, then lift out the crank. (Courtesy Land-Rover)

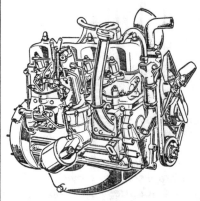

ES40. The Land-Rover diesel ▲ engine first appeared in Series I models. There are a number of detail differences to the 'internals' and huge differences to the 'externals' and you really need to refer to the special Haynes Land-Rover (Diesel engined models) Manual or the relevant sections of the official Land-Rover manuals (Courtesy Land-Rover)

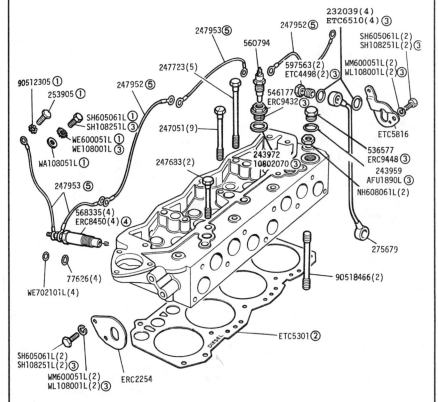

232039(4)
ETC6510(4) ③
247952 ⑤
247953 ⑤
560794
SH605061L(2)
SH108251L(2) ③
247723(5)
597563(2)
ETC4498(2) ③
247952 ⑤
WM600051L(2)
WL108001L(2) ③
90512305 ①
253905 ①
546177
ERC9432
SH605061L ①
SH108251L ③
247051(9)
WE600051L ①
WE108001L ③
ETC5816
WA108051L ①
247633(2)
243972
10802070
536577
ERC9448 ③
243959
AFU1890L ③
247953 ⑤
NH608061L(2)
568335(4)
ERC8450(4) ④
275679
90518466(2)
77626(4)
WE702101L(4)
SH605061L(2)
SH108251L(2) ③
WM600051L(2)
WL108001L(2) ③
ERC2254
ETC5301 ②

ES41. The Series III diesel cylinder head and heater plugs. (Courtesy Land-Rover)

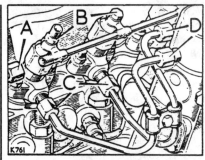

ES42. The Series II and IIA's injector pipes – truly a head like Medusa's!

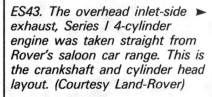

ES43. The overhead inlet-side ▶ exhaust, Series I 4-cylinder engine was taken straight from Rover's saloon car range. This is the crankshaft and cylinder head layout. (Courtesy Land-Rover)

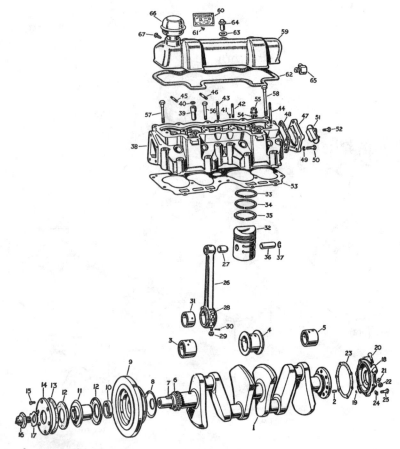

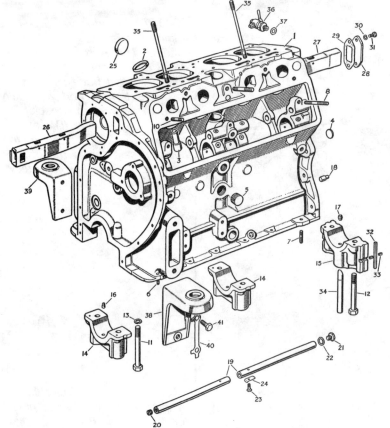

ES44. The Series I OI-SE engine's cylinder block. (Courtesy Land-Rover)

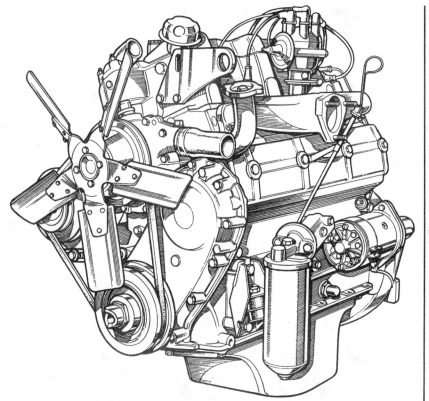

ERA1. Here, we are fitting a shell bearing while pointing out the tongue on the bearing – you can see the receiving notch on the block.

ES45. The 6-cylinder, 2.6 litre engine is a real slogger, with great pulling power and a distinct family resemblance to the Series I's 4-cylinder OI-SE unit. (Courtesy Land-Rover)

ES46. The 2.6-litre engine's cylinder block. (Courtesy Land-Rover)

Engine re-assembly

Author's Note: Please take account of my comments at the start of the previous section – in a nutshell: use this in conjunction with a Manual and use *only* Genuine Land-Rover or reputable Dunsfold Land-Rover parts. Here, again, is the benefit of Brian Bashall's experience:

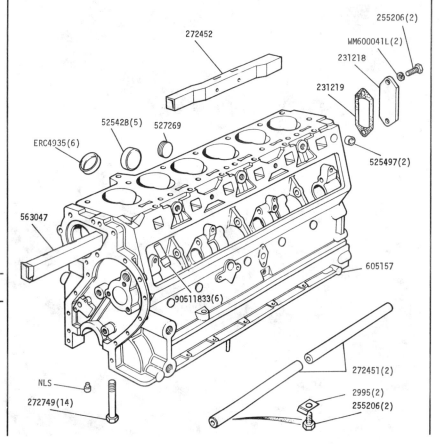

272452

255206(2)

WM600041L(2)

231218

231219

525428(5)

527269

525497(2)

ERC4935(6)

563047

605157

90511833(6)

272451(2)

NLS

2995(2)

272749(14)

255206(2)

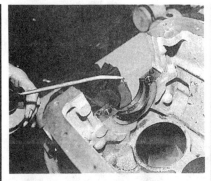

ERA2. Plenty of oil must be used at this stage – really flood it, because when the engine starts up there will be nothing else there.

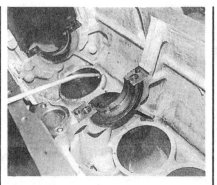

ERA3. However, it's best not to use an engine oil treatment, such as Slick 50 at this stage. Save it until later, when the engine has 'bedded in' a little.

ERA4. Clear picture of the tongues in their respective grooves.

ERA5. Replacing the crank-shaft. Very gently so that you don't disturb any of the shell bearings. It pays to give the crankshaft a good scrub if it has been reground, get a pipe cleaner into all the oilways, or use an airline to give it a good blow-out. This is where the Clarke compressor featured earlier proves to be useful in more ways than one – but wear goggles! Make sure there is no swarf left over, otherwise it will tear the shells out straight away.

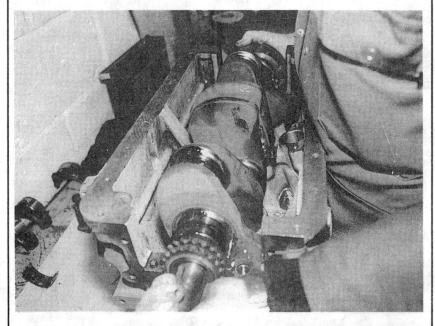

ERA6. Copious quantities of oil on the journals.

ERA7. The crankshaft thrusts; there are two of them. You have got to eliminate any float in the crankshaft because when the clutch pedal is depressed, the first action is to try to push the crankshaft through the front of the engine, in effect!

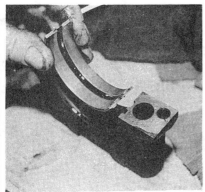

ERA8. Here, there's a shell bearing going in the front cap.

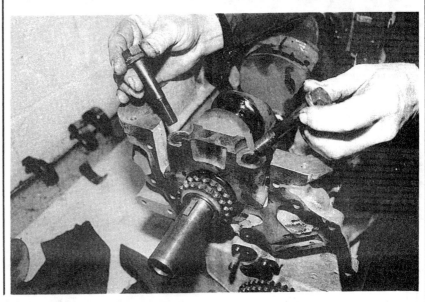

ERA9. Front cap in position. ▲ It is very useful to have the two bolts to manoeuvre the cap into the final position before you torque it down. You have to locate the cap on the two pegs that are in the block.

ERA10. Torquing down the centre bolts, making sure that the crankshaft can still turn. A word of warning: be very careful not to have your hands round the webs of the crank, because it has a lot of momentum and can cause a great deal of damage to hands if they get trapped.

ERA11. Now the bolts in the rear cap are being fitted loosely, prior to tightening with the torque wrench. Check the manual for your specific model of engine for the correct figures. When you have checked that the crank still turns, you can fit the oil seals.

ERA12. Rear main seal kit which is a Rover part with very comprehensive fitting instructions. It shows the metal rubber backed carriers, the split rear main seal, two types of rear main cap corks, the six cylinder and the four cylinder 'T'-shape; the spring that goes into the rear main seal, just loosely hooked together. You must be very careful that you don't stretch the spring or the seal will be useless. The white tube on top of the packet is silicone grease, which must be smothered everywhere. It is a heat resistant grease and does a grand job.

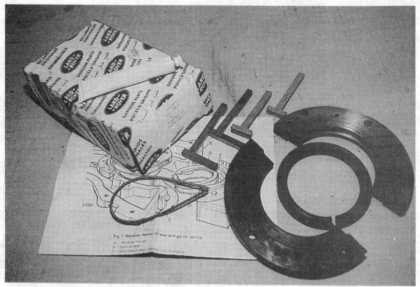

ERA13. Split the seal, opening it up as little as possible and feed it on very carefully so that you don't break the back of it. Again smother in silicone grease.

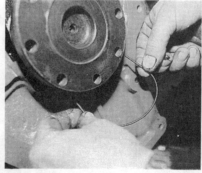

ERA14. Fitting the spring – an awkward job!

ERA15. The seal in position with the spring. Refer to the instructions. You must not have the spring joint and the split in the seal together in the same position.

ERA16. *The oil seal carrier going on to the lower bearing cap, the seal is located by pegs.*

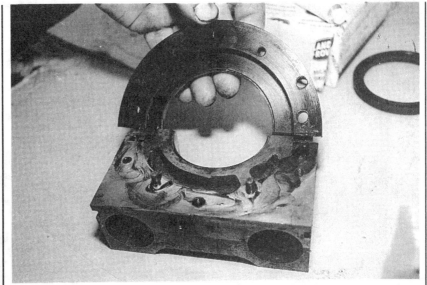

ERA17. *The cork seals (for four-cylinder and six-cylinder engines) being put into their grooves having cleaned them out first.*

ERA18. *Another view of the cap with the seal retainer ready for assembly.*

ERA19. *Upper bearing carrier in position, bearing in mind we are working with the engine upside down. There is a notch in the crankshaft flange through which the little bolts are fitted. Get a socket on there so that the crankshaft can be turned gently, so as not to disturb the existing shell bearings.*

ERA20. *The wedges in position, to stop the corks being dragged or cut.*

ERA21. *Both wedges in position and all ready to go.*

ERA22. *More oil can be wiped onto the bearing shell and a thin smear of non-setting gasket sealant wiped onto the faces of the main bearing cap where it fits against the block – not on the bearing shell, of course!*

ERA23. *Rear bearing cap being put in position.*

ERA24. *Nearly home and dry and being torqued down.*

ERA25. *You must cut off the little nibs of the cork seal, otherwise the sump gasket won't fit and you will have a leak at the back.*

ERA26. Piston ring fitting. Be very careful! If the piston is held upside down the conrod will flop to one side and you will break the skirt off the piston, so support the conrod in a vice and make sure the piston is firmly supported. The bottom ring can be a one piece type or a composite ring which consists of spring steel spreader, main body and upper and lower chromed rings (see ERA27)

ERA27. This is one of the two chrome steel piston rings.

ERA28. Fitting the support section of the scraper ring having already fitted the spreader as shown in the previous picture.

ERA29. A way of putting the ring on without damaging the piston or the ring, using a thin metal feeler gauge to slide it over the grooves.

ERA30. Lower compression ring being positioned. The upper ring already having been fitted.

ERA31. All the rings in position. The compression rings are not composite ones and have very sharp edges which can tear your thumbs to pieces unless you are very careful. These rings usually have a little 'T' etched into them to show which is top and bottom.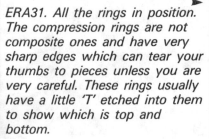

ERA32. A piston ring clamp compresses all the rings nicely. These can be bought or hired. Use plenty of oil at this stage to avoid broken rings. Don't forget to stagger all of the ring gaps.

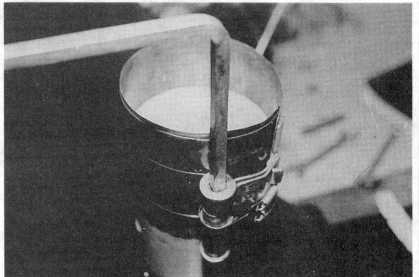

ERA33. Conrod shell being put in. The nib and groove must coincide. Make sure that the conrod hasn't been filed and that there is no dirt on the receiving side of it.

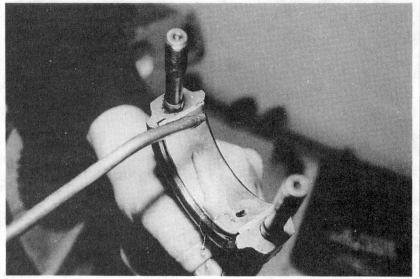

ERA34. Bags of oil, once again!

ERA35. This hole in the side of the conrod is the oil feed which splashes the bores. It has got to be the camshaft side of the engine.

ERA37. Assemble the bottom ▲ of the conrod on to the crank journal...

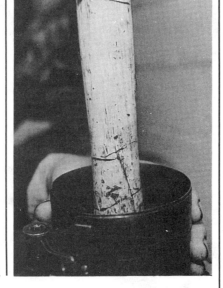

ERA36. Enter the piston into the bores and gently, with the shaft of a hammer, knock down with the minimum of force. Be very careful that you don't damage the crank. The journal should be at the top so that the big end bolts aren't damaging the journal.

ERA38. ...oil, oil and more ▲ oil! – this is the big end cap, complete with new shell.

ERA39. Tighten up with new locknuts, turning the engine after each fitting.

ERA40. Turning the engine over with the pistons in now represents a problem through drag. It pays to put a couple of the flywheel bolts in and with the minimum leverage you can turn the engine over. This should be done to ensure that everything is free and that you aren't going to have a lock-up situation when you come to put the timing chain on.

ERA41. The camshaft and the camshaft thrust which goes in the front. This must be put in very carefully, supporting it all the way, because the sharp journals are liable to pare the bearings that are in the block unless care is taken. One way is to stand the engine on its end so that you are putting it in vertically.

ERA42. These are the markings on the camshaft sprocket. There is a 'P' marked on the outer teeth and there is also a 'P' by one of the keyways. This should be put adjacent to the woodruff key on the camshaft. The outer 'P' lines up with the high stud on the block at 11 o'clock, looking from the front of the engine.

ERA43. You can see these markings clearly. You can choose from a variety of keyways to give the timing chain the correct tension.

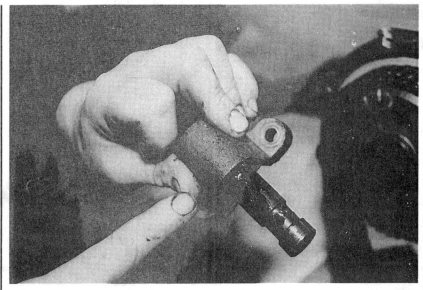

ERA44. The timing chain has ▲
now been put on loosely,
bearing in mind that the pulling
side is to the right, so that must
be straight and tight with the
crankshaft at top dead centre.
Note that, with the pistons 1 and
4 at the top of their stroke, the
keyway is vertical on the
crankshaft and the camshaft
markings are as they should be.

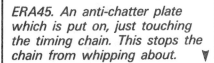

ERA45. An anti-chatter plate
which is put on, just touching
the timing chain. This stops the
chain from whipping about. ▼

ERA46. This is the piston of ▲
the timing chain tensioner.

◄
ERA47. The piston is entered to
the cylinder and the sprocket
and the spring attached. Again
thorough cleanliness is absolutely
vital. Oil pressure tensions the
timing chain initially and, as
wear takes place, there is a
ratchet that clicks up so that oil
pressure carries out the fine
adjustment of the chain tension.
Who says that Land-Rovers are
not sophisticated!

ERA48. In order to put the
timing chain tensioner in place,
hook the aluminium sprocket in
first. There are three bolts
holding the tensioner assembly
there.

ERA49. The toothed tensioner rack.

ERA50. Notice where the spring goes. If it is in the wrong position, the teeth won't engage the ratchet. ▼

ERA51. A general view of the▲ whole assembly from the front of the engine.

ERA52. Timing cover oil seals, usually go age hard or heat hard. They are easily knocked out and this is the easy way to do it. Don't forget to put it in the right way round, so that the lip is inside the engine.

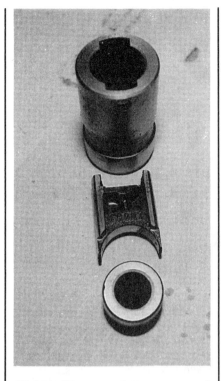

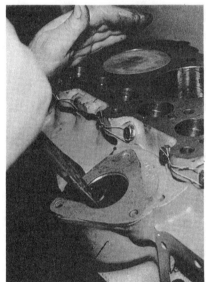

ERA53. The cam follower assembly. The outer body, the tappet and the roller. The roller follows the cam lobes, the tappet moves up and down in the body and works the push rods. Be careful not to drop the rollers in the camshaft chest, so use long nosed pliers and don't force anything.

ERA54. The locating bolts in position and neatly locked up. If these come loose the tappet body drops on to the camshaft and makes a hell of a mess! Buy the correct type of wire from your Land-Rover dealer.

ERA55. The worst job of the lot in an engine assembly: fitting the skew gear which has a bush on it with a hole which must be lined up with the oilways, while the skew gear has, at the same time, got to engage with the skew gear on the camshaft. Refer to the manual.

ERA56. The distributor body being lowered in the right position to stop the skew gear from riding up.

ERA57. You have to get the skew gear located with this little grub screw through the filter housing, a very fiddly job.

ERA58. It is essential that you ► rebuild or replace the oil pump at this stage if you are doing an engine overhaul.

ERA59. The oil pump gears the way they should be. Another thing to watch out for is the strainer pipe which sometimes fractures, so the pump sucks rubbish from the sump as well as oil. ◄

ERA60. The non-adjustable oil relief valve. There should be no ridges and the spring should be clean and undistorted. Put a new copper washer on before you assemble it.

ERA61. The oil pump, ready to go back, and the oil pump drive. While the engine is stripped out at this stage it is well worth renewing the core plugs.

ERA62. This core plug is badly corroded and probably seeps. Take no chances! Drift it out.

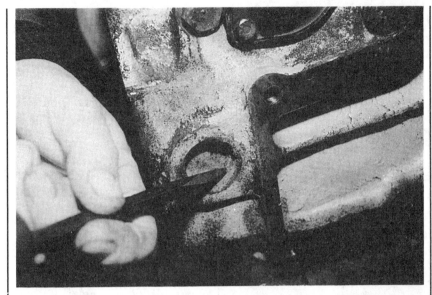

ERA63. Lever the old core plug out, but be very careful not to damage the aperture it fits in. You must not ridge or burr the edge, or damage it in any way, or the new core plug will not seat properly. Clean the seating thoroughly, however.

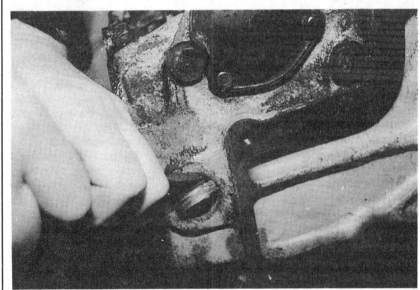

ERA64. Side core plugs being put in with a suitable drift. Don't forget to put lots of Hylomar on them first! While at this stage it is well worth having the water drain tap out and clean the block out thoroughly, getting rid of all the old rusty sediment.

Flywheel overhaul

If the face of the flywheel has become badly scored by the clutch, you can have it refaced by an engineering company with a lathe. Land-Rover recommend that the maximum amount of metal which may be removed from the flywheel face is 0.030in. Check with the original specification for your particular model of Land-Rover to ensure that the flywheel has not already been refaced in the past.

FL1. When, on petrol models, the starter ring has become excessively worn, it is possible to remove it and replace with another one as follows:
1. Either drill through the starter ring or hacksaw down as far as you can go, in both cases without touching the flywheel itself.
2. Use a sharp cold chisel and a heavy hammer and chisel through the flywheel as shown.
3. Place the starter ring in a domestic oven at maximum temperature – usually about 225 degrees C., the temperature to which Land-Rover recommend the starter is heated. Do not exceed this temperature.
4. While the ring is heating, (15 to 20 minutes should be enough once the oven is up to temperature), clean the inner face of the flywheel where the starter ring will sit so that it will be a good tight fit. Place the flywheel on a suitable flat surface.
5. When the starter ring is fully done to a turn, take it from the oven using oven gloves and taking great care not to be burnt or to cause any burns. There should now be a clearance of $\frac{1}{16}$ to $\frac{1}{8}$ in. between the starter ring and the flywheel because of the expansion that will have taken place in the starter ring. Naturally, the longer you take to find out, the more the ring will take to cool down and shrink back to its original size! Press the starter ring firmly against the flange of the flywheel until the ring contracts sufficiently to grip the flywheel. Keep a close eye on it and if necessary, tap the ring down tightly into the flange. Allow the whole thing to cool gradually; do NOT cool the starter ring down rapidly or you will cause internal stresses in the ring which may well cause it to fracture at some time in the future.
(Courtesy Land-Rover)

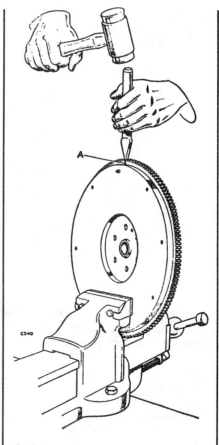

Safety note
On rare occasions, flywheel rings have been known to shatter when split. Wear goggles and gloves and place a heavy cloth over the flywheel and starter ring with a small slit for the chisel to pass through.

Clutch overhaul

CL1. Clutch overhaul is covered thoroughly in your workshop manual but the key point is that you will need a mandrel in order to align the clutch plate so that the first motion shaft on the gearbox will enter the back of the engine when refitting gearbox to engine.

CL2. Note that if the flywheel has been badly scored by a worn clutch in the past, it will be necessary to have it re-faced. You will have to remove the clutch pressure plate studs.

CL3. A tip from Dunsfold Land-Rover is to lubricate the splines on the first motion shaft - clean them out thoroughly first - using, Copper Ease, so that the clutch moves freely on it.

CL4. You can follow the instructions in your manual to rebuild the clutch master and slave cylinders or, for the ultimate in longevity, you can fit new master and slave cylinders from Land-Rover Parts. Don't forget also to renew the flexible hose and also to replace the steel pipe with Automec's copper version, which will never corrode.

Re-fitting the engine

Note – Engine removal and refit for Land-Rovers, Series I to III, is broadly the same in principle as the Series IIA 2¼-litre featured above.

The following notes outline the principles in refitting an engine. Refer to the illustrations under 'Engine Removal'. Mark well the 'Safety Notes' under that section!

Ensure that the top of the crossmember is totally clean, otherwise there is a chance of debris being trapped between the flywheel housing and bell housing – very expensive!
1). Engage a gear to prevent gear shaft rotation. Offer the engine to the gearbox – it may be necessary to rotate the engine sufficiently to align the gearbox primary pinion with the clutch plate splines. When aligned, push the engine fully to the rear and secure the bell housing to the flywheel housing, tightening the fixings evenly.
2). Lift the engine sufficiently to remove the packing or jack from beneath the gearbox and insert the engine front mounting rubbers. Then lower the engine and fit the upper and lower fixings to the engine mountings.
3). Remove the sling supporting the engine. Secure the speedometer drive cable in the cable clip adjacent to the fuel pump.
4). Connect the engine electrical leads at the snap connectors at the right-hand rear side of the engine compartment. Also connect the following:
A) The fuel inlet pipe to the fuel pump and secure the battery lead in the adjacent cable clip.

B) The dynamo and starter motor leads at the dash panel.

C) The carburettor linkage.

D) The engine earth cable.

E) The distributor leads at the ignition coil.

F) The heater hoses (if fitted with a heater) in the engine compartment.

G) The front exhaust pipe to the exhaust manifold.

5). Once all this has been completed, the front floor, radiator and grille panel, air cleaner and bonnet can be refitted.

The cooling system

The Land-Rover's radiator is generally more than adequate for European use, being the same radiator used on export models destined for Africa, apart from the addition then of a heavy duty cooling fan. We decided to fit a Genuine Series III radiator to FVJ, our 'project' Series IIA vehicle – one of the subtle modifications designed to make the vehicle more user-friendly without detracting from its basic character. Brian Bashall recommended the Series III rad. as an even more efficient replacement for the original part.

RAD1. The radiator should give few problems, although corrosion and clogging up of the galleries can occur. On the older-model radiators (shown here), the flat-topped design was very useful for kneeling on when working on the engine, but this often resulted in a collapsed header tank. Through expansion and contraction, these early radiators often used to leak from the top indentations, where the metal is thinner. Solder repairs are not successful long-term, again due to the amount of flexing.

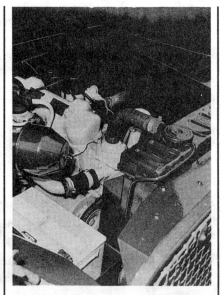

RAD2. Seen here is a 'second generation' flat-topped radiator (on the left of the photograph), with the indentations running lengthways instead of across the width; despite this modification, leaks still occurred! Next to it is a later Series III radiator, with rounded header tank (as from 1972) – at last a cure had been found!

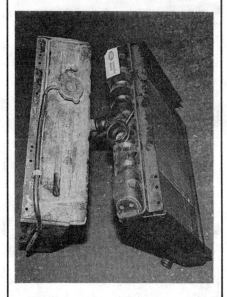

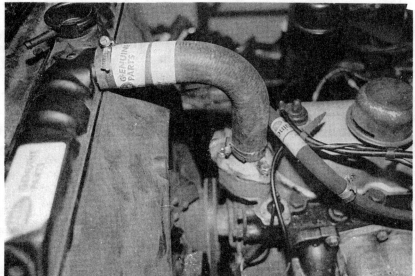

RAD3. A Series III radiator in position. If fitting it to an earlier engine (as in this case), you will have to alter the fan shroud behind the radiator for a Series III type. The hoses will also need to be changed as the radiator connections are of a larger diameter (top and bottom hoses will need updating).

RAD4. This system relies on an overflow bottle, and the bottle carrier can be seen here in the centre of the photograph.

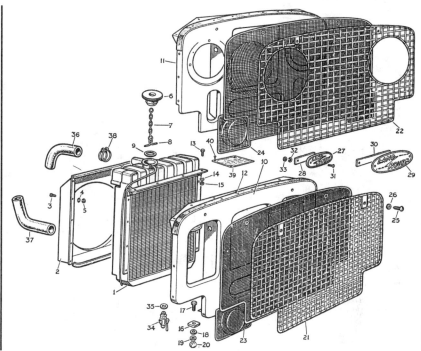

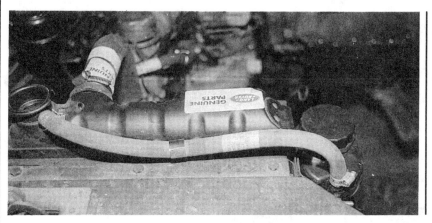

RAD7. Series I radiator grille assemblies with radiator and fixings. Note the rubber pads (item 16), referred to in RAD6 and fitted to all models. (Courtesy Land-Rover)

RAD5. The pipe going to the overflow bottle is clearly visible; when the water expands, it will go into this 'expansion tank', returning to the radiator again once it has cooled.

RAD6. A good view of the shroud behind the radiator, with the radiator and headlamp panel removed from the vehicle. There are three rubber pads on the front chassis supports that hold the radiator; these are vital, for without them the radiator will fracture (due to distortion) and will simply need replacing all over again.

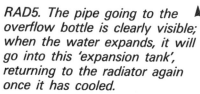

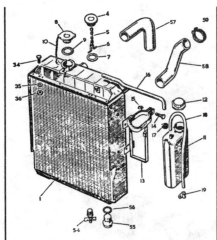

RAD8. *The Series II and IIA radiator and fittings, clearly derived from the Series I component. (Courtesy Land-Rover)*

RAD9. *The Series III radiator and fittings, some of which have UNC threads and some with metric. Dunsfold Land-Rover or your local dealer will advise which part number to order. (Courtesy Land-Rover)*

RAD10. *Removal of the Series II-III water pump and thermostat housing was shown earlier. This is the Series I assembly, showing the steel inlet pipe for the water pump. (Courtesy Land-Rover)*

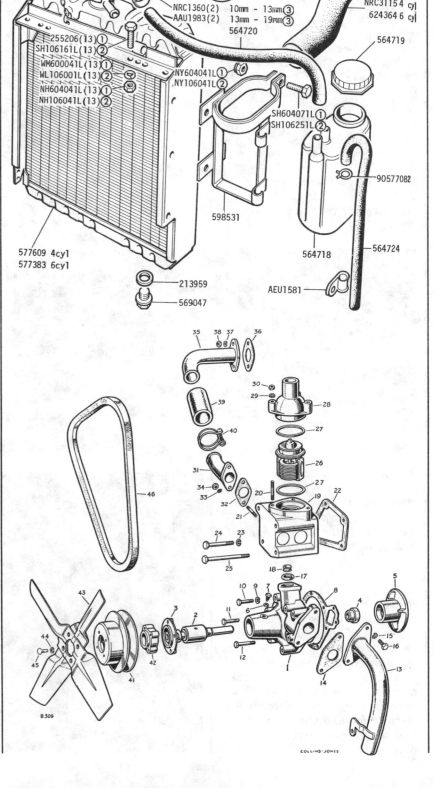

COLLINS-JONES

Exhaust system

EX1. This diagram shows the Series II and IIA exhaust systems; the former is similar to that fitted to Series I vehicles. Series I 80 in Land-Rovers have exhaust straps mounted on 'cotton-reel' mountings, while the 86 in and 107 in onwards front pipe has a different shape to those shown here, up to and including vehicle with the suffix 'B' in the chassis number. The units shown in this diagram comprise:
1. gasket
2. front pipe (prior to 1961)
3. front heat shield
4. rear heat shield
5. manifold heat shield assembly (this is fitted to all models of Series II and IIA 4-cylinder Land-Rovers)
6. front pipe (1961)
7. intermediate pipe (88 in models)
8. bracket
9. silencer (left-hand drive models)
10. intermediate pipe (109 in models)
11. silence (right-hand drive models)
12. support bracket

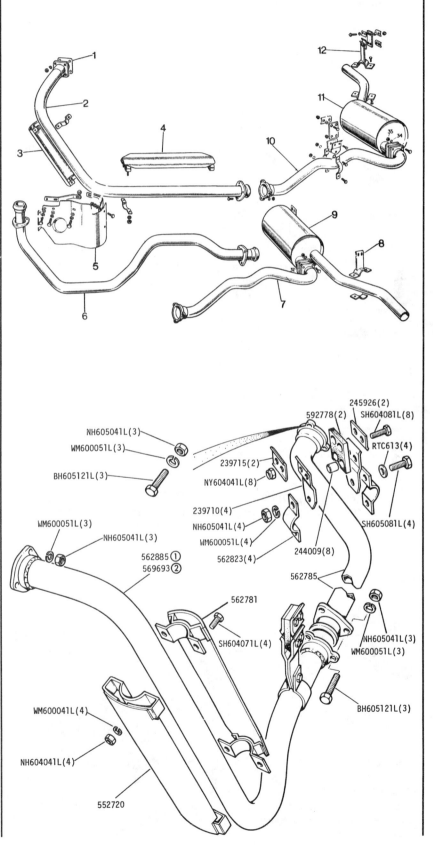

EX2. The Series III V8 exhaust system is, naturally enough, completely different – this is the down pipe and front pipe assembly. (Courtesy Land-Rover)

EX3. ... while the 2.6 litre exhaust system is different again – these are the front and intermediate types. (Courtesy Land-Rover) ►

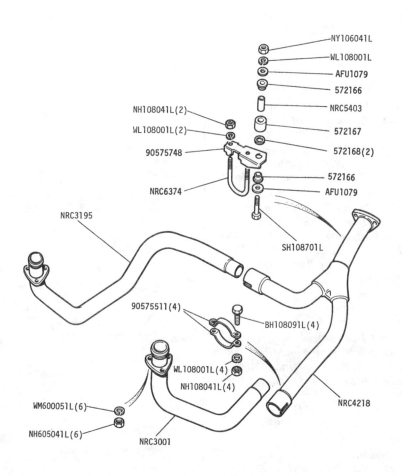

NY106041L
WL108001L
AFU1079
572166
NRC5403
572167
572168(2)

NH108041L(2)
WL108001L(2)
90575748

572166
AFU1079

NRC6374

NRC3195

SH108701L

90575511(4)

BH108091L(4)

WL108001L(4)
NH108041L(4)

WM600051L(6)

NH605041L(6)

NRC3001

NRC4218

EX4. On all the engines the front pipe bolts to the manifold via four studs which are threaded into the manifold itself. It is not unknown for the manifold to break at this point, necessitating renewal.

▼

EX5. An 88 in exhaust system bolted to a new chassis with all new Land-Rover Parts fittings...

EX6. ... and more of the same at the far end of the exhaust pipe where it is routed above the right hand spring and behind the rear crossmember.

Gearbox types and troubleshooting

Potted history

The Land-Rover main gearbox remained virtually the same basic unit from 1948 through to 1970. The transfer box incorporated a free wheel unit to the front axle until 1950. This was a lockable unit – when you wanted to go backwards or required engine braking downhill, you either pulled a chain on the floor to lock it, or you had a yellow knob on the later ones. In 1950 the free wheel unit was scrapped and a two or four-wheel drive facility was offered. This continued until 1983 in the four-cylinder vehicles. There were also some specially built Land-Rovers which were two wheel drive only. The Series II Land-Rover had the same 'innards' as Series I, with a modified casing to suit the engine, and in 1961 the early type of gearbox was modified, with the introduction of the Series IIA. The main gearbox had a beefed up lay shaft and front bearing as well as a repositioned reverse gear idler: these used to break sometimes. The idler pin in the transfer box was also enlarged.

In late 1971 an entirely new main box was introduced. This was introduced together with the Series III model. Basic differences were that this had a larger diaphragm clutch and 4-speed synchromesh. In September 1980 the V8 option became available on the long wheelbase 109s and this was coupled to the permanent four-wheel drive Range Rover type of gearbox with a centre diff. In 1983 the 4-cylinder 110 had a new 5-speed gearbox in an iron casing; this is model LT77. This had a totally new transfer box, the LT230R, with a mechanical diff-lock. The V8 110 retained the 4-speed one-piece Range Rover type of 'box, (the LT95) until 1986, and this had the servo operated diff-lock. The Land-Rover 90 came on the scene in late 1984 and it had the 5-speed gearbox. In 1986 a very heavy duty Santana Spanish 5-speed 'box known as the LT85, was introduced to the V8s and the transfer box was modified to Timken bearings as opposed to roller bearings and this was known as LT230T. The 5-speed boxes have proved to be very trouble free in use, a pleasure to drive, although they do need service tools to dismantle and rebuild when the time comes!

The gearbox in use

The Series I gearboxes, driven by the 1½ or 2-litre engines, had very few problems because of the low power of the engine and the relative light weight of the Land-Rover in those times. The common faults were the engagement dogs on second gear, bearing in mind there was no synchromesh on second gear, chipped first gear on the lay shafts and a broken main shaft. All these were the fault of clumsy driving or overloading, because the small engine just didn't overload the gearbox. With the introduction of the 2¼ engine in late 1958, the extra power caused the same problems, made worse by the larger carrying capacities of the Series IIs. In 1961 a beefed up gearbox was introduced to handle the power of the 2¼ and the loading capacity, could even cope with the 6-cylinder outputs. In 1971 4-speed synchromesh gearbox was introduced which made for easier driving but had to be treated sensibly. The massive baulk ring system did not like being rushed. All these gearboxes had aluminium cases including the transfer box, so were always a little noisy when hot. The gearboxes in the 110 and 90 models caught up with the power outputs of the various engines and are no longer the weak link in the transmission train.

Specific faults in the gearbox

by Brian Bashall of Dunsfold Land-Rover

Problems in service can be divided into three main pigeon holes: a) the 'keep an eye on it' type of problem; b) preventive action; c) major problems, which mean you have to get the tools out but consult the workshop manual first! Before you start the series of tests, you must a) check the oil levels, b) get the engine and gearbox to working temperature.
1. Put the high/low lever into neutral and run through the gears. There should be no noise other than the gentle whirr of gears beating the oil.
2. Put the main box into neutral so press and release the clutch pedal. There should be no grumbling or heavy whirring noises, just the rotating shaft noise. If there is a noise when the clutch pedal is depressed it will probably come from the clutch release bearing, or if the noise is only there when the pedal is released it will probably be coming from the primary or lay shaft bearings.
3. If there is a squeal or grunt as the clutch is slipped for manoeuvring, it is probably caused by a dry primary shaft crankshaft bush in the flywheel. They are sealed-for-life graphite bushes and dry out or get damaged when you put a new gearbox in.
4. Whilst on the run, if you put your hand on the main gear

lever and keep in 3rd gear, check that there is no rock in the gear lever between the drive and overrun condition. A worn or broken main shaft bush will allow the gears to move. Another cause is a loose rear main shaft nut, which will allow the main shaft to shunt.

5. Is the oil transferring from the main box to the transfer box? Possibility of a seal worn through or the bearing fretting in the bearing housing which separates the main box from the transfer box. This happens especially on the Series IIIs where the bearing housing is unpegged and the housing actually turns and wears the case. Another cause for this oil transfer is the breather plate on top of the gearbox or on the earlier ones it's the filler cap which has a little hole to let the gearbox breathe. This can sometimes get blocked by mud on top of the 'box.

6. If when driving there is a heavy rushing noise in 1st, 2nd and 3rd, but all is quiet in top gear, the indication will be that the lay shaft bearings have failed. If there is a gritty noise take immediate action!

7. If you are unable to select 3rd and top, this is a common problem. There are little detent springs in the 3rd and 4th

synchromesh, which break and fail to drop away but jam instead.

8. If you have only got 4th gear accompanied by expensive clattering noises the chances are you have got a broken lay shaft.

9. If you can drive in 1st and 2nd gear but not in 3rd and 4th, the mainshaft will have broken up at the front end.

10. If you can select all the gears with a great deal of noise but with no drive to the transfer box, the main shaft has broken at the rear end.

11. If you are unable to select reverse gear on the pre-1978 models this usually means that the brass bush of the reverse idler has moved out of the gear and is allowing the gear to tilt and jam.

12. Occasional inability to engage gears can occur when one of the reverse selector springs on the selector gate breaks and drops down and fouls the selector shaft. To diagnose the problem finally, it pays to drain off the oil into a clean container and look at what comes out. If you have got red powder coming out – you are in trouble. If the oil is a golden colour it usually means that a brass bush has worn somewhere. If a silver colour it means that something is in

touch with the gearcase and this is aluminium in the oil. If it is mayonnaise it normally means there is water in the oil and if you have been wading, drain out the oil and replace it at once. Finally, the plop of pieces of steel means expense! Stop driving, strip the gearbox and use the workshop manual.

Gearbox removal

GBR1. Because the gearbox can only be removed from inside the vehicle through the passenger doorway, it is strongly recommended that a wheeled hoist with an extended lifting arm is use. It is not recommended that one or more people attempt to lift out the gearbox manually. The unit is extremely heavy, injury could result and the interior of the vehicle could easily be damaged. The entire floor of the vehicle has to be removed (see appropriate section in the Bodywork Chapter of this book) and the seat base also has to be taken out. Drain the transfer box and gearbox oil into a suitable container.

GBR2. *You will be taking out the engine and transfer box complete and, in brief, the following components should be removed.*
– Front and rear propeller shaft and winch drive shaft, if fitted.
– Transmission brake operating mechanism and, on left hand drive models, the brake lever cross-shaft.
– Speedometer cable from transfer box.
– The two bolts from each of the transmission mountings and, on some models, the front exhaust pipe which passes over the left hand mounting.
– The tie rod between chassis and gearbox, when fitted.
– The clutch slave cylinder, leaving hydraulic connections connected and placing carefully so as not to strain the hydraulic pipes.
– The earth strap between gearbox and chassis, if fitted. You can now lightly take of the weight of the gearbox on the hoist and remove each of the bell housing nuts holding the gearbox to the engine. (See spanner in photograph, arrowed)

GBR3. *The complete transmission assembly can now be lifted from the vehicle. Note that the main gear change lever has here been removed from the gearbox. It is often convenient to leave it in place until after the gearbox has been taken out as an extra "something" to take hold of as the gearbox is being pulled out.*

The Series I freewheel unit

The freewheel unit, fitted to very early Series I vehicles can be removed from beneath without removing the main gearbox.

1. Drain the oil, move the transfer lever to the rear position and disconnect the front propeller shaft.
2. On right hand drive models only, you remove the clutch return spring, front end first; disconnect the operating rod from the clutch cross-shaft; disconnect the connecting tube and slide the cross-shaft towards the chassis.
3. Then remove the freewheel control pivot and eyebolt and withdraw the freewheel operating rod.
4. A nut and washer hold the transfer control link to the selector shaft: disconnect and slide the link up the transfer gear change lever.

5. Take off the front propeller shaft drive flange.
6. Carefully remove the transfer selector spring and bore.
7. You can unbolt the complete output shaft housing and lower it, but on gearboxes numbered 860001 to 861988 it is essential that the locking dog remains in the output shaft housing, otherwise the unit will not clear when it is being removed.
8. Jack the gearbox unit upwards slightly from beneath. Unbolt the freewheel housing from the transfer casing and lift it away. Adjust the angle of the gearbox to enable the freewheel housing to clear the chassis. Reassembly is a reversal of the above procedure.

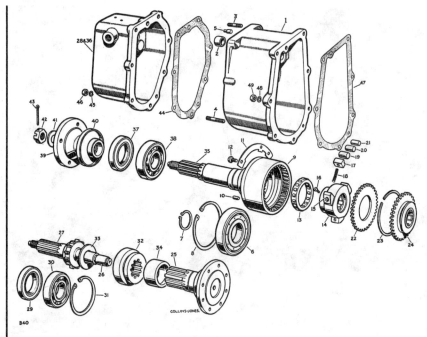

F1. The freewheel unit, as fitted to Series I vehicles.

Strip down

1. Remove the freewheel locking dog (Part No. 24) and take off the circlip (Part No. 8) holding the output shaft rear bearing (Part No. 6) in the freewheel housing. Drive the shaft and freewheel from the housing. You can now remove the output shaft rear bearing.
2. On gearboxes numbered 860001 to 861988, remove the bush (Part No. 26) from the front bore of the output shaft.
3. Remove the spring ring (Part No. 23) and retaining plate (Part No. 22) holding the inner to the outer member. Remove the inner member (Part No. 14) complete with the fixed cam roller shoes (Part Nos. 17 to 21) and remove the inner member pilot bearing (Part No. 13) from the outer member (Part No. 9).
4. Take out the set bolts (Part No. 12) and remove the two locking plates (Part No. 11) holding the freewheel outer member to the output shaft. Disconnect the freewheel outer member from the output shaft.

Re-assembly notes

1. If a new operating shaft bush (Part No. 2) is required, it should be pressed into the housing and reamed to 0.625in when in place.
2. Gearboxes numbered 860001 to 861988. The bush (Part No. 26) in the front bore of the output shaft must be a driven fit. The transfer shaft must be an easy fit in the bush.
3. Start by fitting the outer member to the front output shaft and secure with the bolts.
4. Place the inner member pilot bearing in the outer member.
5. Fit the inner member (Part No. 14) complete with three fixed cam roller shoes (Part No. 15) in the bearing. Place the nine rollers, large medium and small (Part Nos 19, 20 and 21) in position and fit the free cam roller shoes and springs (Part Nos 17 and 18)
6. Fit the toothed retaining plate (Part No. 22) in the outer member and fit the shaft rear bearing into the housing. Fit the freewheel unit into the housing

(Part No.1) and press or lightly drive the output shaft (Part No. 25) through the bearing. Secure with a circlip.
7. Complete the assembly procedure by reversing the dismantling process outlined above.

Fitting a SIII 4-synchromesh gearbox to a SII/IIA

The two synchromesh gearbox fitted to Series II and IIA Land-Rovers is as tough a gearbox as you will get, so if you do a lot of heavy work with your Land-Rover you would be well advised to stick with the two synchro unit and learn how to double-declutch. However, many of us prefer the advantages of having an all synchromesh gearbox fitted to the vehicle and this can be simply done by fitting a Series III gearbox to a Series II or IIA Land-Rover. (Do bear in mind that the very last of the Series IIAs were fitted with a 4-synchro. gearbox as standard.) A word of warning though when it comes to purchasing a Series III 'box for installation into an earlier vehicle. Most well used 4-synchro. gearboxes will have obvious signs of wear in one or more places and you would be well advised to either only buy a gearbox which you can thoroughly road test first or to buy one and have it reconditioned before fitting it to your vehicle. Keith Harris, a reconditioner of gearboxes who lives close by the author, devised the following means of fitting a Series III gearbox to a Series II or IIA Land-Rover.

The main problem stems from the fact that the Series II/IIA and III clutch slave cylinder, operating mechanism and clutch components are incompatible with one another. Bell housings on the two types of gearbox are different to accommodate these different clutches, although you can easily fit a II/IIA bell housing to a Series III gearbox. What you can *not* do is to transfer the Series III first motion shaft, which fits into the bell housing end plate, into the Series II/IIA bell housing because the oil sealing arrangement in the back of the bell housing is different between the two different models. Moreover, the gear on the back of the first motion shaft and the primary gear that engages it have different numbers of teeth between Series II/IIA and Series III gearboxes.

FSG1. The trick is, according to Keith Harris and as confirmed by the work carried out on the author's Series IIA, to take the first motion shaft and primary gear, part numbers 606880 and RTC2684 from the Series II/IIA gearbox and use them with the Series III gearbox. The first motion shaft will be transferred as part of the bell housing while the primary gear must be removed after tapping out the lay shaft. See your workshop manual for details.

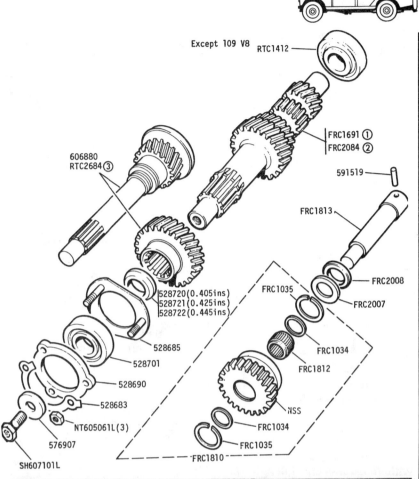

FSG2. The Series II/IIA bell housing will have to be taken from the II/IIA gearbox and fitted to the Series III gearbox.

FSG3. The transfer box also is taken from the II/IIA gearbox and is also bolted on as a direct replacement to the Series III unit. See your workshop manual for details.

FSG4. Keith Harris points out that when you buy your Series III gearbox, it must come complete with the correct top and selectors because they are not transferable between Series II/IIA and Series III gearboxes. (Courtesy Land-Rover)

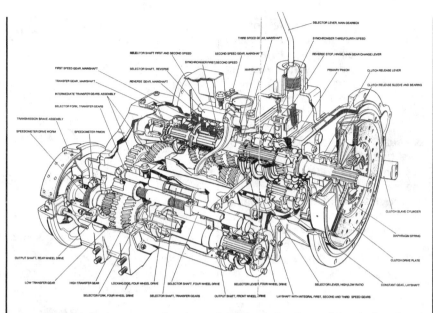

Fitting an overdrive

The Land-Rover overdrive is a quite extraordinary affair being no more or less than an extra gearbox with its own, separate gear change lever. With an overdrive unit fitted, you too can have sixteen forward gears and four reverse! But seriously, the Land-Rover overdrive unit is one of the most desirable of Land-Rover accessories along with free wheeling hubs, and provides some significant benefits. Land-Rover quote, in their usual conservative manner, an improvement in fuel consumption of up to 15% and a road speed increase of 27.8% at the same engine speed. In practice, the saving in wear and tear on mechanical components and on the aural components of the driver make this an accessory that is well worth having. It can be used in any gear although in practice, it will rarely be used in any gear other than third or fourth. In theory, the vehicle could be left in overdrive and driven as a slightly over geared vehicle when lightly laden.

However, Brian Bashall of Dunsfold Land-Rover recommends that you start away from rest with the overdrive "out" to avoid putting undue strain on the overdrive unit itself. The author uses his by shifting into overdrive whilst in third or fourth gear once the open road has been attained and then only shifting out of overdrive on reaching a town or a junction where it is necessary to come to a halt. The overdrive contains its own "slow!" synchromesh and you change in and out by depressing the clutch in the normal way. It quickly becomes second nature to feel down and back for that second gear stick!

OD1. The overdrive unit is supplied by Land-Rover Parts as a complete kit, ready to fit, except for the special spanner which is quoted as being necessary to remove and tighten up the mainshaft nut.

OD2. After removing the rear ▲
bearing housing and the top
cover plate from the transfer
box, the special mainshaft nut
has to be removed and the lock
washer and gear withdrawn.

OD3. The overdrive unit clutch
sleeve and a new lock washer
are fitted to the transfer box,
ensuring that the distance piece
and shim (if fitted) are
re-assembled in the correct order.
If you are unable to make up
your own special spanner for
removing the mainshaft nut, note
that you may be able to beg,
borrow or buy one and that it
has Land-Rover Part Number
600300. The nut has to be re-
tightened to the figure shown in
the workshop manual for your
model of Land-Rover.

OD4. The overdrive unit is now
fitted to the back of the transfer
box using the studs on which
the rear bearing housing was
originally mounted.

OD5. The change linkage as
supplied with the kit is fitted up,
utilising the special bracket
which is bolted to the top of the
gearbox. You have to cut a two
inch hole in the transmission
tunnel to allow the gearchange
lever to pass through and a
rubber grommet and sealing
plate are supplied as part of the
kit. Full instructions for fitting an
overdrive unit are supplied with
every kit.

Transfer box problems

Problems referred to here are
relevant to Series I, II and III
only.

1. The yellow knob will not stay
down. This means you have no
front wheel drive lock-up in the
high range. If you slacken the
yellow knob lock-nut and undo
it sufficiently to stop the spring
getting coil bound, this will
allow the lever to drop and stay
engaged.

2. If you are unable to get front
wheel drive, the selector rods
may have rusted in the nose
casing through lack of use or
because of mud build up.

3. Speed related whine from the
idler gearbox is acceptable. If
this should become too audible

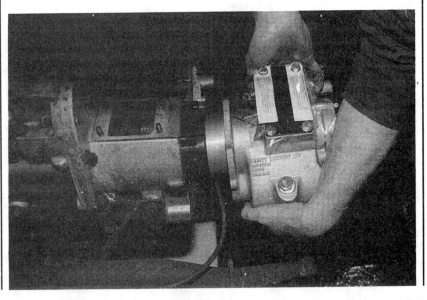

on the drive over-run, it should be checked. Drain the oil and check the colour and contents, remove the tin sump and check the idler gear end float and tooth condition.

4. If you have a problem in the idler gear you have to remove the rear propshaft, the handbrake drum and flange and the back plate, to withdraw the idler pin. *Beware of the next stage* The idler gear is very heavy and the teeth are very sharp. Remove the idler pin keeper and pull out the pin. Lower the gear and thrusts, examine the pin for pitting or wear and check the thrust surfaces. Refer to the workshop manual for exploded diagrams.

5. Speedometer reads normally when cold but reads slower after a few miles, this indicates that the output flange nut on the transfer box is loose, allowing the handbrake hub to move, trapping the speedo drive gear and allowing the speedo drive gear scroll to slip. This is cured by tightening the nut up.

6. If there is a dull rumble on light driving conditions, it is usually loose transfer box output shaft bearings again and they need adjustment, by removing the shims – in conjunction with the workshop manual once more.

Note: Everything must be done in conjunction with the workshop manual and the line drawings. These are just practical hints, produced with the aid of the vast experience of Dunsfold Land-Rover's Brian Bashall and his son Philip. They are intended to help to diagnose the problem.

Differentials and Half Shafts

It is most emphatically not a DIY job to rebuild your own differential but you could save money by removing your own and taking it along to a Land-Rover dealer to exchange it for a reconditioned one. Three types of differentials have been used on Land-Rovers. Series I, II and IIA models are fitted with either the Rover type front and rear or, on later vehicles, with the ENV type front and rear. Series II vehicles are equipped with the Rover type front and rear on short wheelbase versions and the Rover type front and Salisbury type rear on long wheelbase models.

Safety
Follow all the usual safety procedures when working beneath a vehicle, as outlined elsewhere in this book. Note that the handbrake will be ineffective once the half shaft has been removed and so it is doubly important that the wheels remaining on the ground are carefully and adequately chocked to prevent movement.

DHS1. The upper set of drawings shows an exploded view of the front axle and the lower set of the rear axle of vehicles fitted with the earlier Rover type differentials.

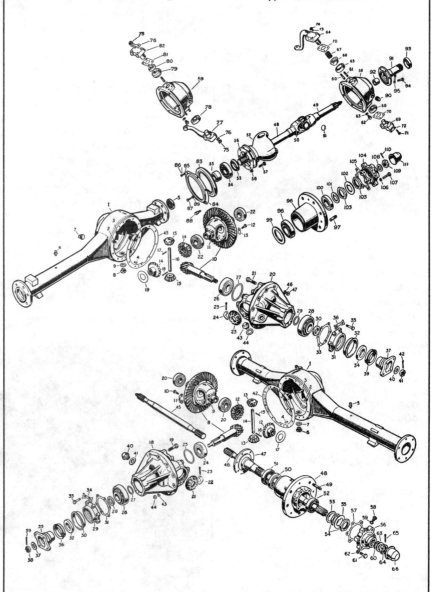

208

Differentials of the Rover and
ENV types can simply be
unbolted from the axle casing
after first partially withdrawing
the half shafts as described
below. Work on the Salisbury
differential is best left to your
Land-Rover dealer.

Rear axle half shafts – Rover
type axle.

1. Chock the front wheels and
support the rear of the vehicle
on axle stands.

2. Remove the six bolts securing
the half shaft driving flange to
the hub.

3. Withdraw the driving flange
and half shaft together, tapping
the driving flange with a soft
faced mallet to encourage it to
come out if necessary. The half
shaft does not need to be
totally removed.

Rear axle half shafts – ENV type
axle.

1. Support the vehicle as
described above.

2. Withdraw the driving flange
and half shaft as described
above but note that if you wish
to remove the half shaft totally,
it is held to the driving shaft
with a circlip which will require
the use of circlip removing pliers
to undo it. It is clearly visible
beneath the hubcap which is
fitted with an oil sealer 'O' ring.

DHS3. The Salisbury type of rear
axle casing used on 109 in
vehicles from suffix "H"
onwards.

Front axle half shafts

The front half shafts are a little
more complex to remove. Refer
to earlier sections:

1. Remove the front hub.

2. Unbolt the brake back plate
and hang it carefully out of the
way, taking care not to stretch
the brake hose. The brake hose
itself should be secured to the
back of the swivel housing.

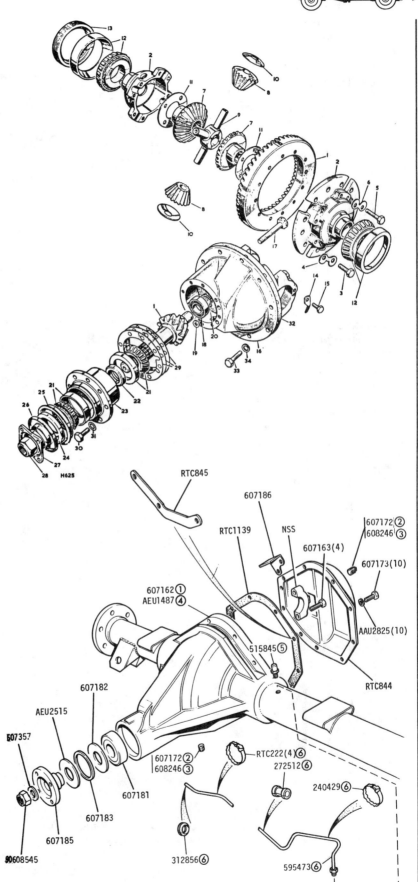

Take out the two bolts to allow the back plate to be moved. The half shaft assembly, complete with universal joint, can now be pulled partially or fully out.

Copper brake pipes and silicone brake fluid

CBP1. For restoration work, both the author and Dunsfold Land-Rover recommend the use of ▶ Automech's copper brake pipe kits. They come ready to fit and, in theory, require no more effort than to screw both ends in place, although in practice, pipes occasionally need to be cut to length and the ends flared before they can be made to fit neatly. Copper has the enormous advantage that it will never corrode and it is also easy to bend to shape. Also available and just as useful are Automech's copper fuel lines.

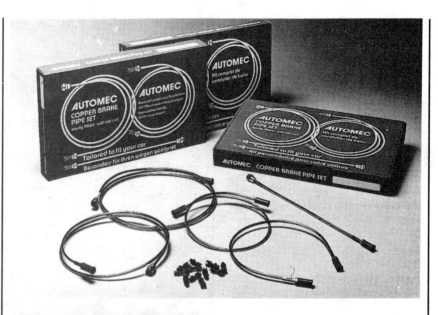

CBP4. New Land-Rover Parts flexible hoses have been fitted to this new chassis and the Automech brake pipe screwed in place on the other side of the bracket. The new fuel line has been neatly clipped in place along the top of the chassis. When stripping down your old Land-Rover, take very careful note of where the brake pipes should go. It is essential that brake pipes are not squashed by the body when it is fitted; that they do not rub on any moving parts; and that they are not allowed to flex because of axle movement. ◀

CBP2. This Sykes-Pickavant flaring tool is the sort of pro. equipment that Dunsfold Land-Rover use.

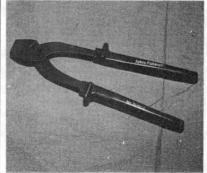

CBP3. Sykes-Pickavant's bending tool is useful, although not absolutely essential where copper is concerned, for very sharp bends especially close to the end of the pipe.

CBP5. Here the new brake pipes have been fitted to the brake light switch.

CBP6. The Automech pipe has ▲ been run to the bracket near the rear axle from where the brake line is taken via a new flexible hose to another bracket mounted on the differential. The copper brake pipe has been bent carefully to follow the shape of the axle, and original Land-Rover clips are used to hold the pipe firmly to the axle casing.

CBP7. Where brake lines cross the rear springs, there should be a bracket on each side, clamped between the spring and axle casing on to which the brake lines are screwed. These are often missing when a vehicle has been restored poorly.

CBP8. Most brake wheel cylinders fail because of the hygroscopic nature of brake fluid: it takes in moisture from the air and this causes corrosion to take place in the wheel cylinder bores. The ideal way of overcoming this problem is to use Automech's silicone brake fluid which is non-hygroscopic and which also has the beneficial side effect of not stripping paint if it is spilled on to it. You can use silicone brake fluid by draining down the old system first and it's really a "must" when a system has been completely rebuilt, such as that on FVJ, the project Land-Rover. It can be mixed with conventional fluid but you then loose the silicone brake fluid's primary benefit, of course! Follow your workshop manual for information on draining the brake fluid and bleeding the brakes.

Brake master cylinders

The various types of master cylinder fitted to Land-Rovers over the years evolved in an easily traceable line. But even so, there are very many detailed differences between the different types fitted and it is essential that you refer to the Parts Book, your vehicle's chassis number and your Land-Rover dealer for the correct information when replacing or rebuilding a master cylinder. Details on overhauling the master cylinder can be found in your workshop manual but you are strongly advised not to carry out any work on the braking system yourself unless you are fully competent and qualified.

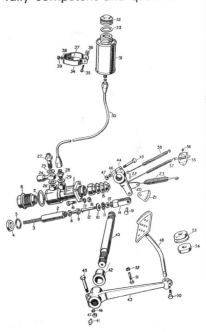

MC1. The Series I brake pedal and master cylinder assembly. Early and later master cylinders looked identical but those used on 80 in models employed BSF fittings while those on 86 in and 107 in models used UNF. At first sight, they look exactly the same and even Brian Bashall confesses that he is often fooled! 109 in Series I master cylinders are the same shape but have a bigger bore. (Courtesy Land-Rover)

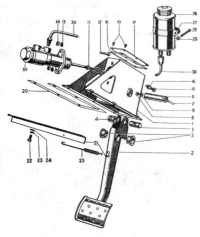

MC2. The earlier Series II and ▲ IIA master cylinder arrangement with the CB type master cylinder. In the late 1960s, the CV aluminium master cylinder was introduced and later still! the transparent fluid reservoir. Short Wheelbase and Long Wheelbase models used different cylinder bores. Master cylinders on vehicles with servo were different again. (Courtesy Land-Rover)

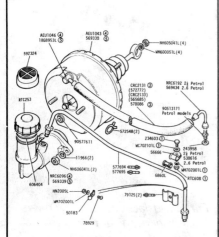

MC3. This is one of the Series III master cylinder and servo arrangements. Note that the correct pipe clips are readily available from Land-Rover Parts. (Courtesy Land-Rover)

Handbrake mechanism

HM1. The handbrake works on the vehicle's transmission and is mounted on the back of the transfer box. The advantage of this system is that the handbrake is totally separate from the footbrake and gives a good supplementary braking system in dire emergency and the mechanism is well protected from the cause of any damage when driving on rough ground. Never use the handbrake to stop the vehicle (unless there is a desperate need for you to do so) because there is a strong risk of damage to the transmission. The brake drum can be removed for the replacement of brakeshoes, although almost by definition, the handbrake will virtually never wear out. The adjuster cone (Part No. 25) may have to be freed off if it seizes in the adjuster housing (Part No. 20). Equally, the plungers (Part No. 33) may have to be freed from their housing (Part No. 26) if seizing up has taken place. Courtesy Land-Rover.

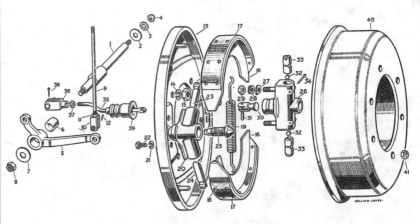

Brake drum removal

▲

BDR1. Before you can remove the brake drum you must slacken off the brake shoe adjuster. On the 88 in short-wheelbase models there was just one adjuster on each back plate up until 1981 when twin leading shoe front brakes were introduced. The 109 in long-wheelbases had twin shoe brakes with twin adjusters on the front, as well as twin adjusters on the rear but only one cylinder.

▼

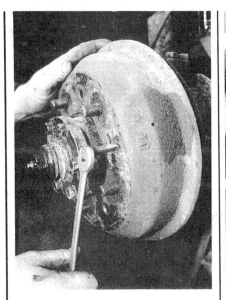

BDR2. This shows a brake drum being removed. There is a tapped thread in each brake drum and with a unified coarse bolt you can pull the drum off. Otherwise you have to run the risk of damaging it by thumping it with a hammer – if you have to do so, use a soft-faced mallet otherwise you might crash the dum with lethal consequences. The dust seal on the back of the drum might well break off the drum.

BDR3. The brake drum is off, revealing the shoes, the cylinder and leaky hub seal.

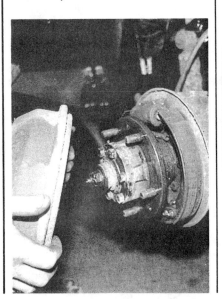

BDR4. When, after assembly, you refit the brake drums, tap them around the perimeter with a soft-faced mallet as you tighten up the two drum retaining screws.

BDR5. This is what can happen if you don't! This wheel stud, from Dunsfold Land-Rover's 'black-musuem', shows how a wheel came loose and rubbed on the studs after a brake drum was fitted but not properly bedded down.

Brake shoe replacement

Safety
Follow the usual safety rules when working on a vehicle lifted off the ground: work only on a firm, level surface; use only stout axle stands to support the vehicle; NEVER go beneath a vehicle supported only on a jack.

Asbestos, which is still used at the time of writing in the manufacture of some inferior brake components, can be most damaging to health. Insist on asbestos-free linings, whenever possible.

BSS1. Spray the shoes, back plate and drums with a proprietary brand of aerosol brake cleaner such as Wurth Sa Besto Brake Cleaner. This non-toxic, CFC-free cleaner washes harmful dust away, for safe disposal. Then you can wipe out thoroughly with a damp cloth; dispose of shoes and wiping materials in sealed plastic bags; wear an efficient face mask. NEVER blow brake dust with your mouth or an airline; don't leave brake dust lying around.

shown in the following Land-Rover diagrams and the same hints and tips can usually be adapted.

BSR1. This delightful 1948 drawing illustrates the entire 80 in braking system. Rear brake shoes (to the left) have only one return spring per side. Dunsfold Land-Rover can supply exchange shoes. (Courtesy Land-Rover)

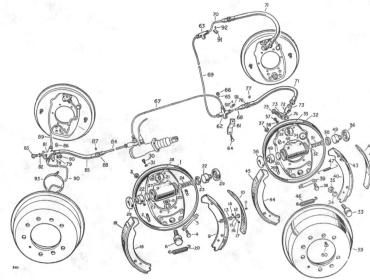

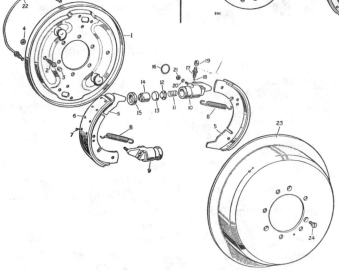

1 Brake anchor plate assembly—lefthand   2 Steady post for brake shoe   3 Bush for steady post
4 Special nut—fixing steady post   5 Brake shoe assembly—lefthand   6 Lining for brake shoe   7 Rivet securing lining
8 Pull-off spring   9 Wheel cylinder assembly   10 Wheel cylinder—lefthand (Part of wheel cylinder assembly)
11 Spring (Part of wheel cylinder assembly)   12 Air excluder (Part of wheel cylinder assembly)   13 Seal (Part of wheel
cylinder assembly)   14 Piston (Part of wheel cylinder assembly)   15 Rubber boot (Part of wheel cylinder assembly)   16 Sealing
ring for cylinder   17 Bleed screw   18 Steel ball for bleed screw   19 Rubber dust cap for bleed screw   20 Spring washer
(Securing wheel cylinder)   21 Nut (Securing wheel cylinder)   22 Conecting pipe for wheel cylinders   23 Brake drum
24 Setscrew fixing brake drum

BSR2. Long Wheelbase Land-Rovers have always had 11 in brakes, unlike the Short Wheelbase's 10 in. This is the Series I, II and III 107 in and 109 in 4-cylinder twin wheel cylinder layout. From June 1980, 88 in Series III models were identically equipped. 6-cylinder and V8 109 in models have a very similar set-up but with wider shoes, a different looking set of wheel cylinders and adjusters that have 'slipped' about 90 degrees around the back plate. (Courtesy Land-Rover)

Exploded view of the rear brake fitted to Series II, LWB models

1 Brake anchor plate
2 Steady post for brake shoe
3 Bush for steady post
4 Special nut for steady post
5 Brake shoe assembly
6 Lining complete with rivets, for
   brake shoe
7 Spring, adjuster end, for brake shoe
8 Spring, wheel cylinder end, for brake shoe
9 Adjuster housing
10 Spring washer, securing adjuster housing
11 Special set bolt, securing adjuster housing
12 Plunger, LH
13 Plunger, RH
14 Cone for adjuster

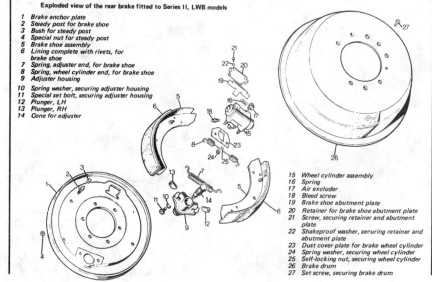

15 Wheel cylinder assembly
16 Spring
17 Air excluder
18 Bleed screw
19 Brake shoe abutment plate
20 Retainer for brake shoe abutment plate
21 Screw, securing retainer and abutment
   plate
22 Shakeproof washer, securing retainer and
   abutment plate
23 Dust cover plate for brake wheel cylinder
24 Spring washer, securing wheel cylinder
25 Self-locking nut, securing wheel cylinder
26 Brake drum
27 Set screw, securing brake drum

BSR3. This is the Long Wheelbase Series I and II rear brake. (Courtesy Land-Rover)

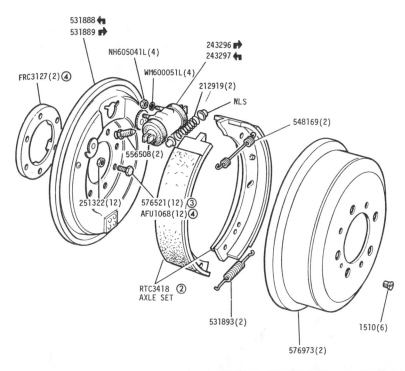

531888 ◄┑
531889 ┍►

NH605041L(4)

243296 ┍►
243297 ◄┑

FRC3127(2) ④

WM600051L(4)

212919(2)

NLS

548169(2)

556508(2)

251322(12)

576521(12) ③
AFU1068(12) ④

RTC3418 ②
AXLE SET

531893(2)

1510(6)

576973(2)

BSR4. This is the rear brake ▲ for all Series IIA and III Long Wheelbase models. (Courtesy Land-Rover)

BSR6. These well oiled-up brake shoes were to be replaced by John, starting with removal of the anchor plate indicated here.

BSR7. John cleaned up the anchor plate and got out of the Dunsfold stores a pair of the special set screws which hold it in place and a new locking plate.

8752

BSR5. The ubiquitous 'stoppers' fitted front and rear to all 86 in and 88 in Land-Rovers, front and rear, up to June 1980. For 88 in Series III from June 1980-on, see BSR2. (Courtesy Land-Rover)

◄ BSR8. Note: John has seen many of these 10 in brakes with a spring fitted between the peg and hole that he is pointing to here. This is a big mistake! If you do fit a spring here, you will have no "pedal" when you first apply the brakes and it will take a good three pumps on the brake pedal to restore any braking efficiency. A spring was never meant to be fitted here. The spring fitted as shown in this picture is however, correct.

BSR9. John uses a pair of mole grips to pull the rear, trailing shoe away from the bottom pivot...

BSR12. With the bottom spring removed the leading shoe can be pulled away from the pivot...

BSR14. ...which can be disconnected leaving the front, leading shoe free to be removed.

BSR10. ...allowing it to pass to one side of the pivot and taking the pressure off the bottom spring.

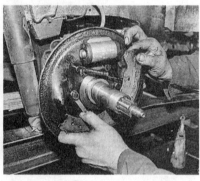

BSR13. ...and swung inwards sufficiently to take the tension off the top spring...

BSR15. Use string or wire to tie the wheel cylinder in the "closed" position, otherwise it will slowly pop itself open.

BSR11. The bottom spring can be unhooked and the trailing shoe lifted away.

◄

BSR16. Take this opportunity to loosen the snail cam brake adjuster, lubricating it thoroughly with Comma Copper Ease lubricant. If it is at all worn, remove the adjuster and fit a new one. If it breaks while the brake shoes are fully adjusted up, you may have to resort to smashing the brake drum in order to remove it.

BSR17. If the brake springs are bent, you will have great difficulty in replacing them later on and if the ends have begun to straighten out, they stand the risk of jumping off the brake shoes. In either case, replace them. The longer spring goes on the top and operates on the leading shoe while the shorter spring goes on the bottom, utilising the two outer holes on the bottom of each brake shoe, and ensures that they both locate properly on the bottom pivot.

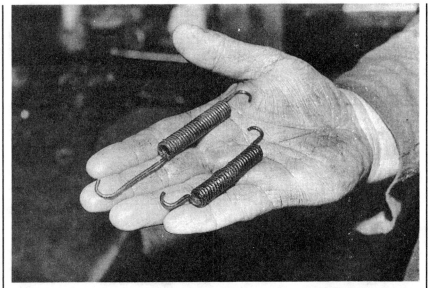

BSR18. You are strongly recommended to only use Genuine Land-Rover Parts brake components, such as those used on FVJ our project vehicle. Before you reassemble, get it straight in your own mind which shoes are which. The two trailing shoes, being pointed to here, can be identified by the absence of adjuster pins (the trailing shoes fit to the rear) while the two leading shoes are handed left and right. The one nearest the camera is a right-hand leading shoe.

BSR19. John reverses the procedure shown in BSR12 and 13 hooking the top spring in place and then locating the bottom of the brake shoe. Note that clean hands are required for this part of the work, to ensure that you don't get any oil or grease on the new brake shoes.

BSR20. Then, the bottom spring is hooked into place on the outer hole of the shoe already fitted...

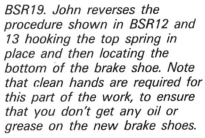

BSR21. . . . and hooked into the outer hole of the complementary shoe.

BSR22. It's back to the self-grip wrench to pull against the force of the bottom spring and locate the bottom of the brake shoe on the pivot.

BSR25. Viewed from low down, John illustrates the way in which it is rather more difficult to achieve all of this with the hub in place. (Brake shoes always have to be replaced when an oil seal hub leaks and it's best done – and easier to photograph! – when the hub is off the car). The job is carried out in a very similar way when the hub is still in place; it's just somewhat more fiddly to fit the return springs.

BSR23. Hand pressure can now be used to locate the top of the shoe against the slot in the wheel cylinder. The tie that had been fitted to the wheel cylinder has already been removed, of course.

BSR24. The anchor plate illustrated earlier is now refitted and the locking plate tabs bent over to secure the special set screws.

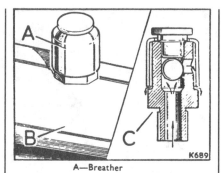

A—Breather
B—Axle case
C—Flow through breather

BSR26. If the brake shoes are ▲ *fouled by oil, check that the axle breather is clear because a blocked breather can cause failure of axle oil seals including those in the hubs.*

Hub removal and wheel bearing replacement

Please note that the following pictures are the result of two separate photo sessions at Dunsfold Land-Rover, which explains the lack of 'continuity' in some shots. The order of working shown here is not the only one you could follow but it is probably the best if you are not working on Land-Rovers every working day!

WB1. Put an oil tray beneath the hub before you start; you'll soon see why!

◄
WB2. Prise off the dust cap with a screwdriver – remember to purchase new ones before you start the job as old dust caps should not be re-used. Beneath the dust cap you can see the castellated nut on the end of the driveshaft. Incidentally, note the stain on the right hand side of the brake drum. Each Land-Rover brake drum has four drain holes and this stain is a sure sign that there's oil or brake fluid in the brake drum from the slave cylinder, or a leaking oil seal. Investigate further!

WB3. The castellated drive-shaft nut split pin is removed. Incidentally, this nut must not be over tightened so, when replacing, don't be tempted to swing on it with part of your socket set!

WB4. Undo the castellated nut but remember to stop the hub from turning by placing something like a tyre lever behind the hub studs, being careful not to damage the threads.

WB5. Unscrew the six drive flange bolts. Place a container on the floor to catch the oil that is in the hub...

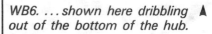

WB6. ...shown here dribbling ▲ out of the bottom of the hub.

WB7. The flange comes out ▲ fairly easily...

WB8. ...but don't forget to catch the washer that goes behind the castellated nut and the felt seal that come out with it. This is a new felt and it goes on after the flange is refitted and before the washer.

WB9. The two large locking ▲
nuts retaining the hub bearings
are now exposed. There is a lock
plate which is bent over both of
the nuts – this must be
straightened before you can
undo them.

WB10. Two almost essential
tools for any DIY Land-Rover
owner are a box spanner, shown
here – and a 'tum' like
Dunsfold's splendid mechanic,
John.   ▼

WB11. The two locking nuts ▲
can now be removed, the outer
one first followed by the lock
plate.

◄

WB12. Here you can see the box
spanner being used 'freehand' –
the nut shouldn't be too tight on
its thread, so the tommy bar
probably won't be needed.
Behind the inner nut is a thrust
washer.

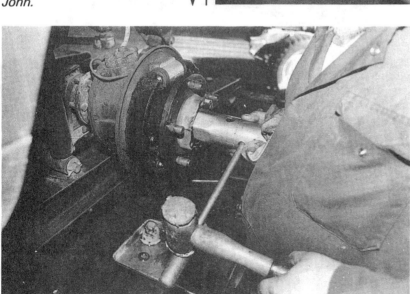

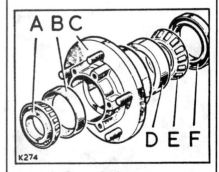

A—Outer roller bearing
B—Outer race for outer bearing
C—Hub
D—Outer race for inner bearing
E—Inner roller bearing
F—Oil seal

WB13. The outer bearing (Part A)
is now loose and can be
removed. (Courtesy Land-Rover)

WB14. The whole hub can now start to be removed. The trick is to pull it away without dropping the inner bearing on the floor or in any dirt! ►

WB15. The inner oil seal (WB13, Part F) can now be levered out of the back of the hub using John's favourite method...

WB16. ...and the inner roller ► bearing (Part E) and oil seal (Part F) lifted away. Both hardened steel bearing races (Parts B and D) are still within the hub.

WB17. Both races must be minutely examined for the smallest trace of scoring, shiny stripes, swarf or pitting, assuming that you have stripped the hub for a purpose other than replacing the bearings...
◄

WB18. ...and if damaged, they ► can be drifted out, working around with the drift so that they don't jam as they come out.

WB19. John drifts in new races from the Land-Rover Parts wheel bearing kit after scrupulously ► cleaning the hub inside and out – take great care to drive in parallel and not to mark them.

WB20. Loads of Castrol High ▲ Melting Point grease is worked into every nook and cranny of the new roller...

WB21. ...and the bearing cavity greased, but note! John points out that if you over pack with grease, some can get past the seal when hubs become hot. He recommends greasing both sides of the bearing then smoothing off, like so! ▼

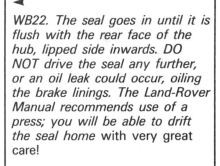

◄
WB22. The seal goes in until it is flush with the rear face of the hub, lipped side inwards. DO NOT drive the seal any further, or an oil leak could occur, oiling the brake linings. The Land-Rover Manual recommends use of a press; you will be able to drift the seal home with very great care!

WB23. So that it doesn't start ▲ its life running dry, add a smear of grease to the inside of the seal.

WB24. *It is vital that the seal is entered with this, the lipped side, facing inwards.*

WB28. *When fitting a new land, it must have some sealant on the inner edge...*

WB25. *The bearing distance piece often gets damaged by the hub seal rubbing a groove in it and causing an oil leak. Crack the distance piece (or land) with a large chisel, being careful not to damage the bearing surface on the stud carrier.*

WB26. *The land should now be loose and is ready to pull off.*

WB27. *A new land is shown here, though obviously this should not be fitted until everything is clean and tidy.*

WB29. *...and a tubular drift may be needed to knock it on square to prevent any future oil leak.*

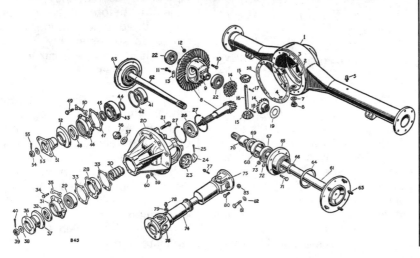

WB30. N.B. THE LAST SERIES III VEHICLES, WITH SO CALLED 'RATIONALISED' AXLE, AS FITTED TO 110, DOES NOT HAVE A REMOVABLE LAND. DON'T TRY TO CHISEL IT OFF; IT'S PART OF THE STUB AXLE! ('Rationalised' axles can be identified by their use of an offset sump drain plug). Two separate oil seals are fitted to these vehicles.

WB31. When reassembling, note that the washer behind the inner hub nut has a tab which locates in a keyway in the stub. End float on the inner nut should be adjusted with a dial gauge. John recommends, as an alternative: tighten a flat at a time, turning the hub each time. When the hub starts to tighten up, go back one flat, then go forwards again just enough to take out the backlash. Use new split pins and refer to your manual for torque settings. The outer nut should be then tightened (with lock washer between nuts) so that it is just more than hand tight. Knock the lock washer over the rear nut first, to stop it twisting and tearing the keyway tab off. Then tighten the outer nut to the recommended torque and lock the washer over that as well. Use new lock washers each time. Thanks, John!

WB32. The Series I 'semi-floating' rear axle, showing the rear hub arrangement, where 64 is the oil seal (not shown on later Land-Rover drawings); 66 is a distance washer; 67 is the bearing 68 oil seal sleeve; 69 oil seal; 70 retaining collar. Front hubs are virtually identical on all Series I models, except that wheel studs screw in to the hub, rather than push in from the rear. When they come unscrewed with the wheel nut, clean the stud and hub threads and Loctite them back into place.

Later Series Is have the Series II/IIA/III fully-floating axles and rear hubs are virtually identical. (Courtesy Land-Rover)

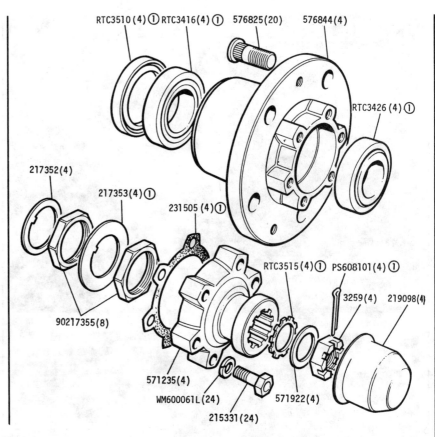

WB33. Front and rear 88 in hub assemblies up to June 1980. Always use a new driving member gasket (231505) when reassembling. (Courtesy Land-Rover)

RTC3510(4) ① RTC3416(4) ① 576825(20) 576844(4)

RTC3426 (4) ①

217352(4)

217353(4) ①

231505 (4) ①

RTC3515(4) ① PS608101(4) ①

3259(4) 219098(4)

90217355(8)

571235(4)

WM600061L (24)

571922(4)

215331(24)

WB34. 88 in front hubs from July 1980 and 109 in front assembly, except V8. (Courtesy Land-Rover)

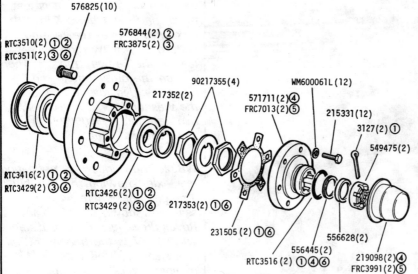

576825(10)

576844(2) ②
FRC3875(2) ③

RTC3510(2) ①②
RTC3511(2) ③⑥

90217355(4)

217352(2)

571711(2)④
FRC7013(2)⑤

WM600061L (12)

215331(12)

3127(2)①

549475(2)

RTC3416(2) ①②
RTC3429(2) ③⑥

RTC3426(2)①②
RTC3429(2) ③⑥

217353(2) ①⑥

231505 (2) ①⑥

556445(2)

RTC3516 (2) ①④⑥

556628(2)

219098(2)④
FRC3991(2)⑤

Fitting freewheeling hubs

Freewheeling front hubs were fitted to our project vehicle by Dunsfold Land-Rover using Genuine Land-Rover Parts freewheeling hub kits. This accessory is one of the most

useful and cost effective that can be fitted to your Land-Rover. With the hubs set to '4 x 2' the wheels are disconnected from the vehicle transmission. Only the wheels rotate while the front propshaft, differential and drive shafts remain stationary. This saves wear and tear on the front transmission and also saves a considerable

amount of fuel and makes a noticeable difference to the vehicle's performance.

The only disadvantage is that, in order to engage four wheel drive, you have to stop the vehicle and turn the hubs outer casing – they turn easily by hand – so that they are set to '4 x 4' before engaging four wheel drive or low range. If you fail to do so, severe transmission damage can result. In bad weather, the usual thing is to drive around with the front hubs set to '4 x 4' so that four wheel drive can be engaged without having to stop and get out of the vehicle. The makers recommend strongly that the vehicle is run for approximately 20 miles out of every 500 with the free wheeling hubs in a '4 x 4' position so that the swivel housing oil is enabled to circulate and do its job.

FWH1. The hub kit as supplied by Land-Rover Parts. Disappointingly, the outer surface of the hubs are not protected in any way and the aluminium quickly becomes dull and pitted when salty roads are encountered. You are strongly recommended by the author to give the outer surfaces of the hubs two or three coats of Smoothrite paint before fitting them.

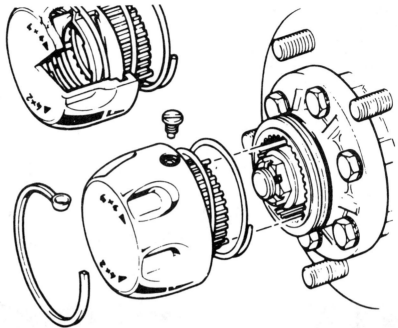

FWH3. Remove the locking screw and holding the hub body and cover firmly together, withdraw the retaining strip using the plastic rod provided. Note that there is a great deal of spring pressure there and the components must be separated carefully. Grease the hub bearing, the cam face and the splines of the actuator assembly (Parts No. 4) – see arrows – with a molybdenum disulphide bearing grease.

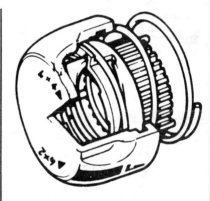

FWH4. Position the actuator assembly on top of the cams and place them inside the cap...

FWH2. Different kits are available for Series IIA and III 88 in, IIA 109 in and Series III 109 in. Parts numbered 7 are the service kit required when you need to remove the hubs and parts number 10 comprise the replacement bearing kit. Part number 2, the Spirolox ring is only needed for 109 in models. To install the kit, you start by removing the hub driving member as described in an earlier section. Check the bearings for end float and adjust as necessary.

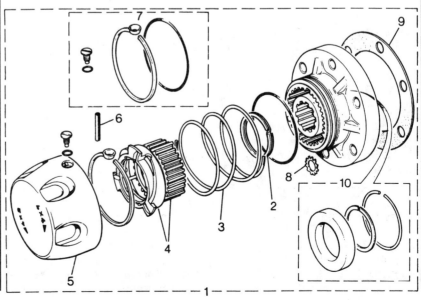

FWH5. ...and offer these parts to the hub body ensuring that the three pins enter the three large splines. Push fully home and secure with retaining strip and locking screw. Check the operation of the hubs, that they turn to left and right to engage and disengage '4 x 4' and check the oil level in the swivel housing. Run them for the first few miles in the '4 x 4' position to lubricate the hubs thoroughly. Affix the warning notice supplied with the kit inside the vehicle.

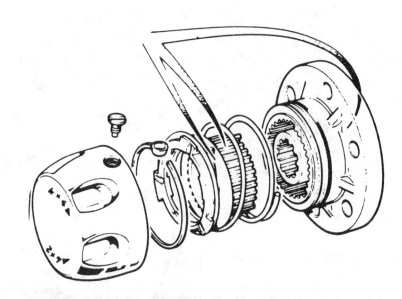

Removing a brake back plate

BPR1. The back plate is held on by six bolts with three lock plates. To remove the back plate, the ears of the lock plates must be knocked back first...

BPR2. ...and then the bolts should be loosened. ◄

BPR3. Loosen ALL the bolts, ► remove them and...

BPR4. ... the back plate can now be lifted off, being careful not to damage the stub axle. The back plate is still connected to a flexible brake pipe and you must support this pipe and be sure not to strain it.

BPR5. When removing the back plate, have a piece of wire handy to thread through one of the bolt holes and then hang the back plate out of the way under the wing so that the flexible brake hose is not being strained. There should be some conveniently placed brackets to attach the wire to! The back plate is rather heavy, so make sure the wire you use is up to the job.

Swivel hubs

Safety notes
Ensure, when working underneath the vehicle, that the wheels remaining on the ground are well chocked and that the vehicle is supported on substantial axle stands designed for the weight of the vehicle. Only raise the vehicle on a smooth, level, hard surface.

SH1. The swivel hubs – the ► chrome balls on the front axle – can corrode, the chrome tearing the seals and causing oil leaks.

SH2. With the vehicle jacked up and the brakes removed (covered elsewhere), place a drip-tray under the swivel hub. The stub axle carrier is shown here being removed.

SH3. The driveshaft with the universal joint pulls out from the differential and it is essential to check that the UJ is intact.

SH4. The collar in a bearing track (in the back of the swivel housing) and the shrunk-on collar which traps it all together are shown here. Note that the oil is still dripping!

SH5. The track rod should be removed by taking out the split-pin and castle nut...

SH6. ... followed by a swift blow on the fore-and-aft position on the eye of the steering arm. This should shock the steering joint out. Don't hit it on the threaded portion!

SH7. It may be preferable to use a ball joint splitter such as this one from Sykes-Pickavant. You might have to shock the joint with a spanner as well.

SH8. The top swivel bearing can be seen here; a plain pin in a bush which is fitted in the swivel.

SH9. The top pin is removed and is fairly rusty due to condensation. The pin often dries out of oil, mainly due to lack of use on the freewheel hubs.

SH10. One of the shims is shown, a form of adjustment on the top pin to give a 12lb drag with a spring balance on the eye of the steering arm (arrowed). Refer to the workshop manual for full details.

SH11. On the back of the swivel housing carrier is the oil seal retainer plate. This has six bolts, one of them longer than the others with the lock-stop on it. Undo the lock nut first to prevent it shearing off!

SH12. Remove the oil seal ▲ retainer and hook out the seal. With the top pin removed, the swivel housing carrier can be pulled out.

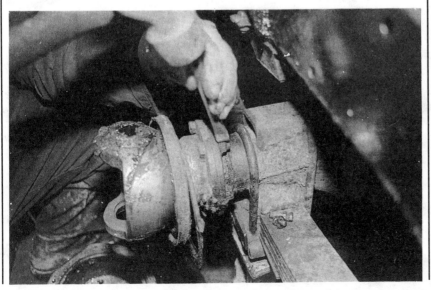

SH13. When the balls are corroded like this, you will probably find that the nuts are also corroded. A ring spanner can't be used because of the machining and welding on the axle to the flange, so you will need to crack the nuts with a chisel.

SH14. You can *try* removing them with a spanner but you probably won't be successful!

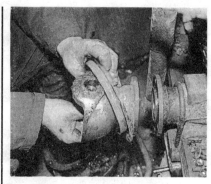

SH15. The swivel housing is now ready for withdrawal.

SH16. Shown here is the oil seal in the axle tube, this stopping the differential oil getting into the swivel. The swivel housing holds a pint of oil to lubricate the wheel bearings and top and bottom joints, and this also has to be kept out of the differential.

SH17. The new seal is back in position in the axle tube, something which must not be overlooked.

SH18. The new chrome ball in all its splendour! The Railko top bush can be seen in its housing, having been carefully pressed in place. The Railko thrust must be put in the bottom – you can see the hole for the oil to get into it. Don't overlook the thrust washer when reassembling.

SH19. The bottom Timken bearing (from your Land-Rover dealer) is in the bottom of the chrome ball, which again needs pressing in carefully.

SH20. The half shaft bearing, a sliding roller bearing, is often overlooked but must be put in fairly early on in the reassembly process. ▶

SH21. Likewise, carefully grease the big oil seal (a twin track seal so grease must be put between both tracks). The aperture in the swivel housing carrier must be meticulously clean or the seal won't be seated properly.

SH24. The aperture for receiving the oil seal has been cleaned and must now be sealed. On this Series IIA, there are no shims in the bottom to worry about, unlike the Series I variant.

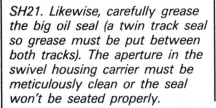

SH25. Another view of the Timken bearing, all greased and ready to go in.

SH22. Don't forget the retainer at this stage, shown here going into place.

SH23. The ball is going back into the position and the forward centre bolt should have a lock-stop (an L-shaped bracket) fitted. (See Workshop Manual)

SH26. The housing is carefully offered up to the swivel ball...

SH27. . . . and secured, with an assortment of shims and seals. The Railko bush is a form of damper coupled with the idler, forming the damping system on the steering; hence the accuracy of the 12lb drag mentioned earlier is vital. ▶

SH30. . . . and fully secured. Don't forget the lock-stop, the nut and bolt seen here lying against the spring mounting, which goes in the middle forward mounting.

SH28. The seal is ready to go back in and the locks on the bolts are now locked over.

SH29. The seal and retainer are now put back in . . .

SH31. The half shaft goes back in, being careful not to damage the seal in the axle case. Gently line it up with the diff when fitting.

SH32. The half-shaft is now fitted and the stub carrier is shown going back on, complete with new gasket. The back-plate can also be refitted now, and the whole lot can be bolted back together.

Road spring replacement

RS1. How little they changed! This is the earliest Series I road spring arrangement, with tab washers on the U-bolt nuts. Part No. 68 is the combined left-hand rear shock absorber and exhaust pipe mount. Parts 99 to 107 are for, 'fixing engine unit to chassis frame front and rear'. (Courtesy Land-Rover)

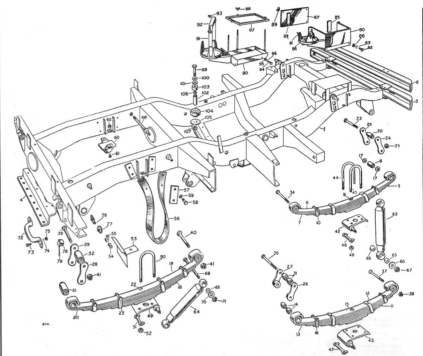

RS2. This was the author's Series I with sagged suspension, caused by a broken leaf in the road spring. Here's how to replace. The procedure is ▶ virtually identical on all models.

RS3. Unscrew the nuts holding the U-bolts to the bottom plate. On later models, they are fitted with lock nuts. Nothing can drop at this stage because the axle is resting upon the springs. Remove the bottom plate. You may be able to get away with leaving it attached to the lower end of the shock absorber; if not, disconnect it. ▼

RS4. Before going any further, ▲ the axle itself must be supported with an axle stand. The front shackle pin nut can be removed and the pin itself drifted out with a large drift.

RS5. The rear shackle can be removed by taking out either the top or bottom pin, although if you remove the top pin, it will be simpler to work on the bottom shackle pin with the spring off the vehicle.

RS6. The spring – which adds up to a very heavy lump! – was dragged out from beneath the vehicle.

RS7. Taking off the shackle from the nut side was no problem...

RS8 ... but removal of the bush ▲ from the spring eye can be incredibly difficult. A company by the name of R. H. Engineering Services produce the 'Bushwaka', a purpose made press for the removal and insertion of road-spring bushes. They also produce 'polybushes', polyurethane bushes providing greater life expectancy than the rubber originals. Rubber bush life can be extended by not tightening shackle bolts until the vehicle's weight is back on the ground. Polybushes are not to be confused with another far stiffer type of alternative bush which is on offer. At the time of writing polybushes have not seen a great deal of service life and so it is not possible to comment on their longevity in use.

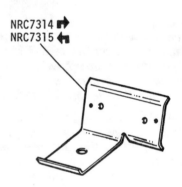

NRC7314 ➡
NRC7315 ⬅

RS10. When refitting a rear spring remember to use a brake pipe shield. This is the correct pattern for all but the very early vehicles. New shields are available from Land-Rover Parts and are handed, left and right.

RS9. Road springs from the left hand and right hand side of Land-Rovers are not interchangeable; they are specially shaped so that the driver's side, both front and rear, sits a little higher than the passenger's to compensate for the extra weight on that side of the vehicle. ▲

Check strap and rubber buffer replacement

CS1. Dunsfold Land-Rover ▶ emphasise that broken check straps should always be replaced to avoid damage from excessive suspension travel. As well as the strap itself, use new bolts, large flat washers and nuts for mounting the strap to the mounting points welded on to the rear chassis.

CS2. This is an alternative check strap mounting point and is similar to that on Series I vehicles. Note how the brake pipe shield defends the brake pipe against possible rubbing by the check strap.

Also ensure that all four rubber suspension stop buffers are in good condition. See Part No. 60 in RS1.

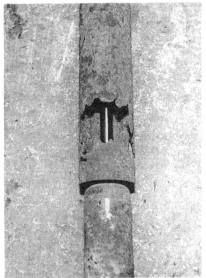

Shock absorber replacement

SAR1. Shock absorber casings can rust through like this, or they can simply stop working. Because of the strength of Land-Rover springs, it is impossible to test the shock absorbers whilst fitted to the vehicle. Take them off, place one end in the vice and judge for yourself the resistance available when trying to open and close the shock absorber. If in doubt, simply replace with new Land-Rover parts.

SAR2. The mounting is identical on every model of Land-Rover up to the end of Series III. Take out the top mounting bolt...

SAR3. ...taking note of the correct order of washers and bushes. Renew the bushes if at all worn.

SAR4. On later models, remount the new shock absorber with new split pins, where appropriate. When removing the fixing nuts from earlier models, it is all too easy for the nut to seize and for the bottom plate to be ruined. If there is any evidence that this is likely to happen, use a nut splitter or saw down one side of the nut and chisel through the thin metal remaining.

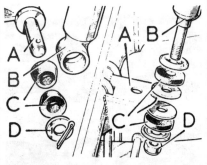

A Chassis   C Rubber bushes
B Shock absorber   D Securing nut (or washer)

SAR5. Two alternative mounting methods for Series II to III shock absorbers, lower end.

Steering system

There are so many items to wear in a Land-Rover steering system that a small amount of wear in several of them can add up to a vehicle that is very unpleasant to drive. However, it is worth bearing in mind that one other factor in particular can lead to poor steering: stiffness in the front swivels can stop the front wheels from returning readily to the straight ahead position and can render the Land-Rover extremely difficult to drive in a straight line! It is essential that the swivels are fitted exactly in accordance with the manual. Replacement of ball joints is a DIY proposition, as is replacement of the steering idler. Series I worm-and-nut steering boxes are easily removed, although not so easily overhauled, because the availability of reproduction parts is, at best, intermittent. Contact Dunsfold Land-Rover for the latest news. Unfortunately, overhaul of steering box and steering idler and removal of the steering box on all but the early models is at best a job for the workshop manual, with little to add here. At worst, there are jobs on the steering that simply cannot be carried out at home. For instance, removal of the steering drop arm from the steering box is described (even in the Haynes manual where short cuts are sought wherever practicable), to be a job for a Land-Rover special tool.

SS1. Layout of the Land-Rover steering gear with the steering column very considerably foreshortened!

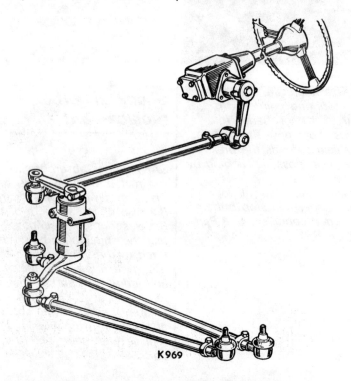

K969

SS2. The Series I worm-and-nut steering box. Early versions, with an aluminium casing, had a nasty habit of shearing off just beneath the top collar due to electrolytic action between aluminium and steel. They are then broken beyond redemption. Being topped up with oil and regular use should help to prevent this problem. (Courtesy Land-Rover)

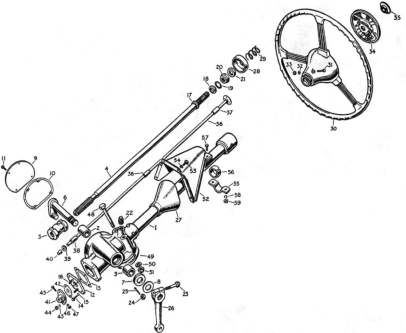

Steering joint replacement

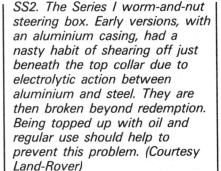

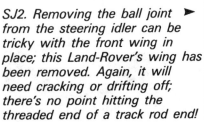

SJ1. Use a track rod tapered fork used for cracking the ball joint away from the steering arm, having obviously removed the nut, washer and split-pin (or lock nut) first.

SJ2. Removing the ball joint ▶ from the steering idler can be tricky with the front wing in place; this Land-Rover's wing has been removed. Again, it will need cracking or drifting off; there's no point hitting the threaded end of a track rod end!

SJ3. Each track rod has a left-handed and a right-handed thread ball joint for adjustment to the rod. Make sure you're getting the right one started and make sure the slot in the track rod tube is clear as there is a clamp that goes on to squash the rod tight against the shoulder of the track rod joint. Ensure it's a good fit and use lots of grease. The clip is not shown in the photograph.

SJ4. The steering tube clamp and bolt be seen here, ready to go on to the steering tube.

SJ5. The track rod is shown here with the clamp fitted. On this front joint above the steering idler, check that the bolt is correct for the clamp and that it can't foul the battery box pedestal, thereby leading to jammed steering.

SJ6. A split-pin goes into the ► castle-nut – a small but vital point to remember! Some non-original track rod ends use self-locking nuts but many experts prefer the split-pin arrangement.
The steering box is a recirculating ball system and simply requires adjustments as per the workshop manual.

Steering relay removal

◄
SR1. With body removed, the position of the steering idler in the chassis can be seen here clearly. Undo the pinch bolts that hold the top and bottom relay arms in place and lever them off their splines. Take out the two long bolts that pass front to rear and hold the relay into the chassis.

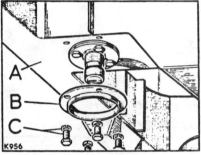

A—Underside of chassis
B—Flange plate
C—Fixings for flange plate

SR2. Remove the relay ▲ mounting flange plate from the underside of the chassis and ensure that there is no equipment fitted above the relay before you attempt to remove it. (Courtesy Land-Rover)

◄
SR3. A well rusted in relay will be a swine to remove because of the accumulation of corrosion and dirt between relay body and chassis.

SR4. With the Land-Rover four-square on the ground, Dunsfold's John uses a hydraulic jack underneath the relay body to push it up out of the chassis against the weight of the vehicle. *ENSURE THAT THE SMALL SHAFT ON THE BOTTOM OF THE RELAY CAN NOT SLIP OFF THE JACK AND CAUSE AN ACCIDENT.*

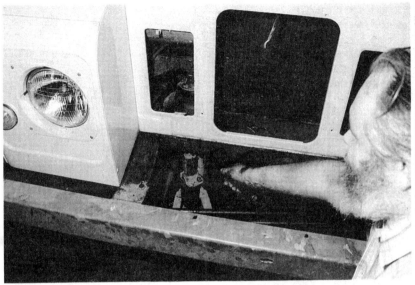

SR5. It's now simply a matter of persuading the relay to emerge from its hiding place.
DO NOT STRIP DOWN THE RELAY UNDER ANY CIRCUMSTANCES! It contains an extremely strong spring and no matter what advice any of the manuals may give, it should be sent to a Land-Rover agent for overhaul or replacement.

Wheels and tyres

Land-Rovers, along with most dual-purpose vehicles, place great stresses on their tyres as they operate under various loads and conditions.

A large selection of tyres are produced by a variety of manufacturers providing the owner with the task of choosing which particular design and pattern they prefer. As with any other vehicle, the brand chosen normally relates to personal preference and experience. Those chosen by the author for FVJ, the project vehicle, are made by Michelin, one of the suppliers of OE (original equipment) tyres to Land-Rover and manufacturers of very fine tyres for 4x4 vehicles.

In addition to a choice of tyre, we also felt that it would be a good idea to examine the availability of wheel types. Early Land-Rovers were fitted with either 6.00 x 16 or 7.00 x 16 Dunlop tyres and, even though Dunlop is now Japanese owned, very many original tread patterns are available from Vintage Tyre Supplies who advertise widely through the classic car journals.

Our project vehicle was fitted with 6.00 x 16 tyres on 5 in rims. We decided to go for 5.5 in rims and to use the wheels fitted by Land-Rover to the 90 and 110, the models that superseded the Series III, the models that superseded the Series III. This was Brian Bashall's idea, and an excellent one it has proved to be. The extra track width has added valuable extra stability and the wider wheels have enabled the use of some very fine tyres indeed.

The Michelin XM + S244 tyres might be a bit of a mouthful to ask for, but they have transformed the dynamics of the vehicle beyond all recognition when compared with previous Series II owned by the author which was shod with the cheapest remould cross-ply tyres available! The new Michelins give tremendously encouraging reserves of grip, they improve the ride quality beyond recognition – gone are the spine-jarring thumps that were previously the norm, and tyre noise is greatly reduced. Of course, they cost more to buy, but they outlast cross-ply tyres many times over. In addition, they have the benefit conferred by all radial tyres over cross-ply: the steering is less liable to require constant correction. This is because cross-plys are notorious for 'following' marks and undulations in the road surface, while radials are far better at not doing so.

The other huge improvement over the old-style tyres is the extra grip experienced in really bad snow conditions. In conditions where the old cross-plies would not have stood a chance, the XM + S244 Michelins enabled the Land-Rover to keep going without slipping a wheel – which is as well, because, with

the absence of diff. locks, a Land-Rover will loose its footing in very slippery conditions before some other 4 x 4s (or at least, the older ones), without the latest diffs. will do so. The remainder of this section consists of some general and worthwhile advice from Dunsfold's Brian Bashall on Land-Rover tyre care.

W&T1. The author's IIA, equipped with Michelin XM+S244 radial ply tyres and in the sort of conditions that make you glad to be a Land-Rover owner!

W&T4. For ultimate non-studded grip in poor going, while still retaining good on-road use, there is the Michelin XC4/XCM+S4 (another mouthful!), which is best reserved for winter use. Most owners are not, of course, able to run to the expense and extra storage space of swappable sets of tyres, but if you live in a place where winter conditions are habitually dreadful, you may wish to consider it.

General advice

First, all Land-Rover tyres are equipped with inner tubes, but it is essential that the correct type and size is fitted. Its presence enables the tyre to retain air if damage to the rim flanges occurs, provided of course that the inner tube is not itself punctured!

Second, you must contemplate the choice of tyre casing construction you require:

Cross-ply tyres

Where Land-Rovers are used on rough terrain and facilities to repair damages are few and far between, cross-ply tyres are probably the safest choice, as it is much simpler to make a home-repair to a cross-ply tyre than to a radial.

W&T2. The XM+S244 is described by Michelin as being ideal for someone who drives the vehicle mainly in ideal conditions, giving crisp handling on tarmac, but with superb off-road performance. It easily lives up to its claims.

W&T3. The XM+S100 and S200 tyres are also described by Michelin as being suitable for all-year-round use but the XM+S200 (illustrated) is particularly effective on muddy or other soft surfaces. These tyres have specially angled self-sharpening tread blocks for extra grip and traction in poor conditions and they can be expected to be noisier on the road than S244s.

Radial tyres

Where, however, a Land-Rover is used primarily on road-like surfaces, the radial tyre comes into its element.

Radial tyres allow cooler running at maximum speed and load than cross-plies, providing the driver with good handling abilities on road-surfaces, but without impairing off-road performance. Cross-ply tyres operating under these conditions would incur irregular tread wear and a reduced life, thus requiring regular changes as recommended by the manufacturer.

Low pressure tyres

Low ground pressure tyres, such as the Michelin XS, are ideal in bad conditions, for use on soft sand where maximum 'flotation' is required, or for use in crop fields, for example, when damage to crops must be minimised.

Mixing tyres

NEVER fit radial and cross-ply tyres on the same axle.

NEVER fit cross-plies to the rear of the vehicle if radials are fitted to the front. Check local regulations. In some parts of the world it is illegal to use both radial and cross-ply tyres on the vehicle in any position. It is NEVER to be recommended.

To maximise the performance obtained from your tyres, a full set of either radial or cross-ply should be fitted.

A mixed set of tyres will impair your vehicle's handling abilities, as both tyres will react differently under the same circumstances. The UK tyre safety rules, Section 108(2) of the Construction and Use Regulations, November 1983 ensures that all original fitments are correct; it's best to stick with them or a more modern version of them, as described above.

Pressures

Tyre pressures are of paramount importance with any vehicle, but particularly with Land-Rovers with their multiple uses.

Uneven or quick tread wear is a symptom of incorrectly inflated tyres, which may also lead to weakening of the casing. The most common problem is under-inflation rather than over-inflation, invariably due to pressures not being restored to the correct level after off-road use, for example, or when rear pressures are not increased sufficiently to cope with towing heavy loads.

Lowering tyre pressures for off-road driving will provide you with better grip, and you may go as low as 13psi with conventional inner-tube tyres and an astounding 5psi with Tredlite tyres. However, it is essential that tyre pressures are restored to the correct level when returning to normal road conditions. Failure to do so may result in poor braking, cornering ability and even straight-line stability, whilst the excessive movement which occurs puts a strain on the casing and contributes towards a very damaging heat build up.

Abnormal tread wear

Over-inflation of cross-ply tyres could promote speedy centre tread wear, whilst under-inflation of cross-ply and radial tyres will result in excessive flexing and wear at the tread shoulders. Poor tracking or failure to alternate tyres at pre-determined service intervals of 6,000 miles (10,000 km) will promote uneven wear around and across the circumference of the tread area. If all tyres have these symptoms then a diagonal interchange is suggested; however, if it is only the front tyres then these should be swapped over (provided that you are not using uni-directional tyres). To ensure that you maximise the life of your tyres, regular checks should be made to pressures, wheel alignments and positions.

6: Interior and electrics

SAFETY NOTE: Before commencing any work on the car's electrical system ensure the battery is disconnected.

Fitting an alternator in place of a dynamo

Why alternators? Brian Bashall of Dunsfold Land-Rover points out that alternators have been in the electro-generating world for years, but they started to arrive on the automotive scene in the mid-'40s and were fairly commonplace on the passenger bread-and-butter market in the late '50s. Land-Rovers didn't have them as standard until 1971 but they were available as an optional extra in the mid-'60s. There's one snag for the Land-Rover owner: all the alternators are negative earth whereas our vehicles until 1968 were positive earth.

Fortunately, although dynamos and alternators are mounted on opposite sides of 4-cylinder and 6-cylinder engines, they are the same units, so your replacement can be sourced from either engine type. One does away with the voltage regulator, so it will pay to get some heavy cable as the basic alternator will turn out 30 – 35amps and the heavy duty ones will be producing 65amps. The alternator shown here fitted to the project Land-Rover is the standard, Genuine Land-Rover Part. Some of the following photographs were taken on another vehicle.

AF1. The dynamo in position with the fan belt removed. You can see the top adjuster bolt here; this has to be removed.

AF2. The bottom mounting. This is quite often a problem as it is about 4 inches long and goes through a casting on the crank case block. On the early Land-Rovers, up to 1962, this also went through an aluminium mounting to the front of the dynamo and this long bolt quite often seized up in this mounting, and was difficult to remove. If you need to drift out this bolt, you will have to remove the radiator, undo the engine mounting bolts and lift the front of the engine. Remember to lubricate it once it has been disturbed. Copper Ease is ideal.

AF3. The later type of front mounting – a composite bracket for the Land-Rover – just a simple bolt and lock nut on the front. You can see the boss on the crank case where the rear side bolt goes. ▶

AF4. The top of the composite mounting bracket is locked up with a tag which has to be released. The bottom bolt (partly hidden by the spanner) is behind the flywheel pulley so this will have to be removed.

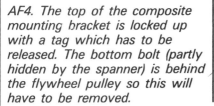

AF5. The top mounting for the adjuster slider, which has to come out.

AF6. Undoing the lock-plate on the crankshaft.

AF7. It needs a sharp blow! Don't just try to turn it or you will simply turn the engine backwards. Crack it with a hammer and it will normally come undone. If the worst comes to the worst, you may have to drop the sump and lock the crank with a piece of hardwood.

AF8. The starter dog and crankshaft pulley nut coming undone.

AF11. Here is the long bolt mentioned earlier in its boss on the crankcase. It's always well worth lubricating this when you have the chance to get it off.

AF13. A new long bolt!

AF9. The pulley partially extracted. It is a cast pulley – so be careful not to damage it when getting it out.

AF12. This is the special alternator bracket which fits the existing holes in the block.

AF14. The new alternator mounted on its bracket.

AF10. Now you can get at that bottom bolt and withdraw the front of the mounting bracket.

AF15. The field and the dynamo wires – refer to your workshop manual for wiring loom details for your model of Land-Rover. Note: The earlier alternators did in fact have a potted voltage regulator unit – from a transistorised Lucas Type No. TR5 or TR6 – and later alternators had their own diodes, acting as a regulator, built into them. ◄

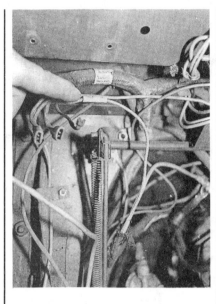

AF16. The bulkhead with the old fashioned voltage regulator and control box removed. The smaller wire from the alternator has to be joined to the ignition warning light by means of a sleeve connector.

AF17. The heavy brown wires are gathered together with an insulated bolt (a Land-Rover part), illustrated here. ►

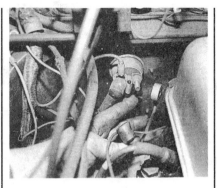

AF18. The old type of starter switch. The brown wires have to go on to the battery feed.

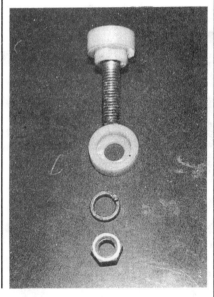

AF19. The right hand terminal is the starter lead.

AF20. Changing over the wires on the ammeter to give the correct reading, but beware! The average ammeter is only good for about 22amps and the alternator is likely to be charging at 30amps. You may have to swap for one from a later model. Note: Wiper motors are OK. If you have had a radio fitted it needs to be positive earth. The other problem with negative earth is that the fuel gauge and transmitter will not work when connected the wrong way round. Negative fuel gauges and transmitters are a different system, known as 'slow-readers' and they work on a stabilised voltage of about 8 volts. You have to get a new gauge, tank unit and voltage stabiliser and go on to slow reading instruments. This system will also give you water temperature and oil pressure gauges on the stabilised voltage system which could be an advantage over the old style capillary activated gauges. Look into all the ramifications before going into such a conversion. It was worth it on our model of IIA; on yours it might not be! ◄

Speedometer restoration

by John Philpott of Renown Instruments

In general, the repair and restoration of an instrument such as this is best left to the experts, as the special equipment and spare parts required are not readily available to the home mechanic. Here is an overview of the way in which Renown Instruments restored the author's Land-Rover's speedometer.

SR3. The bezel glass is removed...

SR4. ...followed by the inner spacer ring.

SR1. The speedometer which is need of refurbishment arrives at the instrument workshops for visual and mechanical check-over.

SR5. The movement mounting screws are removed.

SR2. The strip down begins with the removal of the bezel. The fixing lugs are easily broken and so great care must be taken at this stage if the bezel is to be re-used.

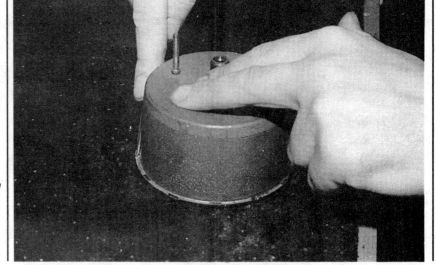

SR6. *This enables the entire mechanism to now be removed from the case as a complete unit. At this point great care must again be taken. The unit comprises many small, delicate parts, which may be easily damaged. Also, the magnet assembly could be damaged. This would affect the calibration and without specialist equipment it would be impossible to restore the instrument to its original accuracy.*

SR7. *Here the instrument's main components are shown disassembled prior to cleaning and replacement of any worn parts.*

SR8. *The main magnet drive spindle is refitted into the base casting . . .*

SR9. *. . . and secured with the fixing screws – the unit must rotate freely.*

SR10. *The spindle cup is reassembled onto the magnet top.*

SR11. *Here the clips which secure the cam gear and hold the operating arms for odometer are being checked for security before the initial testing.*

SR12. *The test shows some 5mph high on the reading at 60mph...*

SR14. *...and the result is spot-on.*

SR16. *The finished reconditioned and recalibrated instrument.*

SR13. *...so the magnet is de-magnetised using special equipment...*

SR15. *The new, shining instrument with the old, rusty case alongside.*

Dashboard and instruments

DI1. *Remove the five retaining screws securing the instrument panel to the dashboard. The top row are held in by captive nuts.*

DI2. *The panel is then pulled forward to expose the wiring, etc.*

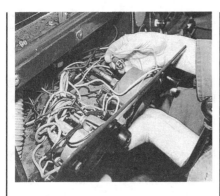

DI3. The speedo lamp bulb is simply pulled out.

DI4. Unscrew and pull away the speedo drive cable.

DI5. Unscrew the knurled nuts securing the speedo to the instrument panel. This nut also attaches the earth wire.

DI6. Remove the speedo securing bracket.

DI7. The speedometer can now be pulled free from the instrument panel.

DI8. The warning lamps are simply pushed through the instrument panel and the bulb holder pulled out.

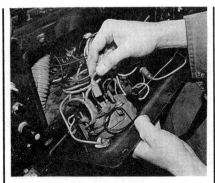

DI9. Remove the wiring connections from the combined fuel gauge/ammeter, making sure to label every one in turn.

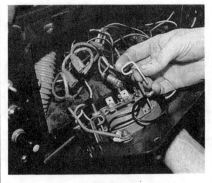

DI10. The combined fuel gauge/ammeter is secured in a similar manner to that of the speedo, first unscrewing the knurled nut and removing the two single retaining brackets.

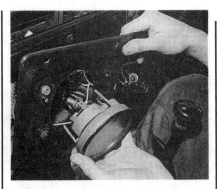

DI11. The instrument is then pulled clear from the panel.

DI12. Fitting the new speedometer, the procedure is a direct reversal of removal. Refit the instrument panel to the dashboard.

Front seat removal

On all models, the seat base lifts up after unclipping the leather fixing strap, when fitted. Bolted-in backrest: unbolt in an obvious fashion. Folding backrests: unclip the leather strap, when fitted.

On charge!

BAT1. These are quite different from conventional batteries. The plates are coiled and the acid is sealed-in gel. As a result, an Optima battery is smaller, more powerful and can be recharged in an hour without damaging it. It can be mounted at any angle – even upside down! Well, you never know . . .

BAT2. When a car stands, its battery can quickly go flat which is irritating and shortens a battery's life. The Exide 12V Charger Battery Saver Plus provides a constant trickle charge from the sun – free and continuous!

FSR1. Take out the split pins holding the seat base pivots in place.

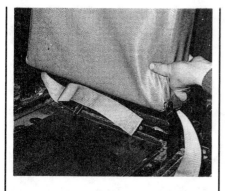

FSR2. Philip Bashall pushes hard to one side until the pivot comes out of the back rest bracket.

FSR3. The backrest is then lifted on that side and pulled out of the bracket on the opposite side.

Rear seat fit and removal

The seats shown here are bench seats fitted into the rear of an 88 in model.

RSF1. Philip Bashall points to one of the two "hooks" that clip beneath the waist rail as the seat is slotted into position in the back of the vehicle.

RSF2. The seat is held to the rear body with two bolts, one at each end of the frame, which simply pass through and are secured beneath with flat washer, spring washer and nut. A job for two people!

Fitting Series III Seat bases to a II/IIA

The seats fitted to FVJ, our project vehicle, are of lovely original fleck material which is not now available and so we decided, at Dunsfold Land-Rover, that we would fit new seat bases and back rests, still available from Land-Rover Parts, so that the originals will not be damaged in daily use.

LSB1. What we didn't know was that the back rests would go in as a direct replacement but that the seat bases now available are designed for a different location arrangement and that the position of the leather retaining straps is different.

LSB2. On the Series IIA Land-Rover, there is a channel either side of the seat base which prevents the base from slipping sideways and which has a lip at the front end of each channel to stop it from slipping forwards. Our later seat bases had flat bottoms that just slithered about. ▶

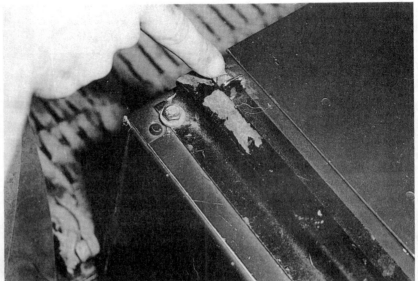

LSB3. We decided to fit wooden strips to enable the seats to be located properly. Here woodworkers' adhesive is being applied to the bottom of one of the strips, already cut to length.

LSB5. The timber strips are now pinned down to the seat base.

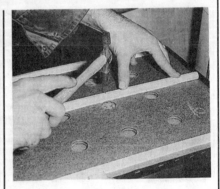

LSB6. The two outer strips enable the correct location to take place while the middle strip prevents the seat base from sagging.

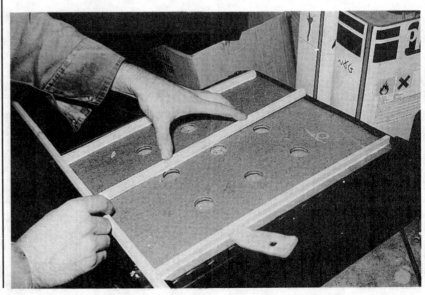

LSB4. The long piece of wood at the bottom of this picture is held there temporarily to ensure that the three strips of wood being fitted are lined up correctly.

LSB7. Next, it was on to that misplaced leather strap. With some careful levering with a screwdriver, the leather strap and the plastic plug which located, it were levered out of the hole in the seat base. ▶

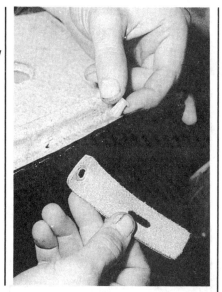

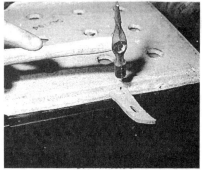

LSB10. The plastic nail was then driven down into the plug, expanding it and fixing firmly as before.

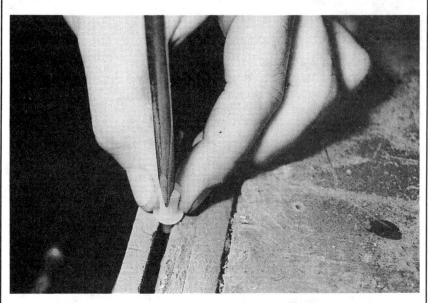

LSB11. With all three seats fitted out with newly positioned retaining straps and wooden strips that now located on the channel shown here...

LSB8. The plug contained a ▲ special plastic nail that had been driven into when it had been fitted to expand the plug and hold it firm. The plastic nail was now pushed out with a screwdriver.

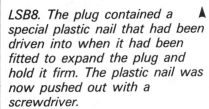

LSB9. The correct position for the leather strap was now marked on the seat base and a hole drilled in the composite material. The plastic nail was located in the plug and the plug pushed down firmly through the leather strap and into the seat base. ▶

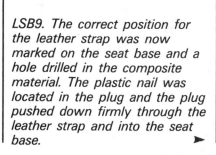

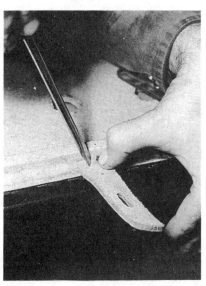

LSB12. ...the new seats could now be fitted into position.

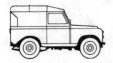

Re-covering seats

In 1984 and 1985, *Practical Classics* magazine – *the magazine for classic car, DIY and restoration enthusiasts –* restored their own Series I Land-Rover. Since, as you would expect, replacement seats are not available for Series I vehicles, *Practical Classics* carried out their own seat overhaul. The author is very grateful to *Practical Classics* magazine for giving permission for the use of their line drawings for this section.

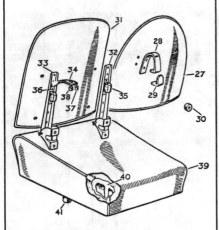

RCS1. The two types of seat back fitted to Series I Land-Rovers 1948-53. 1954-58 models' seat bases had special tongues in their rear lower corners which slotted into the bodywork while the hinge brackets for the seat backs were of a slightly different construction. For a long time, new Series I seat bases were not available, owners having to resort to cutting up piece of foam to make substitutes. Now however, through their connection with a well-established Birmingham company by the name of Latex Cushion Ltd, Dunsfold Land-Rover can supply new, replacement seat bases, complete with the correct type of base board, for Series I Land-Rovers; quite a breakthrough! (Courtesy Land-Rover)

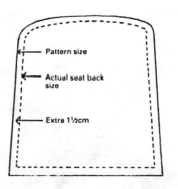

RCS2. Lay seat back onto paper and draw around it – add 1½cm. all round and cut out.

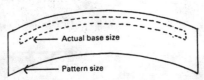

RCS3. Hold the seat back vertically onto the paper, draw along the concave curve at the base of the back, extending the line 4cm beyond the sides. Draw a line parallel with this curve approximately 12cm away, then join these two lines to make the base pattern strip.

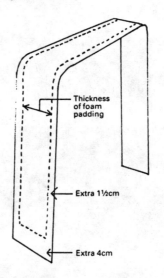

RCS4. Measure the length around the outside of the seat back, excluding the base but adding 4cm either end to allow for 'neat edge' turning under. The width of this Box Section strip is the thickness of the foam padding, plus 1½cm each side.

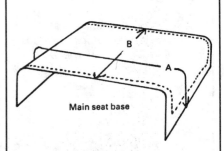

RCS5. Measure the front-to-back length over the top of the seat base adding 4cm to each end for turning under and stapling to the wooden base (dimension A). Measure the width of the seat, adding 1½cm for sewing seams.

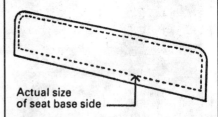

RCS6. Hold the seat base on its side and draw round, adding 1½cm to the top and sides for turning and 2cm at the bottom. In order to calculate the amount of material required, lay all the pattern pieces onto a table, or mark an area on the floor the same width as the fabric to be purchased (usually 150cm). Do not forget to include two seat backs and two seat base sides for each seat.

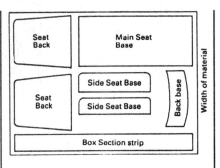

Seat Back	Main Seat Base	
Seat Back	Side Seat Base	Back base
	Side Seat Base	
Box Section strip		

Width of material

RCS7. Make sure that all pattern pieces are parallel to the edge. Buy the correct amount of vinyl using your rough layout as a guide. (It is also a good idea to draw it all out to remind you later where each piece goes.) Lay all the pattern pieces out on vinyl – do not pin in place; pin holes will show. *Sellotape can be used if necessary, but spreading the fingers of one hand to hold the patterns is probably easiest. Cut out using sharp scissors. First set the sewing machine to the longest stitch and note that in the following diagrams the 'wrong' side of the vinyl is shown as the tinted areas.*

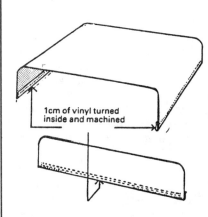

1cm of vinyl turned inside and machined

RCS8. Using the extra 4cm at each end of the Main Seat Base and the extra 2cm on the bottom of each Side Seat Base, turn each up 1cm and machine down onto the 'wrong' side of the vinyl in order to neaten these edges.

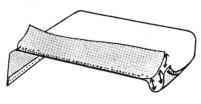

RCS9. The two Side Seat Bases are sewn to the Main Seat Base, beginning with one or other as follows: find the middle points of both pieces (A and B, see next diagram) and paperclip or sellotape these points together ('right' sides of vinyl together).

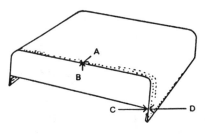

RCS10. Continue to paperclip or pin both pieces together until points C and D are matched, with a small part of the Main Seat Base extending beyond these points. (If pinning make sure that the pins are inside the seam allowance of 1½cm, so that they do not make holes that will be permanently visible in the vinyl).

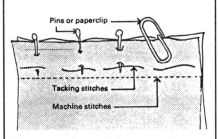

Pins or paperclip

Tacking stitches

Machine stitches

RCS11. Tack using large running stitches inside the seam allowance, so that no marks will show and then machine 1½cm from the edge. Repeat with the other seat side section.

RCS12. Once sewn, trim the seams down to about 7mm...

RCS13. ...and cut 'V' shapes in the curved edges near to the stitching to avoid lumpy seams and pulling. Turn the seat cover 'right' side out, fold the excess seams (now underneath) towards the Main Seat Base piece.

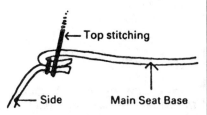

← Top stitching

← Side   Main Seat Base

RCS14. Stitch from the 'right' side close to the edge, stitching through all layers of seam. This is called 'top stitching' and is for strength as well as for decoration.

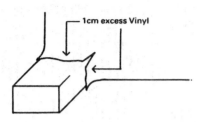

RCS15. Place the seat cover over the foam covered seat base and mark out the position of the wooden slats which protrude. Cut the vinyl 1cm smaller than the size of the slat to allow for turning under.

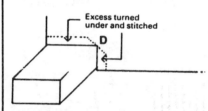

RCS16. Cut into corner (D), turn raw edges under and machine in place.

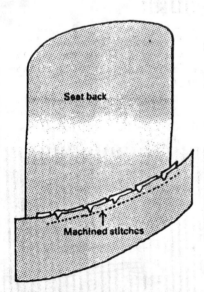

RCS17. Sew the Base Section to the forward facing seat back along the curved bottom edge, keeping 'right' sides together. To help the curvature, cut towards seam stitching every 3cm. The base section should extend beyond the edges of the seat back.

RCS18. Take the other seat back, turn the bottom curved edge over 1cm onto the 'wrong' side and machine in place for a neat edge. Clip the raw edge of the turnback if it puckers.

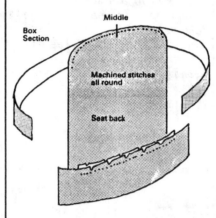

RCS19. Find the middle of both the top of the Seat Backs and the Box Section strip and mark these points. Place 'right' sides together and starting at the centre just marked, place the strip around the outside raw edge of the first Seat Back. Tack and machine 1½cm from the edge. Trim seams to 7mm and clip curves as before.

Turn 'right' side out, push seams away from the Seat Back material towards the Box Section side strip and top stitch close to the edge from the 'right' side as described in RCS14. Note that though the Main Seat Base is top stitched, it is the Side Box Section which carries the top stitching in the case of the seat back.

Turn the work inside out again and tack the remaining Seat Back to the Box Section strip 'right' sides facing. Machine 1½cm from the edge, then trim seams and clip curves as before. Don't try to top stitch; with the whole Seat Back Cover turned correct side out, the envelope thus formed renders this impossible, except by laborious hand stitching.

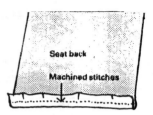

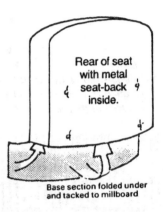

Base section folded under and tacked to millboard

RCS20. Place cover over the padded seat back. Turn under the bottom flap and tuck it under the neatened edge of the seat back and tack to the short strip of millboard riveted to the metal backrest. This is secured by the metal brackets.

At this stage the seat cushions can be offered up for a first fitting. From this the exact position for the leather straps, which secure to seat bases, can be established. At the same time the position for the rubber stops on the seat backs can be determined. The seats will then have to be removed for the fitting of the leather straps and the rubber stops. The seats are then ready for final fitting.

Seat belts

The project vehicle FVJ, was fitted with Land-Rover Parts inertia reel seat belts in place of the somewhat jaded static belts fitted as standard. This was one of the many minor modifications

carried out in conjunction with Dunsfold Land-Rover to make the vehicle safer and more environmentally friendly, without detracting from its original character.

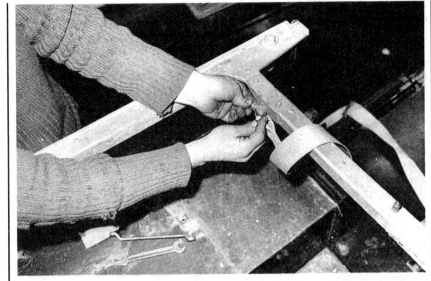

SB1. Philip Bashall unbolts the static seat belt from the waist rail behind the driver's seat...

SB2. ...and from the rear of the seat base. The two other short straps were unbolted from their positions between the seat cushion.

SB3. The Land-Rover Parts kit comes complete with all components necessary for conversion to inertia belts. In place of the short lengths of strap there is a pair of stalks which bolt down to the original mounting position. On the heads of the stalks are quick release catches which protrude only a very short distance above the seat cushion.

SB4. Philip bolted the bracket to take the inertia reel mechanism to the waist rail in the position indicated in the instructions...

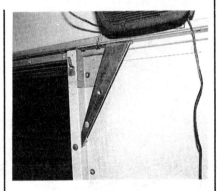

SB5. ...and the reinforcing bracket supplied as part of the kit was fitted to the top corner of the hard top.

SB6. The far end of the inertia reel strap was fitted down to the original mounting point shown in SB2. and the inertia reel belts were in place, ready to fit snugly to the correct size for anyone who might use the vehicle and with the shoulder strap in exactly the right position because of the high bracket shown in this picture. In addition, inertia reel belts are almost impossible to fall over as you dismount from the vehicle! ►

Heaters

Land-Rover heaters are often poor for one of a number of reasons. Suggested solutions follow in brackets:

The engine does not get warm enough (change the thermostat; fit a radiator muff, but also fit a water temperature gauge and watch the temperature!);

The heater tap, heater pipes or heater matrix have become blocked (flush them through or purchase a new heater matrix or tap);

The heater hoses have collapsed internally (replace);

The blower motor has become tired (replace or have it rebuilt);

The heater switch/rheostat has become faulty (replace);

The pre-Series III heater was never particularly good to start with (wear more clothes or save up for a Discovery!).

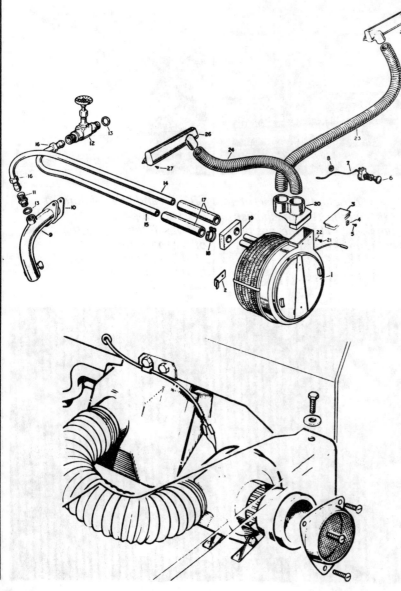

HR1. This is the petrol engine Series I heater layout, although diesel models and II and IIA models are very similar. Removal of each of the components is an obvious process. (Courtesy Land-Rover)

HR2. Series III models had a far more efficient heater, drawing fresh air in through a grille in the front left hand wing. The heater motor is bolted into place with the bolts obviously visible through the engine bay and with two more bolts hidden behind the lower facia panel – take out the trim screws and trim to expose the bolts for removal. (Courtesy Land-Rover)

HR3. A Series III heater tap will seize solid if left in one position for any length of time. Disconnect the cable and try releasing it with lots of releasing fluid and gentle persuasion. Replacement might be the only answer. The cables may also seize: remove the heater controls by taking out the two screws visible on the ends of the facia; disconnect the cables and ensure that they are free. Lubricate or replace the cables as necessary.

Door seals

DRS1. New door seals tend not to do their job when first fitted because the sealing lips pop out from behind the door. ➤

DRS2. The problem is that they have to be trained to "remember" their new shape, after which they will be held flat by the door frame itself. Place masking tape around the door seal where it sticks out from inside the door and leave it there for two to three weeks until the door seal learns to behave itself.

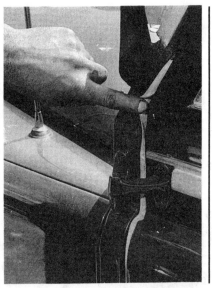

Interior - sundries

IS1. The screws holding down the station wagon door seal and the threshold plate tend to rust immovably into place. You may have to grind off the heads, saw $\frac{1}{8}$in off the end of the plate, move it along by that amount in one direction or the other and drill new holes just to one side of the originals . (The screws are of hardened steel and can't be drilled out).

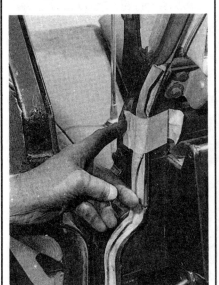

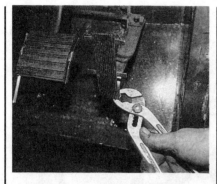

IS2. New pedal rubbers are still available from Land-Rover Parts and are fitted by bending the fixing taps over the back of the relevant pedals.

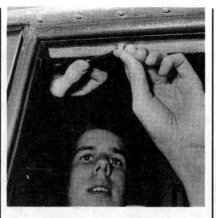

IS4. The relatively luxurious Series III cab trim is held in place with plastic plugs which have to be very carefully levered out...

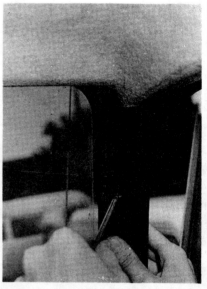

IS5. ...and other sections of trim that are held in place with clearly visible self-tapping screws.

IS3. Series I brake and clutch ➤ pedals benefit enormously from having new felt seals fitted (not seen here; below floor level) and rubber sealing grommets. Otherwise, the draught up your trouser leg has to be experienced to be believed!

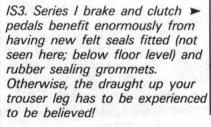

IS6. More headlining fixings ▲ double up as sunvisor mountings...

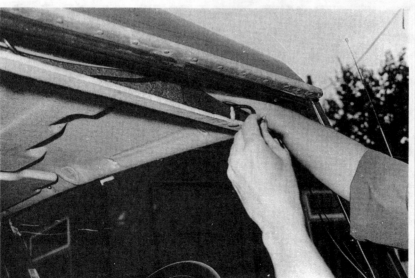

IS7. ...and with those removed, you can begin to lower the headlining. In this case, only one corner was being lowered to install some additional wiring. Do take very great care when handling the headlining boards because they are extremely brittle and liable to break.

Electrical

Windscreen wiper motor overhaul

WW1. Earlier Land-Rovers were fitted with two separate wiper motors and these were rather prone to slow running and to wiping varying segments of the windscreen. Remove the "park" handle and unscrew the outer casing. Ensure that the earth connection to the outer casing and to the body is sound. ▶

WW2. Inside the outer casing, the switch that makes contact via a rather crude rivet. If electrical contacts have broken down completely in this area, you may have to remove the rivet and replace it, using Copper Ease as a corrosion preventative. You may be able to improve matters by tapping the rivet a little tighter. If all else fails, a replacement motor may be called for. Very early windscreen motors, such as those fitted to Series I Land-Rovers with a squared-off casing, can still be purchased from Holden Vintage and Classic (see address at back of this book). ▶

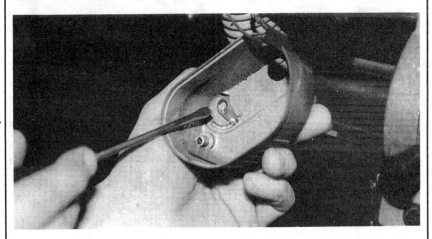

Halogen headlamps

HL1. The rather dim original headlamps on FVJ were replaced with the vastly superior Halogen type from Land-Rover Parts. When a Land-Rover has been fitted with bulb headlamps, the connections on the back of the headlamp have to be changed. Do note that headlamp efficiency is greatly affected by the quality of the wiring and especially the connections all the way along the line. For maximum headlamp efficiency, re-solder any poor connections and disconnect and clean all the existing ones.

Land-Rover mobile telephone

In the U.K., Land-Rover Parts have selected Mercury Telecom to be the suppliers and fitters of Land-Rover mobile telephones. For those of us who take fullest advantage of the Land-Rover's out-and-about ability, a mobile telephone is a great advantage!

MTP1. Mercury Communications can supply a number of different types of mobile 'phone for your Land-Rover through Land-Rover dealerships. For this fitment we chose one that works in the ► conventional manner when installed into the car but which can also be taken out of the vehicle and carried around.

MTP2. The first job was to find somewhere to site the ► transceiver unit which comes complete with battery pack. We decided to place it just behind the passenger seat...

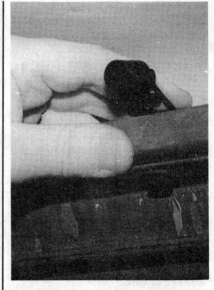

MTP4. To comply with the ▲ regulations, it will be necessary to use a car 'phone "hand-free" and Wayne, Mercury's engineer, fitted the microphone on the top rail in front of the driver.

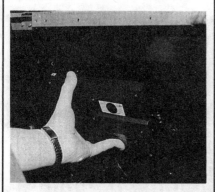

MTP3. ...from where the ▲ transceiver and battery pack could be clipped into and out of place with great ease.

◄
MTP5. There was no need to drill a hole for the aerial because this was glued to the front screen with the signal transmitted through the glass to a receiver on a pad glued to the inside of the screen.

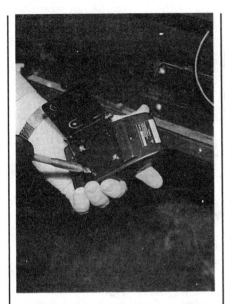

MTP6. Back inside the car, the bracket for taking the hand set was fitted with the integral speaker used in connection with the "hands-free" operation...

MTP7. ...and when the telephone is in place it is situated within easy reach of the driver's left hand. Both Land-Rover and Mercury emphasise that fitting a car phone is not a DIY job! It's all too easy to fit a car 'phone so that it works inadequately or even dangerously and it is a job best left to a trained engineer.

MTP8. The beauty of this particular model is that once the transceiver has been clipped out and the portable aerial screwed on to it, the handset can be unclipped from the vehicle and slotted into place on the transceiver-cum-carrying pack. This particular unit can be carried away from the Land-Rover for a full working day before running out of battery power and it comes fully equipped with all the features that you could possibly want in a mobile telephone. Highly recommended!

Fitting in-car entertainment

A particular set that caught our eye is the Roadstar Off Road Four by Four radio cassette player. Although its visual treatment is, shall we say, perhaps a little lively by Land-Rover standards, the principles behind the Roadstar "Off Road" seem to make it ideal for rugged use. Roadstar claim that the unit is water and dust sealed and there is a cover for the cassette door to protect the mechanism when the player is not in use. The whole unit is shock absorbed and it can be slid out of the vehicle for those occasions when the Land-Rover has to be left unattended. The set boasts a so-called ice hazard signal which is of limited use since it indicates that the temperature has dropped to five degrees Celsius and, by most people's reckoning, that's a long way from the formation of ice! However, the Roadstar "Off Road" delivers a high power output and that makes it particularly suitable for an extremely noisy vehicle like a Land-Rover!

ROR1. Roadstar also produce special speakers to go with the "Off Road" set but there is simply nowhere to put them in a Land-Rover. We chose to fit surface mount speakers.

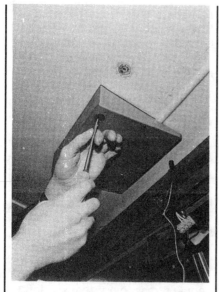

ROR2. You may think that there is nowhere in a Land-Rover to mount the set itself – and you would be right! We fabricated this sheet steel box which was screwed to the inside of the roof of the hardtop, using sealed bolts and nuts passing through the roof from above. As you can see, there were already holes up there where someone had apparently previously fitted a citizens' band radio.

ROR3. We also purchased a ▶ plastic shelf mounting kit from a local accessory store and into this we installed the Roadstar mounting basket...

ROR4. ...which was permanently clipped into place using the Roadstar fixing clips which form part of the kit.

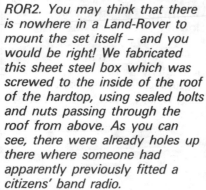

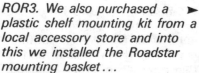

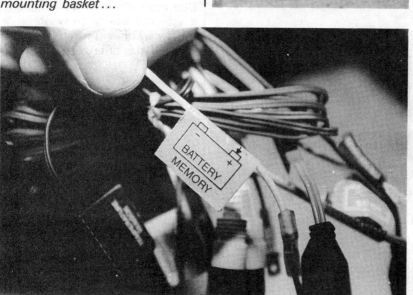

ROR5. Bob of Bluesound National screwed the fixing kit up to the mounting bracket that we had previously fitted to the roof. Without the aforesaid mounting bracket, the radio cassette player would be pointing at the same angle as that of the roof and it would not be possible to see the dials clearly.

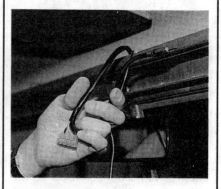

ROR6. Bob routed the power supply and aerial cables up the centre pillar and clipped them neatly to the pillar itself with small wiring clips.

ROR7. Out of the back of the set appeared a veritable viper's nest of cables but each of them is already fitted with a connector and a clear label indicating its use. This particular set has a memory – which is as well in view of the fact that it comes with 18 FM, six medium wave and 6 long wave settings – and the memory must be connected up to a fused permanent feed. Note that this set must only be used with negative earth vehicles.

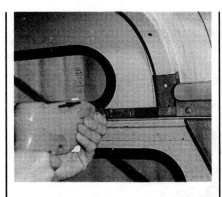

ROR8. Each of the speakers was bolted to the top channelling that runs around the roof after drilling a hole for the single mounting stud. To prevent the speaker from turning, Bob used two pieces of double sided tape...

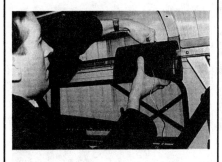

ROR9. ...so that when the speaker is bolted into place, the tape prevents it from twisting. The cable on the back of the speaker was run around the channel and connected up to the set as indicated in the instructions.

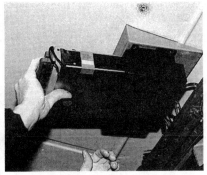

ROR10. With all the wires connected, the set was slid into its cage and clipped into place.

ROR11. When you want to remove the Roadstar "Off Road" set from the vehicle, you press on the handle which allows it to spring half an inch forwards and you can then pull the handle which slides the complete set out of its mounting. Bluesound National, who fitted the set, recommend the use of an FM dipole aerial to allow the FM part of the set to work at its best. When the set is removed from the vehicle, an internal automatically rechargeable battery allows the set to "remember" the wave bands that you have tuned into it. The sound quality is amazingly good for the cost of the set and it copes easily with the din of a Land-Rover on full bore!

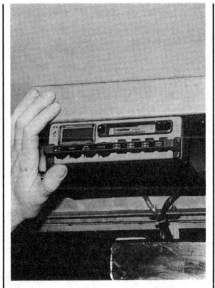

Fitting an electric cooling fan

In temperate climates, Land-Rovers can all too easily run cool which is bad for efficiency and bad for engine wear – although this can only be relative, since Land-Rover engines seem to go on and on in any case! However, matters can only be improved by removing the mechanical cooling fan and fitting an electric one. We fitted a Kenlowe fan to the project vehicle and found that removal of the mechanical fan made the engine quieter and also more economical, because it was not having to waste energy in driving a fan that for most of the time is not required.

KF1. The Kenlowe cooling fan kit comes with a complete set of parts. The kit with which we were supplied was designed to fit behind the radiator and to suck air through it. However, we felt that it would be far simpler to fit it in front of the radiator but this meant that the fan had to reversed on its spindle to operate as a blower. The instructions that come with the kit tell you how to carry out this operation.

KF2. The fan must be fitted with the cable entry at the bottom because this hole also acts as a drain hole. Here, the mounting arms have been fitted to the fan but we discovered that the arms had to be shortened to enable them to fit into the space in front of the radiator.

KF3. There were no shake proof washers for mounting the bracket to the fan body so we added those ourselves, although to be fair, Kenlowe have designed these mountings to be secured by a stud into a threaded plate with a lock nut on top. We added belts to the braces!

KF4. The horizontal plate just ahead of the radiator was marked out, centre punched and drilled so that the mounting brackets could be bolted into place.

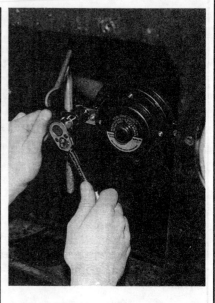

KF5. The whole assembly was ▲ offered up with all the bracket loosely mounted and then tightened in situ so that the fan blade was the thickness of one's fingers away from the radiator core. We chose to mount it just a little further away from the radiator than Kenlowe recommend.

KF6. Two radiator mounting holes are already the correct distance apart for the thermostat's bracket. The holes in the bracket had to be drilled out slightly in order to take the existing Land-Rover bolts.

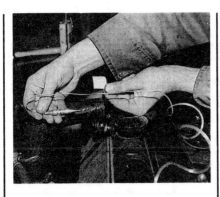

KF7. Following the Kenlowe instructions, the sensor has to be placed into the stub on the top of the radiator header tank and the capillary tube bent so that it comes out of the stub as shown.

KF8. Kenlowe's patented seal is then placed on the stub and the capillary tubes slid into the slit in the top of the seal. The top hose can be eased over the stub, the seal and the capillary tube and then clamped down in the normal way. This is an excellent system and, without recourse to any sealer, we experienced no leaks from the top hose.

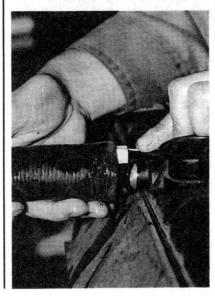

KF9. Using the water temperature gauge, if fitted, or following Kenlowe's instructions to the letter, you can set the fan to come on at the appropriate temperature. We found it to be remarkably efficient and that it cooled the engine temperature below the level at which the fan was required in a matter of seconds. As yet, the Kenlowe fan has never had to cut in whilst the Land-Rover has been on the move – which indicates the level of savings in power output that can be experienced! As an added extra, we clipped the capillary tube down to another of the radiator mounting bolts using a normal wiring clip. Finally, the Land-Rover's mechanical fan has to be removed.

Appendices
1 Workshop Procedures and Safety First

Professional motor mechanics are trained in safe working procedures, whereas the onus is on you, the home mechanic, to find them out for yourself and act upon them. However enthusiastic you may be about getting on with the job in hand, do take the time to ensure that your safety is not put at risk. A moment's lack of attention can result in an accident, as can failure to observe certain elementary precautions.

There will always be new ways of having accidents, and the following points do not pretend to be a comprehensive list of all dangers; they are intended rather to make you aware of the risks and to encourage a safety-conscious approach to all work you carry out on your vehicle.

Be sure to consult the suppliers of any materials and equipment you may use, and to obtain and read carefully operating and health and safety instructions that they may supply.

Essential DOs and DON'Ts

DON'T rely on a single jack when working underneath the vehicle. Always use reliable additional means of support, such as axle stands, securely placed under a part of the vehicle that you know will not give way.

DON'T attempt to loosen or tighten high-torque nuts (e.g. wheel hub nuts) while the vehicle is on a jack; it may be pulled off.

DON'T start the engine without first ascertaining that the transmission is in neutral (or 'Park' where applicable) and the parking brake applied.

DON'T suddenly remove the filler cap from a hot cooling system – cover it with a cloth and release the pressure gradually first, or you may get scalded by escaping coolant.

DON'T attempt to drain oil, automatic transmission fluid, or coolant until you are sure it has cooled sufficiently to avoid scalding you.

DON'T grasp any part of the engine, exhaust or catalytic converter without first ascertaining that it is sufficiently cool to avoid burning you.

DON'T allow brake fluid or antifreeze to contact vehicle paintwork.

DON'T syphon toxic liquids such as fuel, brake fluid or antifreeze by mouth, or allow them to remain on your skin.

DON'T inhale dust – it may be injurious to health (see Asbestos below).

DON'T allow any spilt oil or grease to remain on the floor – wipe it up straight away, before someone slips on it.

DON'T use ill-fitting spanners or other tools which may slip and cause injury.

DON'T attempt to lift a heavy component which may be beyond your capability – get assistance.

DON'T rush to finish a job, or take unverified short cuts.

DON'T allow children or animals in or around an unattended vehicle.

DON'T park vehicles with catalytic converters over combustible materials such as dry grass, oily rags, etc., if the engine has recently been run. As catalytic converters reach extremely high temperatures, any such materials in close proximity may ignite.

DON'T run vehicles equipped with catalytic converters without the exhaust system heat shields fitted.

DO wear eye protection when using power tools such as an electric drill, sander, bench grinder, etc., and when working under the vehicle.

DO use a barrier cream on your hands prior to undertaking dirty jobs – it will protect your skin from infection as well as making the dirt easier to remove afterwards; but make sure your hands aren't left slippery. Note that long term contact with used engine oil can be a health hazard.

DO keep loose clothing (cuffs, tie, etc.) and long hair well out of the way of moving mechanical parts.

DO remove rings, wrist watch, etc., before working on the vehicle – especially the electrical system.

DO ensure that any lifting tackle used has a safe working load rating adequate for the job, and is used precisely as recommended by the manufacturer.

DO keep your work area tidy – it is only too easy to fall over articles left lying around.

DO get someone to check periodically that all is well, when working alone on the vehicle.

DO carry out work in a logical sequence and check that everything is correctly assembled and tightened afterwards.

DO remember that your vehicle's safety affects that of yourself and others. If in doubt on any point, get specialist advice.

IF, in spite of following these precautions, you are unfortunate enough to injure yourself, seek medical attention as soon as possible.

Fire

Remember at all times that petrol (gasoline) is highly flammable. Never smoke, or have any kind of naked flame around, when working on the vehicle. But the risk does not end there – a spark caused by an electrical short-circuit, by two metal surfaces contacting each other, by a central heating boiler in the garage 'firing up', or even by static electricity built up in your body under certain conditions, can ignite petrol vapour,

which in a confined space is highly explosive.

Always disconnect the battery earth (ground) terminal before working on any part of the fuel system, and never risk spilling fuel on to a hot engine or exhaust.

It is recommended that a fire extinguisher of a type suitable for fuel and electrical fires is kept handy in the garage or workplace at all times. Never try to extinguish a fuel or electrical fire with water.

Fumes

Certain fumes are highly toxic and can quickly cause unconsciousness and even death if inhaled to any extent. Petrol (gasoline) vapour comes into this category, as do the vapours from certain solvents such as trichloroethylene and those from many adhesives. Any draining or pouring of such volatile fluids should be done in a well-ventilated area.

When using cleaning fluids and solvents, read the instructions carefully. Never use any materials from unmarked containers – they may give off poisonous vapours.

Never run the engine of a motor vehicle in an enclosed space such as a garage. Exhaust fumes contain carbon monoxide which is extremely poisonous. If you need to run the engine, always do so in the open air or at least have the rear of the vehicle outside the workplace.

If you are fortunate enough to have the use of an inspection pit, never drain or pour petrol, and never run the engine, while the vehicle is standing over it; the fumes, being heavier than air, will concentrate in the pit with possibly lethal results.

The battery

Never cause a spark, or allow a naked light, near the vehicle battery. It will normally be giving off a certain amount of hydrogen gas, which is highly explosive.

Always disconnect the battery earth (ground) terminal before working on the fuel or electrical systems.

If possible, loosen the filler plugs or cover when charging the battery from an external source. Do not charge at an excessive rate or the battery may burst.

Take care when topping up and when carrying the battery. The acid electrolyte, even when diluted, is very corrosive and should not be allowed to contact the eyes or skin.

If you ever need to prepare electrolyte yourself, always add the acid slowly to the water, and never the other way round. Protect against splashes by wearing rubber gloves and goggles.

Mains electricity

When using an electric power tool, inspection light, etc., which works from the mains, always ensure that the appliance is correctly connected to its plug and that, where necessary, it is properly earthed (grounded). Do not use such appliances in damp conditions and, again, beware of creating a spark or applying excessive heat in the vicinity of fuel or fuel vapour.

Also, before using any mains powered electrical equipment, take one more simple precaution – use an RCD (Residual Current Device) circuit breaker. Then, if there is a short, the RCD circuit breaker minimises the risk of electrocution by instantly cutting the power supply. Buy from any electrical store or DIY centre. RCDs fit simply into your electrical socket before plugging in your electrical equipment.

Ignition HT voltage

A severe electric shock can result from touching certain parts of the ignition system, such as the HT leads, when the engine is running or being cranked, particularly if components are damp or the insulation is defective. Where an electronic ignition system is fitted, the HT voltage is much higher and could prove fatal. Consult your handbook or main dealer if in any doubt. Risk of injury while working on running engines, e.g. adjusting the timing, can arise if the operator touches a high voltage lead and pulls his hand away on to a projection or revolving part.

Welding and bodywork repairs

It is so useful to be able to weld

when carrying out restoration work, and yet there is a good deal that could go dangerously wrong for the uninformed – in fact more than could be covered here. **For safety's sake** you are strongly recommended to seek tuition, in whatever branch of welding you wish to use, from your local evening institute or adult education classes. In addition, all of the information and instructional material produced by the suppliers of materials and equipment you will be using must be studied carefully. You may have to ask your stockist for some of this printed material if it is not made available at the time of purchase.

In addition, it is strongly recommended that *The Car Bodywork Repair Manual,* published by Haynes, is purchased and studied before carrying out any welding or bodywork repairs. Consisting of 292 pages, around 1,000 illustrations and written by Lindsay Porter, the author of this book, *The Car Bodywork Repair Manual* picks the brains of specialists from a variety of fields, and covers arc, MIG and 'gas' welding, panel beating and accident repair, rust repair and treatment, paint spraying, glass-fibre work, filler, lead loading, interiors and much more besides. Alongside a number of projects, the book describes in detail how to carry out each of the techniques involved in car bodywork repair with safety notes where necessary. As such, it is the ideal complement to this book.

Compressed gas cylinders

There are serious hazards associated with the storage and handling of gas cylinders and fittings, and standard precautions should be strictly observed in dealing with them. Ensure that cylinders are stored in safe conditions, properly maintained and always handled with special care and make constant efforts to eliminate the possibilities of leakage, fire and explosion.

The cylinder gases that are commonly used are oxygen, acetylene and liquid petroleum gas (LPG). Safety requirements for all three gases are: Cylinders must be stored in a fire resistant, dry and

well-ventilated space, away from any source of heat or ignition and protected from ice, snow or direct sunlight. Valves of cylinders in store must always be kept uppermost and closed, even when the cylinder is empty. Cylinders should be handled with care and only by personnel who are reliable, adequately informed and fully aware of all associated hazards. Damaged or leaking cylinders should be immediately taken outside into the open air, and the supplier and fire authorities should be notified immediately. No one should approach a gas cylinder store with a naked light or cigarette. Care should be taken to avoid striking or dropping cylinders, or knocking them together. Cylinders should never be used as rollers. One cylinder should never be filled from another. Every care must be taken to avoid accidental damage to cylinder valves. Valves must be operated without haste, never fully opened hard back against the back stop (so that other users know the valve is open) and never wrenched shut but turned just securely enough to stop the gas. Before removing or loosening any outlet connections, caps or plugs, a check should be made that the valves are closed. When changing cylinders, close all valves and appliance taps, and extinguish naked flames, including pilot jets, before disconnecting them. When reconnecting ensure that all connections and washers are clean and in good condition and do not overtighten them. Immediately a cylinder becomes empty, close its valve.

Safety requirements for acetylene: Cylinders must always be stored and used in the upright position. If a cylinder becomes heated accidentally or becomes hot because of excessive backfiring, immediately shut the valve, detach the regulator, take the cylinder out of doors well away from the building, immerse it in or continuously spray it with water, open the valve and allow the gas to escape until the cylinder is empty. If necessary, notify the emergency fire service without delay.

Safety requirements for oxygen are: No oil or grease should be used on valves or fittings. Cylinders with convex bases should be used in a stand or held securely to a wall.

Safety requirements for LPG are: The store must be kept free of combustible material, corrosive material and cylinders of oxygen.

Cylinders should only ever be carried upright, securely strapped down, preferably in an open vehicle or with windows open. Carry the suppliers safety data with you. In the event of an accident, notify the Police and Fire Services and hand the safety data to them.

Dangerous liquids and gases

Because of flammable gas given off by batteries when on charge, care should be taken to avoid sparking by switching off the power supply before charger leads are connected or disconnected. Battery terminals should be shielded, since a battery contains energy and a spark can be caused by any conductor which touches its terminals or exposed connecting straps.

When internal combustion engines are operated inside buildings the exhaust fumes must be properly discharged to the open air. Petroleum spirit or mixture must be contained in metal cans which should be kept in a store. In any area where battery charging or the testing of fuel injection systems is carried out there must be good ventilation, and no sources of ignition. Inspection pits often present serious hazards. They should be of adequate length to allow safe access and exit while a car is in position. If there is an inspection pit, petrol may enter it. Since petrol vapour is heavier than air it will remain there and be a hazard if there is any source of ignition. All sources of ignition must therefore be excluded.

Lifting equipment

Special care should be taken when any type of lifting equipment is used. Lifting jacks are for raising vehicles; they should never be used as supports while work is in progress. Jacks must be replaced by adequate rigid supports before any work is begun on the vehicle. Risk of injury while working on running engines, e.g. adjusting the timing, can arise if the operator touches a high voltage lead and pulls his hand away on to a projection or revolving part. On some vehicles the voltage used in the ignition system is so high as to cause injury or death by electrocution.

Consult your handbook or main dealer if in any doubt.

Work with plastics

Work with plastic materials brings additional hazards into workshops. Many of the materials used (polymers, resins, adhesives and materials acting as catalysts and accelerators) readily produce very dangerous situations in the form of poisonous fumes, skin irritants, risk of fire and explosions. Do not allow resin or 2-pack adhesive hardener, or that supplied with filler or 2-pack stopper to come into contact with skin or eyes. Read carefully the safety notes supplied on the tin, tube or packaging.

Jacks and axle stands

Special care should be taken when any type of lifting equipment is used. Any jack is made for lifting the car, not for supporting it. NEVER even consider working under your car using only a jack to support the weight of it. Jacks are only for raising vehicles, and must be replaced by adequate supports before any work is begun on the vehicle; axle stands are available from many discount stores, and all auto parts stores. These stands are absolutely essential if you plan to work under your car. Simple triangular stands (fixed or adjustable) will suit almost all of your working situations. Drive-on ramps are very limiting because of their design and size.

When jacking the car from the front, leave the gearbox in neutral and the brake off until you have placed the axle stands under the frame. Make sure that the car is on level ground first! Then put the car into gear and/or engage the handbrake and lower the jack. Obviously DO NOT put the car in gear if you plan to turn over the engine! Leaving the brake on, or leaving the car in gear while jacking the front of the car will necessarily cause the jack to tip (unless a good quality trolley jack with wheels is being used). This is unavoidable when jacking the car on one side, and the use of the handbrake in this case is recommended.

If the car is older and if it shows signs of weakening at the jack tubes while using the factory jack, it is best

to purchase a good scissors jack or hydraulic jack – preferably trolley-type (depending on your budget).

Workshop safety – summary

1 Always have a fire extinguisher at arm's length whenever welding or when working on the fuel system – under the car, or under the bonnet.
2 NEVER use a naked flame near the petrol tank.
3 Keep your inspection lamp FAR AWAY from any source of dripping petrol (gasoline); for example, while removing the fuel pump.
4 NEVER use petrol (gasoline) to clean parts. Use paraffin (kerosene) or white (mineral) spirits.
5 NO SMOKING!

If you do have a fire, DON'T PANIC. Use the extinguisher effectively by directing it at the base of the fire.

Paint spraying

NEVER use 2-pack, isocyanate-based paints in the home environment or home workshop. Ask your supplier if you are not sure which is which. If you have use of a professional booth, wear an air-fed mask. Wear a charcoal face mask when spraying other paints and maintain ventilation to the spray area. Concentrated fumes are dangerous!

Spray fumes, thinners and paint are highly flammable. Keep away from naked flames or sparks.

Paint spraying safety is too large a subject for this book. See Lindsay Porter's *The Car Bodywork Repair Manual* (Haynes) for further information.

Fluoroelastomers – Most Important! Please Read This Section!

Many synthetic rubber-like materials used in motor cars contain a substance called fluorine. These substances are known as fluoroelastomers and are commonly used for oil seals, wiring and cabling, bearing surfaces, gaskets, diaphragms, hoses and 'O' rings. If they are subjected to temperatures greater than 315°C, they will decompose and can be

potentially hazardous. Fluoroelastomer materials will show physical signs of decomposition under such conditions in the form of charring of black sticky masses. Some decomposition may occur at temperatures above 200°C, and it is obvious that when a car has been in a fire or has been dismantled with the assistance of a cutting torch or blow torch, the fluoroelastomers can decompose in the manner indicated above.

In the presence of any water or humidity, including atmospheric moisture, the by-products caused by the fluoroelastomers being heated can be extremely dangerous. According to the Health and Safety Executive, 'Skin contact with this liquid or decomposition residues can cause painful and penetrating burns. Permanent irreversible skin and tissue damage can occur.' Damage can also be caused to eyes or by the inhalation of fumes created as fluoroelastomers are burned or heated.

If you are in the vicinity of a vehicle fire or a place where a vehicle is being cut up with cutting equipment, the Health and Safety Executive recommend the following action:
1 Assume unless you know otherwise that seals, gaskets and 'O' rings, hoses, wiring and cabling, bearing surfaces and diaphragms are fluoroelastomers.
2 Inform firefighters of the presence of fluoroelastomers and toxic and corrosive fume hazards when they arrive.
3 All personnel not wearing breathing apparatus must leave the immediate area of a fire.

After fires or exposure to high temperatures:
1 Do not touch blackened or charred seals or equipment.
2 Allow all burnt or decomposed fluoroelastomer materials to cool down before inspection, investigation, tear-down or removal.
4 Preferably, don't handle parts containing decomposed fluoroelastomers, but if you must, wear goggles and PVC (polyvinyl chloride) or neoprene protective gloves whilst doing so. Never handle such parts unless they are completely cool.
5 Contaminated parts, residues, materials and clothing, including protective clothing and gloves, should be disposed of by an approved contractor to landfill or by incineration according to national

or local regulations. Original seals, gaskets and 'O' rings, along with contaminated material, must not be burned locally.

Symptoms and clinical findings of exposure:

A Skin/eye contact:
Symptoms may be apparent immediately, soon after contact or there may be considerable delay after exposure. Do not assume that there has been no damage from a lack of immediate symptoms; delays of minutes in treatment can have severe consequences.
1 Dull throbbing ache.
2 Severe and persistent pain.
3 Black discoloration under nails (skin contact).
4 Severe, persistent and penetrating burns.
5 Skin swelling and redness.
6 Blistering.
7 Sometimes pain without visible change.

B Inhalation (breathing):
– immediate
1 Coughing.
2 Choking.
3 Chills lasting one to two hours after exposure.
4 Irritation.

C Inhalation (breathing) – delays of one to two days or more:
1 Fever.
2 Cough.
3 Chest tightness.
4 Pulmonary oedema (congestion).
5 Bronchial pneumonia.

First aid

A Skin contact:
1 Remove contaminated clothing immediately.
2 Irrigate affected skin with copious amounts of cold water or lime water (saturated calcium hydroxide solution) for 15 to 60 minutes. Obtain medical assistance urgently.

B Inhalation
Remove to fresh air and obtain medical supportive treatment immediately. Treat for pulmonary oedema.

C Eye contact
Wash/irrigate eyes immediately with water followed by normal saline for 30 to 60 minutes. Obtain immediate medical attention.

2
Major Development Milestones

The Land-Rover project began in the spring of 1947 after much study of the Jeep design; in fact a Jeep chassis was used for the first prototype which was completed that summer. The first twenty-five trial vehicles were ready for testing by the autumn.

The first vehicle was launched at the Amsterdam Motor Show in April 1948. It had an 80 in wheelbase, pick-up body and 1595cc Rover "P3" type four-cylinder engine, with permanent four-wheel drive and freewheel in the front drive line. It was spartan, and was priced at £450.

Forty-eight of these vehicles were produced, and the real production run started in July 1948 – same price but better fittings!

In October a light-alloy panelled station wagon was introduced at a price of £959. This style was built until 1951.

In 1950 an alternative top was offered, now both metal or canvas being available. Also the freewheel feature was discontinued, and the transmission had optional four-wheel or rear-wheel drive with cockpit control.

From the beginning of 1952 the engine was bored out to 1997cc, and in 1954 the wheelbase was increased from 80 in to 86 in. A long-wheelbase version (107 in) was produced with an extra 41 in of loading platform.

In 1956 the wheelbase of each version was extended to 88 in and 109 in respectively, and these measurements were to remain standard for about thirty years. It was introduced to take new engines, both diesel and petrol. The station wagon remained at 107 in until September 1958.

The diesel engine, of 2052cc, with overhead valves was introduced in June 1957, and was very quickly available for the export market.

The Series II Land-Rover replaced all previous models in April 1958. The chassis remained unchanged, but wheel tracks were increased, also front wheel lock, and turning circles were reduced. There was a new style, which included "barrel" body sides and panels beneath the doors. A new engine of 2286cc was announced, with overhead valves.

A important milestone was reached in November 1959 when, eleven years after the Land-Rover had been launched, a total of 250,000 vehicles was recorded.

Series IIA Land-Rovers replaced the previous models in 1961. The main mechanical difference was that the diesel engine was increased to 2286cc, the same as the bore and stroke of the petrol engine.

A big change was accomplished with the introduction of the forward-control vehicle, based on the 109 in frame, with a new overframe, adapted cab, and 1,525kg payload, (1,270kg when driving over rough country). The 2286cc petrol engine became standard, with no option of diesel.

Although it had taken eleven years to produce the first 250,000 vehicles, the next 250,000 were achieved in only $6\frac{1}{2}$ years, to April 1966.

In September of that year the suspension was modified, and the wheelbase of the forward-control extended to 110 in. There was a choice of three engines, 2286cc petrol, 2286cc diesel and (for the first time) 2625cc six-cylinder petrol engine. Wheeltracks were enlarged by $2\frac{1}{2}$ in to improve stability and roadholding.

The following year the 2625cc six-cylinder engine was produced on the 109 in chassis normal control Series IIA Land-Rovers. Also some internal improvements were made with more comfortable seat padding.

After twenty years of the original styling, some

modifications were made in the headlamp position for the export market – they were remounted on the front wings. (This was introduced into the UK market in February 1969.)

In September 1968 a special heavy-duty "1 ton" version was produced, using the 109 in chassis and the six-cylinder 2625cc engine.

Also around this time the "Rover 1" or "half-ton" was introduced, available only for the Army. It had a standard 88 in chassis, but a lightweight body (lighter than the standard Army Land-Rover, but still heavier than the civilian version) for ease of transportation.

In June 1971 the 750,000th Land-Rover was completed.

In October, the forward-control Land-Rovers became described as Series IIB, and Series III replaced the Series IIA normal-control machines. Series III had a synchromesh gearbox, and new styling of grilles, instrument panels and added comfort. The wheelbases remained at 88 in and 109 in with the same choice of engines, petrol and diesel.

The Commercial Vehicle Show in London in September 1972 saw the introduction of a new specialised military Land-Rover, the 101 in wheelbase machine, produced for the British forces only. It was produced in 1974, and used the Range-Rover's V8 3528cc engine with permanent four-wheel drive central transmission on a new chassis. The cab and pick-up body was simple, and there was a rear power take-off drive for the hitching up of trailers,

providing a 6 x 6 combination.

Civilian forward-control Land-Rovers ceased production after the last export order in 1973.

In August 1974 an optional Fairey overdrive was announced, for the transfer box of all types of Land-Rovers.

By June 1976 the millionth Land-Rover was produced and presented to the British Motor Industry Heritage Trust collection, to join R.01, the first pilot vehicle.

By this time it was hoped to double the Solihull based production, but Leyland's financial problems delayed these plans until the end of 1978. By 1980 an investment cost of £280 million was made for these projects.

In March 1983 a new Land-Rover One Ten was announced, with 110 in wheelbase, coil spring suspension, and five-speed all-synchromesh gearbox on all four-cylinder models.

The following year a 2495cc diesel four-cylinder engine directly replaced the 2286cc on all relevant models. Later in 1984 the Land-Rover Ninety was introduced with a shorter version of the One Ten chassis, coil spring suspension, (but a

wheelbase of 92.9 in) four-cylinder engine and five-speed all-synchromesh gearbox.

In May 1985 the Spanish-built "Santana" gearbox was introduced for the V8 vehicles; also this engine became available for the Ninety model, ending the Series III assembly.

A new petrol engine, 2495cc four-cylinder, replaced the 2286cc type on all models in September 1985.

In October the 1,500,000th vehicle came off the production lines at Solihull.

In June 1986 the new forward-control Land-Rover, V8 engine with five-speed manual gearbox was shown, and by October the 85 bhp turbocharged 2.5 litre diesel engine became optional for all models.

3 Technical Specifications

Land-Rover Series I 1948 – 1951

Engine
4-cylinder 69.5 x 105mm 1595cc CR 6.8:1
Solex carb. 50 bhp (net) at 4,000 rpm
Max torque 80 lb ft at 2,000 rpm

Transmission
Permanent 4-wheel drive with free wheel in front drive.
Front and rear differentials
High and low range of gears
Axle ratios 4.7:1 High range step down ratio 1.148:1;
Overall gear ratios 5.396, 8.039, 11.023,
16.165, Reverse 13.743:1
Low range step down ratio 2.89:1;
Overall ratios 13.578, 20.229, 27.738,
40.676, Reverse 34.581:1.
Synchromesh on top and third gears.

Suspension and brakes
Live front axle, half elliptic leaf springs,
telescopic dampers,
live rear axle,
half elliptic leaf springs,
telescopic dampers,
worm and nut steering.
10 x 1.5in front and rear drum brakes
6.00 – 16in or 7.00 – 16in tyres

Dimensions
Wheelbase 6.8in (80in)
Front and rear track 4ft 2in
Length 11ft 0in
Width 5ft 1in
Height (hood up) 5ft 10.5in
Unladen weight 2,594 lbs
Max payload 1,000 lbs

Series 1 (80 in model) produced 1952 – 1954

Specification as for original 80in model except for:

Engine
77.8 x 105mm 1997cc CR 6.8:1
52 bhp (net) at 4,000 rpm
Max torque 101 lbs ft at 1,500 rpm

Transmission
(introduced 1950)
Optional 4-wheel or rear wheel drive
No freewheel

Dimensions
Height (hood up) 6ft 1.5in
unladen weight 2,604 lbs

Series 1 (86 in model) produced 1954 – 1956

Specification as for final 80in model except for:
Dimensions

Wheelbase 7ft 2in (86in)
Length 11ft 8.7in
Width 5ft 2.6in
Height (hood up) 6ft 4in
Unladen weight 2,702 lbs

Series 1 (107 in model) produced 1954 – 1958 (Station Wagon 1956 – 1958 only)

Specification as for final 80in model except for:
Dimensions

Wheelbase 8ft 11in (107in)
Length 14ft 5.5in
Width 5ft 2.6in
Height (hood up) 6ft 11.5in
Unladen weight 3,031 lbs
Max allowable vehicle weight 4,151 lbs

Series 1 (88 in model) produced 1956 – 1958

Specification as for final 80in model except for:
Dimensions

Wheelbase 7ft 4in (88in)
Length 11ft 8.75in
Width 5ft 2.6in
Height (hood up) 6ft 4in
Unladen weight from 2,740 lbs
Max allowable vehicle weight 4,190 lbs

Series 1 (109 in model) produced 1956 – 1958

Specification as for final 80in model except for:
Dimensions

Wheelbase 9ft 1in (109in)
Length 14ft 5.5in
Width 5ft 2.6in
Height (hood up) 6ft 11.5in
Unladen weight 3,080 lbs
Max allowable vehicle weight 5,185 lbs

Alternative Diesel Engine 2052 cc produced 1957 – 1958

Engine

85.79 x 88.9mm 2052cc CR22.5:1
CAV fuel injection
55 bhp (net) at 3,500 rpm
Max torque 87 lbs ft at 2,000 rpm

Dimensions

Extra weight 196 lbs

Series II (88 in model) produced 1958 – 1961

Engine	4 cylinder 90.47 x 88.9mm 2286cc CR 7.0:1 Solex carb 70 bhp (net) at 4,250 rpm Max torque 124 lbs ft at 2,500 rpm
Transmission	Optional 4-wheel or rear wheel drive Front and rear differentials High and low range of gears Axle ratios 4.7:1 High range step down ratio 1.148:1 Overall gear ratio 5.396, 7.435, 11.026 16.171, Reverse 13.745:1 15.1 mph/1,000 rpm in top gear Low range step down ratio 2.888:1 Overall ratios 13.578, 18.707, 27.742, 40.688, Reverse 34.585:1 7.3mph/1,000 rpm in top gear Synchromesh on top and third gears
Suspension and brakes	Live front axle, half elliptic leaf springs, telescopic dampers, live rear axle, half elliptic rear springs, telescopic dampers, Recirculating ball steering 10 x 1.5 front and rear drum brakes 6.00 – 16in tyres
Dimensions	Wheelbase 7ft 4in (88in) Front and rear tracks 4ft 3.5in Length 11ft 10.4in Width 5ft 4in Height (max) 6ft 5in Unladen weight from 2,900 lbs Max allowable vehicle 4,453 lbs

Series II (109 in model) produced 1958 – 1961

Specification as for 88in model except for:

Suspension and brakes	11 x 2.25 front and rear brakes 7.50 – 16in tyres
Dimensions	Wheelbase 9ft 1in (109in) Length 14ft 7in Height (max) 6ft 9in Unladen weight from 3,294 lbs Max allowable vehicle weight 5,905 lbs

Alternative Diesel Engine 2052 cc produced 1958 – 1961

Engine	85.7 x 88.9mm 2.052cc CR 22.5:1 CAV fuel injection 51 bhp (net) at 3,500 rpm Max torque 87 lbs ft at 2,000 rpm
Dimensions	Extra weight 195 lbs

Series IIA (88 in model) produced 1961 – 1971

Specification as for Series II 88in model except for:

Dimensions
    Unladen weight from 2,953 lbs
    Max allowable vehicle weight 4,453 lbs

Series IIA (109 in model) produced 1961 – 1971

Specification as for Series II 109in model except for:

Dimensions
    Unladen weight from 3,301 lbs
    Max allowable vehicle weight 5,905 lbs

Alternative Series IIA Diesel Engine 2286cc produced 1962 – 1971

Engine
    90.47 x 88.9mm 2286cc CR 23.0:1
    CAV fuel injection
    62 bhp at 4,000 rpm
    Max torque 103 lb ft at 1,800 rpm

Dimensions
    Extra weight 144 lbs

Series IIA (109 in 6-cylinder model) produced 1967 – 1971

Specification as for normal Series II Series IIA 109in petrol model except for:

Engine
    6-cylinder 77.8 x 92.1mm 2625cc CR7.8:1
    SU carb 83 bhp (net) at 4,500 rpm
    Max torque 128 lbs ft at 1,500 rpm

Transmission
    High range step down ratio 1.148:1
    Overall gear ratios 5.396, 8.09, 11.98
    19.43, Reverse 16.30:1
    16.5 mph/1,000 rpm in top gear
    Low range step down ratio 1.35:1
    Overall ratios 11.05, 16.57, 24.51
    39.74, Reverse 33.34:1
    8.0 mph/1,000 rpm in top gear

Suspension and brakes
    Front brakes 11x 3in drums

Dimensions
    Unladen weight from 3,459 lbs
    Max allowable vehicle weight 5,905 lbs

Series IIA (109 in "1 ton" model) produced 1968 – 1971

Specification as for normal Series IIA 109in model except for:

Transmission
    High range step down ratio 1.53:1
    Overall gear ratios 7.19, 10.80, 15.96
    25.90 Reverse 21.7:1
    13.3 mph/1,000 rpm in top gear
    Low range step down ratio 3.27:1
    Overall ratios 15.40, 23.10, 24.10
    55.3 Reverse 46.4:1
    6.25 mph/1,000 rpm in top gear

Suspension
    9.00 – 16in tyres

Dimensions
    Unladen weight from 3,886 lbs
    Max allowable vehicle weight 6,750 lbs

"Half Ton" Air Portable Military Land-Rover (88 in model) produced 1968 – 1985

Specification as for appropriately engined (4-cylinder, petrol or diesel) Series IIA or Series III civil Land-Rovers except for:

Dimensions	Length 12ft 0in
	Width 5ft 0in
	Height 6ft 5in
	Unladen weight (petrol engine) 3,210 lbs
	In stripped out form for air transportation 2,660 lbs
	Max allowable vehicle weight 4,450 lbs

Series III (88 in model) produced 1971 – 1985

Engine	4-cylinder 90.47 x 88.9mm 2286cc
	CR 8.0:1
	Zenith carb 70 bhp (din) at 4,000 rpm
	Max torque 120 lbs ft at 1,500 rpm
Transmission	Optional 4-wheel or rear wheel drive
	Front and rear differential
	High and low range of gears
	Axle ratios 4.7:1
	High range step down ratio 1.148:1
	All synchromesh gear box
	overall gear ratios 5.396, 8.05, 12.00,
	19.88, Reverse 21.66:1
	15.1 mph/1,000 rpm in top gear
	Low range step down ratio 2.35:1
	Overall ratios 11.10, 16.50, 24.60
	40.70, Reverse 44.30:1
	7.4 mph/1,000 rpm in top gear
Suspension and brakes	Live front axle,
	half elliptic leaf springs,
	telescopic dampers,
	live rear axle,
	half elliptic leaf springs,
	telescopic dampers,
	recirculating ball steering.
	10 x 1.5in front and rear drum brakes
	6.00 – 16in tyres
Dimensions	Wheelbase 7ft 4in (88in)
	Front and rear tracks 4ft 3.5in
	Length 11ft 10.6in
	Width 5ft 6in
	Height (max) 6ft 5in
	Unladen weight from 2,953 lbs
	Max allowable vehicle weight 4,453 lbs

Series IIIB (109 in models) produced 1971 – 1985

Specification as for 88in model except for:

Transmission	16.5 mph/1,000 rpm in high range
	8.0 mph/1,000 rpm in low range
Suspension and brakes	11 x 2.25in front and rear drum brakes
	7.50-16in tyres
Dimensions	Wheelbase 9ft 1in (109in)
	Front and rear tracks 4ft 4.5in
	Length 14ft 7in
	Height (max) 6ft 7in
	Unladen weight from 3,301 lbs
	Max allowable vehicle weight 5,905 lbs

Series III (109 in 6-cylinder model) produced 1971 – 1985

Specification as for Series 109in model except for:

Engine	6-cylinder 77.8 x 92.1mm 2625cc CR 7.8:1 Zenith-Stromberg carb 86 bhp (din) at 4,500 rpm Max torque 132 lbs ft at 1,500 rpm
Brakes	3in x 11in front 2.25in x 11in rear
Dimensions	Unladen weight from 3,459 lbs Max allowable vehicle weight 5,905 lbs

Alternative Series III Diesel Engine 2286cc
produced 1971 – *1985*

Engine	90.46 x 88.9mm 2286cc CR 23.0:1 CAV fuel injection 62 bhp (din) at 4,000 rpm Max torque 103 lbs ft at 1,800 rpm
Dimensions	Extra weight 144 lbs

Series III (109 in "one ton" model) produced 1971 – 1985

Specification as for normal Series III 109in model except for:

Transmission	High range step down ratio 1.53:1 Overall gear ratios 7.19, 10.80, 15.96, 26.46, Reverse 28.91:1 13.3 mph/1,000 rpm in top gear Low range step down ratio 3.27:1 Overall ratios 15.40, 23.10, 34.10, 56.56 Reverse 61.78:1 6.25 mph/1,000 rpm in top gear 9.00-16in tyres
Brakes	3in x 11in front 2.25in x 11in rear
Dimensions	Unladen weight from 3,886 lbs Max allowable vehicle weight 6,750 lbs

Forward Control (109 in model) produced 1962 – 1966

Engine	4-cylinder 90.47 x 88.9mm. 2286cc CR 7.0:1 Solex carb 67 bhp (net) at 4,000 rpm Max torque 116 lbs ft at 1,500 rpm
Transmission	Optional 4-wheel or rear wheel drive Front and rear differentials High and low range of gears Axle ratios 4.7:1
Dimensions	Wheelbase 9ft 1in (109in) Front and rear tracks 4.5in Length 14ft 9in Height (max) 6ft 7in Width 5ft 6in Unladen weight from 3,396 lbs Max allowable vehicle weight 5,976 lbs

Land-Rover One-Ten introduced in 1983

Engines

4-cylinder petrol 90.47 x 88.9mm
2286cc CR 8.0:1
Weber carb 74 bhp (din) at 4,000 rpm
Max torque 120 lbs ft at 2,000 rpm

4-cylinder diesel 90.47 x 88.9mm
2286cc CR 23.0:1
CAV fuel injection
60 bhp (din) at 4,000 rpm
Max torque 103 lbs ft at 1,800 rpm

V8-cylinder petrol 88.9 x 71.1mm 3528cc
CR 8.13:1
2 Zenith Stromberg 175 CDSE carbs
114 bhp (din) at 4,000 rpm
Max torque 185 lbs ft at 2,500 rpm

Transmission

Permanent 4-wheel drive,
Three differentials
High and low range of gears
Axle ratios, all derivatives, 3.54:1
4-cylinder cars
High range step down ratio 1.66:1
Overall gear ratios (5 forward ratios)
    4.90, 5.89, 8.89, 13.57, 21.14
    Reverse 21.82:1
Low range step down ratio 3.31:1
Overall gear ratios (5 forward ratios)
    9.76, 11.74, 17.70, 27.02, 42.11
    Reverse 43.47:1
V8-cylinder cars
High range step down ratio 1.34:1
Overall gear ratios (4 forward ratios)
    4.72, 7.11, 11.57, 19.23,
    Reverse 17.32:1
Low range step down ratio 3.32:1
Overall gear ratios (4 forward ratios)
    11.74, 17.68, 28.76, 47.81
    Reverse 43.05:1

Suspension and brakes

Live front axle, coil springs
Radius arms, Panhard rod
Telescopic dampers
Live rear axle, coil springs
Radius arms, (A), optional self-levelling (standard on "County" station wagons)
telescopic dampers recirculating ball steering (optional power assistance)
11.8in front disc brakes
11.0in rear drum brakes with vacuum servo assistance
7.50-16in tyres on 5.5in rims

Dimensions

Wheelbase 9ft 2in (110in)
Front and rear tracks 4ft 10.5in
Length 14ft 7in
Height 6ft 8.1in
Width 5ft 10.5in
Unladen weight from 3,799 lbs
Max allowable vehicle weight 6,724 lbs or 6,504 with self-levelling suspension

From January 1984 an enlarged diesel (but not petrol) engine was fitted:
    90.47 x 97mm 2495cc CR 21.0:1
    BPS fuel injection
    67 bhp (din) at 4,000 rpm
    Max torque 114 lbs ft at 1,800 rpm

From May 1985 a new 5-speed all synchromesh gear box (type LT 85) was fitted to the V8 engined derivatives:
High range step down ratio 1.410:1
Overall gear ratios (5 forward ratios)
3.97, 4.99, 7.165, 10.88, 18.22
Reverse 19.085:1
Low range step down ratio 3.32:1
Overall gear ratios (5 forward ratios)
9.34, 11.95, 16.87, 25.61, 42.99 Reverse 44.93:1

From August 1985 the 4-cylinder petrol engine was also enlarged to 2495cc (bore x stroke as for diesel)
83 bhp (din) at 4,000 rpm
Max torque 133 lbs ft at 2,000 rpm

Land-Rover Ninety introduced 1984

Engines

4-cylinder petrol as One-Ten, 4- cylinder.
Diesel, as 2.5 litre 1984 One-Ten
V8-cylinder engines (from May 1985 only) as One-Ten

Transmission

Permanent 4-wheel as One-Ten, but:
4-cylinder cars:
High range step down ratios 1.41:1
Overall gear ratios (5 forward ratios)
4.14, 4.99, 7.52, 11.49, 17.91
Reverse 19.46:1
Low range as One-Ten
V8-cylinder cars (from May 1985 only):
High range step down ratio 1.19:1
Overall gear ratios (5 forward ratios)
3.355, 4.22, 6.06, 9.20, 15.40 Reverse 16.14:1
Low range step down ratio 3.32:1
Overall ratios as for V8-cylinder 5-speed
One-Ten

Dimensions

Wheelbase 7ft 8.9in (92.9in)
Front and rear tracks 4.10.5in
Length 12ft 2.5in
Height 6ft 5.6in (max)
Width 5ft 10.5in
Unladen weight from 3,540 lbs
Max allowable vehicle weight 5,513 lbs

4
Production Figures

Year	Annual sales	Cumulative sales

1948-51 Land-Rover Series I 80-inch introduced:

1947-1948	48	48
1948-1949	8,000	8,048
1949-1950	16,085	24,133
1950-1951	17,360	41,493
1951-1952	19,591	61,084

1952-54 Land-Rover Series I 80-inch produced with increased engine size:

1952-1953	18,570	79,654
1953-1954	20,135	99,789

1954-56 Land-Rover Series I 86-inch produced:
1954-58 Land-Rover Series I 107-inch produced:

1954-1955	28,882	128,671
1955-1956	28,365	157,036

1956-58 Land-Rover Series I 88-inch produced:
1956-58 Land-Rover Series I 109-inch produced:

1956-1957	25,775	182,811

1957-58 Alternative diesel engine produced:

1957-1958	28,656	211,467

1958-61 Land-Rover Series II 88-inch produced:
1958-61 Land-Rover Series II 109-inch produced:
1958-61 Alternative diesel engine produced:

1958-1959	28,371	239,838
1959-1960	34,168	274,006
1960-1961	35,148	309,154

1961-71 Land-Rover Series IIA 88-inch produced:
1961-71 Land-Rover Series IIA 109-inch produced:
1961-71 Alternative Series IIA diesel engine produced:

1961-1962	37,139	346,293
1962-1963	34,304	380,597
1963-1964	42,569	423,166
1964-1965	45,790	468,956
1965-1966	47,941	516,897
1966-1967	44,191	561,088

1967-71 Land-Rover Series IIA 109-inch 6-cylinder produced:

1967-1968	44,928	606,016

1968-71 Land-Rover Series IIA 109-inch '1 ton' produced:

1968-1969	50,561	656,577
1969-1970	47,538	704,115
1970-1971	56,663	760,778

1971-85 Land-Rover Series III 88-inch produced:

1971-85 Land-Rover Series III 109-inch produced:
1971-85 Land-Rover Series III 109-inch 6-cylinder produced:
1971-85 Land-Rover Series III diesel engine produced:

1971-1972	52,445	813,233
1972-1973	49,724	862,947
1973-1974	45,169	908,116
1974-1975	54,298	962,414
1975-1976	58,523	1,020,937
1977	41,452	1,062,389
1978	46,172	1,108,561
1979	42,936	1,151,497
1980	51,198	1,202,695
1981	41,059	1,243,754
1982	38,926	1,282,680
1983	28,586	1,311,266
1984	25,562	1,336,828
1985	31,046	1,367,874

5
Chassis Numbering

To date, throughout the Land-Rover's life, a total of seven differing chassis number arrangements have been used. To follow are the various arrangements for their respective years:

1948 – 1949
Prefixed by an L or R indicating left-hand or right-hand drive, were six or seven digits:
The first digit indicates the year – 8 = 1948-1949.
The second digit indicates the type – 6 = Land-Rover.
The third digit (applicable only to seven digit nos) indicates the differing models – 6 = Basic, 7 = Station Wagon, 8 = Welder.
With the exception of the 866 series, whose serial number started at 3001, the last four digits show the serial number starting with 0001 in each series.

1950 – 1953
Prefixed by an L or R indicating left-hand or right-hand drive, only on 1950 models. Eight digits:
The first digit indicates the year – 0 = 1950, 1 = 1951, 2 = 1952, 3 = 1953.
The second digit indicates the type – 6 = Land-Rover.
The third digit indicates the differing models – 1 = Basic, 2 = Station Wagon, 3 = Welder, 6 = completely knocked down CKD.
The fourth digit, excluding 1950 models, indicates the destination – 0 = Home Market, 3 = LHD Export, 6 = RHD Export.
With the exception of 1950 models which have five serial numbers, the last four digits starting at 0001 indicate the serial number.

1954 – 1955
An eight-digit chassis numbering system
The first digit indicates the year – 4 = 1954, 5 = 1955.
The second digit indicates the type – 7 = Land-Rover.

The third digit indicates the differing models – 1 = 86-inch, 2 = 107-inch, 6 = 86-inch CKD, 7 = 107-inch CKD.
The fourth digit indicates the destination – 0 or 1 = Home Market, 3 or 4 = LHD Export, 6 or 7 = RHD Export.
The last four digits starting with 0001 indicate the serial number.

1955
A nine-digit chassis numbering system:
The first digit indicates the type – 1 = Land-Rover.
The second digit indicates model – 7 = Land-Rover.
The third digit indicates destination – 0 = Home Market, 3 = LHD Export, 4 = LHD CKD, 6 = RHD Export, 7 = RHD CKD.
The fourth digit indicates the sanction period – 6 = late 1955 for service.
The last five digits starting with 00001 indicate the serial number.

1956 – 1961
A nine-digit chassis numbering system:
The first digit on all models = 1.
The second and third digits are in pairs in the following sequence indicating model and specification – Series I Models = 11-35, Series II Models = 41-70.
The fourth digit indicates the year – 6 = 1956, 7 = 1957 etc.
The last five digits starting with 00001 indicate the serial number.

1962 – 1979
Eight-digit chassis numbering system with suffix letters:
The first, second and third digits indicate the model and specification. The sequence 241-354 = Series II Models,

901-965 = Series III Models. The last five digits starting with 00001 indicate the serial number. Design modifications are shown by the suffix letters which assist when servicing.
NB. The year or model-year of manufacture have no identification digit.

1980 – date
All these years have the conventional Vehicle Identification Number (V.I.N.).

Where to Locate Your Chassis Number

80-inch chassis numbers
These can be found on the nearside engine mounting and on the brass plate on the nearside of the bulkhead (the latter were positioned inside the cab on later models).

86-inch and 107-inch chassis numbers
These can be found on the bulkhead inside vehicles and on the *right hand front* spring hanger.

88-inch and 109-inch chassis numbers
These can be found on the bulkhead inside vehicles and on the *right hand front* spring hanger.

6 Clubs and Specialists

The following web site details, addresses and telephone numbers were believed to be correct at the time of going to press. However, as these are subject to change, no guarantee can be given for their continued accuracy.

The Land-Rover was arguably one of the first post-war vehicles to attract the sort of enthusiasts keen enough to form an owners' club. As early as the mid-1950s, there were Land-Rover clubs in existence; quite a remarkable achievement for a vehicle designed primarily as an agricultural aid!

Nowadays, there are a number of local and national clubs to cater for the needs of every Land-Rover owner. However, Clubs are almost invariably run by volunteers, and addresses and telephone numbers change fairly regularly. Rather than include addresses which may be out of date by the time you read this, we suggest you refer to your favourite Land-Rover magazine or internet search engine for current club contacts.

National and Local Clubs

There are more Land Rover clubs than you can shake a gearstick at. All offer gatherings, they often have stands at the main Land Rover shows and offer technical advice and merchandise. Lots of local off-roading guaranteed!

Specialists

Dunsfold Land-Rovers Ltd.,
Alfold Road, Dunsfold,
Godalming, Surrey, GU8 4NR
www.dunsfold.com
Tel: 01483 200567

The author has nothing but praise for the efforts and enthusiasm of Dunsfold Land-Rover. If you want to buy parts and have work carried out by Land-Rover Retail Dealers who are also keen enthusiasts – and if you need Series I parts, into the bargain – Dunsfold Land-Rover is *the* place to go!

The Dunsfold Land-Rover Museum, which houses probably the best collection of classic and specialist Land-Rovers in the world, has grown out of a collection first established in 1968.

GM Accident Repairs,
Phillip's Garage, Petworth Road,
Wormley, Surrey, GU8 5TU
Tel: 01428 684165
Gerald Perrett of GM Accident Repairs carry out all of Dunsfold Land-Rover's paintwork and sprayed FVJ, the project vehicle, to a high standard using their low bake oven.

Sykes-Pickavant Ltd.,
www.sykes-pickavant.com
Sykes-Pickavant's range of hand tools is superb! Angle drive extensions give a semi-universal joint effect in tight corners, while the surface drive sockets avoid rounding nuts because effort is applied to the flats, not the points of the nut or bolt.

Holden Vintage & Classic Ltd.,
Linton Trading Estate, Bromyard,
Herefordshire, HR7 4QT
www.holden.co.uk
Tel: 01885 488488
Suppliers of obsolete Lucas electrical equipment of all types. Excellent for overhaul of elderly distributors, especially where new replacements are no longer available, such as on Series I models.

Kenlowe Ltd.,
Burchetts Green, Maidenhead,
Berkshire, SL6 6QU
www.kenlowe.com
Tel: 01628 882 3303
Suppliers of electrically-driven engine cooling fans and the 'Hotstart' engine pre-heater.

Michelin Tyres Plc,
www.michelin.co.uk
Manufacturers of car, truck and
motorcycle tyres and tubes and
suppliers of Land-Rover original
equipment and a full range of
superb specially tyres.

Namrick, The Nut & Bolt Store,
www.namrick.co.uk
Tel: 01273 736963
Nuts, bolts, washers and fixings
of all types and sizes. Mail order
service.

Wurth,
1 Centurion Way, Erith, Kent,
DA18 4AF
Tel: 08705 987841
www.wurth.co.uk
Aerosol zinc-rich primer and
thousands of other items of
workshop materials - all of the
finest quality.

Automec Equipment & Parts Ltd.,
36 Ballmoor, Buckingham,
MK18 1RQ
Tel: 01280 822 818
www.automec.co.uk
Copper brake, clutch and fuel
pipes and fittings. Silicon brake
fluid.

Magazines

Land Rover Monthly,
5 Tower Court,
Irchester Road,
Wollaston,
Northants, NN29 7PJ
Tel: 0207 907 6878
www.lrm.co.uk

Land Rover Owner,
Media House,
Lynchwood,
Peterborough, PE2 6EA
Tel: 01733 468582
www.lro.com

Land Rover World,
Kelsey Publishing Group,
PO Box 978,
Peterborough, PE1 9FL
Tel: 01959 543530
www.landroverworld.co.uk

Haynes
Restoration
Manuals

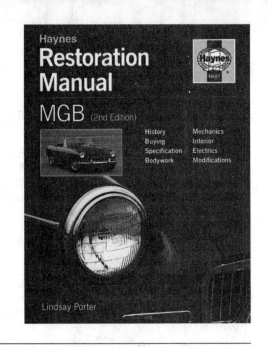

For more information on books please contact: Customer Services,
Haynes Publishing, Sparkford, Yeovil, Somerset BA22 7JJ, UK
Tel. **01963 442030** Fax: **01963 440001**
Int. tel: **+44 1963 442030** Fax: **+44 1963 440001**
E-mail: **sales@haynes.co.uk** Website: **www.haynes.co.uk**